"*Theology and the End of Doctrine* is an important book, long in gestation. Only now, at some distance from the twentieth century, can we see new ways of narrating the story of liberal theology. Helmer's 'end' of doctrine is only the ending of a chapter, not the story itself. Helmer challenges Lindbeck's reading of Schleiermacher as a theologian for whom religious experience displaces the normativity of biblical language and doctrine. The way forward is not merely to analyze the grammar of the language of faith but rather to engage the lived reality that occasions this language. This is a stimulating work in constructive theology that opens up fresh approaches to several problems at once: the dual responsibility of theology to church and academy, the tension between trans-historical truth and historical tradition, and, most of all, the relation of doctrinal language to a theological reality (i.e., God) that, precisely because it is living, invites us to say not only something faithful but also something new."

—Kevin J. Vanhoozer, Research Professor of Systematic Theology,
Trinity Evangelical Divinity School

"Helmer's book is a groundbreaking revitalization of doctrine for Christian theology and faith but also for the academy. It critiques two prominent approaches: authoritarian views of doctrine that deny its constructed character and the reductionist tendencies of religious studies where 'theology' and doctrine are viewed as anti-intellectual. The crucial connection of doctrine to transcendence through human witness, Helmer argues, *requires* recognition of doctrine's socially constructed character and the necessity of change. Reappropriating the contributions of Martin Luther and Friedrich Schleiermacher in enormously enlightening ways, she even shows how the work of Karl Barth supports her case for combining social constructionism and the transcendent."

—Mary McClintock Fulkerson, Professor of Theology,
Duke Divinity School

"Succinct and elegantly written, this book is an unflinching engagement with our contemporary suspicion that doctrine (or theology itself) has come to an end. Drawing on some of the most prominent figures in the Reformed tradition, Helmer sketches a compelling vision of a new end for doctrine—one that is designed to resonate across academy, culture, and church. That she manages to do this in conversation with theology, religious studies, and philosophy (including the neglected neo-Kantian movement in Germany) without ever losing the forest for the trees makes her book an excellent candidate for cross-disciplinary discussion."

—Andrew Chignell, Associate Professor of Philosophy, Susan Linn Sage
School of Philosophy, Cornell University

"Recent discussion on doctrine has often been critical of the theological insights of modernity. Christine Helmer undertakes a careful revision of this discussion, emphasizing the need to take history and religious studies seriously. She demonstrates that this emphasis does not downplay the language and reality of theological doctrine but gives them a new relevance."

—Risto Saarinen, Professor of Ecumenics, University of Helsinki

"The title is deliberately ambiguous: the true 'end' (purpose) of doctrine is to point beyond itself to the relation of the living God to human beings in this world. Where this 'end' is lost to view, we are threatened with the 'end' (demise) of doctrine. Christine Helmer wants to reinvigorate doctrine. To accomplish this goal, she takes us on a historical journey through twentieth-century theology: from the Ritschlian reaction against mysticism and metaphysics and Brunner's critique of Schleiermacher through Barth's theology of the Word to the creation of an epistemic model by the so-called Yale School in which doctrine has lost its referential status altogether and thus its connection to divine and historical reality. Helmer's constructive solution proceeds through a recovery of Schleiermacher's epistemology (exploding a few myths about the great Berliner along the way!) in order to advance an understanding of doctrine as the expression of a socially conceived interaction with the 'real.' What emerges from this fine study is a theological epistemology that expands and deepens Barth's concept of the Word in important ways and an understanding of doctrine that repairs the damage done to its reputation in recent decades."

—Bruce L. McCormack, Charles Hodge Professor of Systematic Theology, Princeton Theological Seminary

Theology and the End of Doctrine

Theology and
the End of Doctrine

Christine Helmer

Jan 9/16
Fu Wuvanee,
with gratitude
ana best wishes
Christine

WESTMINSTER
JOHN KNOX PRESS
LOUISVILLE · KENTUCKY

First edition
Published by Westminster John Knox Press
Louisville, Kentucky

14 15 16 17 18 19 20 21 22 23—10 9 8 7 6 5 4 3 2 1

Scripture quotations are from the New Revised Standard Version of the Bible, copyright © 1989 by the Division of Christian Education of the National Council of the Churches of Christ in the U.S.A., and used by permission.

Book design by Sharon Adams
Cover design by MTW Design/Dilu Nicholas
Cover art: Fragments of Thought *by Filomena de Andrade Booth, provided with permission*

Library of Congress Cataloging-in-Publication Data

Helmer, Christine.
  Theology and the end of doctrine / Christine Helmer.
     pages cm
  Includes bibliographical references and index.
  ISBN 978-0-664-23929-9 (alk. paper)
  1. Theology. 2. Dogma. 3. Schleiermacher, Friedrich, 1768-1834. 4. Luther, Martin, 1483-1546. I. Title.
  BT21.3.H46 2014
  230--dc23

                                                        2013049524

♾ The paper used in this publication meets the minimum requirements of the American National Standard for Information Sciences—Permanence of Paper for Printed Library Materials, ANSI Z39.48-1992.

Most Westminster John Knox Press books are available at special quantity discounts when purchased in bulk by corporations, organizations, and special-interest groups. For more information, please e-mail SpecialSales@wjkbooks.com.

For Robert A. Orsi
My love, companion, conversation partner, co-parent

Contents

Preface   xi

Source Abbreviations   xv

Chapter 1: Theology and Doctrine   1

    I. Theology between Church and Academy   1

    II. Theology's Concern with Doctrine   5

    III. The Lure of Eternity   8

    IV. Historicist Shock   11

    V. Linguistic Turn   14

    VI. A Look Ahead   20

**Chapter 2: From Ritschl to Brunner: Neither Mysticism
nor Metaphysics, but the Problem with Schleiermacher**   23

    I. What Does Doctrine Mean?   23

    II. Ritschl and the Doctrine of Justification   28

        II.1. Righteousness and Justification   29

        II.2. A New Take on Justification   32

        II.3. Justification and the Problem with Schleiermacher   39

III. Mysticism to Mediation   40

   III.1. Mediation in Relationship: Spirit   41

   III.2. Mysticism in Relationship: Nature   44

IV. Brunner and the Word against Schleiermacher   47

   IV.1. The Problem of "Ground": Metaphysics   49

   IV.2. The Problem of Immediate
       Self-Consciousness: Mysticism   52

   IV.3. Theology of the Word   54

  V. The Problem with Schleiermacher   55

**Chapter 3: From Trinitarian Representation
to the Epistemic-Advantage Model:
Word, Doctrine, Theology**   59

PART 1

  I. From Word to Doctrine   59

  II. Theology and Trinitarian Representation   62

    II.1. Word in the Aftermath of War   63

    II.2. Word in the Crisis of National Socialism   72

    II.3. Word in the Prolegomena to Theological System 75

       II.3.1. Word and the Dialectics of Genre   76

       II.3.2. Word and Dogmatics   79

       II.3.3. Word, Trinity, and Dogmatics   81

    II.4. Doctrine and Ground of System?   83

PART 2

  I. The Epistemic-Advantage Model of Doctrine   88

    I.1. Doctrine as Root Assertion   90

    I.2. Christian Beliefs, Communal Identity, God   94

       I.2.1. Christian Beliefs and the Harmonizing Hermeneutic   94

I.2.2. Christian Beliefs and Communal Identity   96

I.2.3. Christian Beliefs and God   98

I.3. Luther's Contribution   99

I.4. Christianity as a Worldview   100

I.5. Conversion to a Worldview   103

II. The End of Doctrine   105

**Chapter 4: Language and Reality: A Theological
Epistemology with Some Help from Schleiermacher**   109

I. At the End, a (Tentative) Beginning   109

I.1. Bible and Doctrine   110

I.2. Reception and Production   111

I.3. Qualifying the Help from Schleiermacher   114

II. Language and Reality in the New Testament   117

II.1. Jesus and the New Testament   118

II.2. Mysticism Again   120

II.3. Total Impression   122

II.4. Acclamation   124

II.4.1. Predication and Intensional Logic   126

II.4.2. Predication in a Linguistic Milieu   128

II.5. Consciousness, Language, and Doctrine   130

III. Theological Epistemology and Doctrine   131

III.1. The Origins of Doctrine   132

III.2. The Development of Doctrine in Intersubjective Milieu 134

III.3. Doctrine in a Global Context   136

III.3.1. Categorization   139

III.3.2. Construction   141

IV. From Epistemology to Content   145

**Chapter 5: Acknowledging Social Construction
and Moving beyond Deconstruction: Doctrine
for Theology and Religious Studies** 149

    I. Doctrine as Inevitable Social Construction 149

    II. Beyond Deconstruction 153

    III. Getting Clear on the Social Construction of Reality 159

       III.1. Conversation with Religious Studies 160

       III.2. The Return to History 162

    IV. Language, Doctrine, Reality 165

Bibliography 171

Index of Ancient Sources 181

Index of Names 182

Index of Subjects 185

Preface

This book's title, as many readers will recognize, alludes to George A. Lindbeck's important book *The Nature of Doctrine*, first published in 1984 and then issued again as a twenty-fifth anniversary edition in 2009 by Westminster John Knox Press. The question about language in relation to reality, which I take to be an intensely theological issue, first gripped me when I read Lindbeck's book in graduate school. The search for an answer has taken me through Luther studies to Schleiermacher, then to the early twentieth century, and finally to contemporary theology. This book documents my travels. The turning point in my quest was my reading of Schleiermacher's *Dialektik* and the *Glaubenslehre* under the generous guidance of two brilliant mentors at the University of Tübingen, Manfred Frank and Eilert Herms. I then began to intuit a theological direction that motivated the concerns of this present work.

The term "end" contains the hope of a vital beginning, and in this sense the "end of doctrine" is meant to have a double meaning. Doctrine's end is an evaluation, a judgment, disclosing an intra-Christian theological concern with the effects that modernity has had on doctrine. I wanted to contribute to this concern by asking a number of questions, historical, epistemological, and theological, in order to turn doctrine itself into a question specifically about the reality with which Christian theology is most concerned. With this comes a second question: how that reality is communicated in a transhistorical way so that doctrine may be an opportunity both for a distinct experience of the living triune God and for inscribing a personal sense of the gospel into the living tradition of Christianity. I wanted to press the referential dimension of doctrine in order to get at the core of the Christian tradition, which, as I understand it, invokes the personal and communal, the contextual and transhistorical. If doctrine were to be regarded as witness to a reality who invites endless conversation, then how might doctrine be pressed to be faithful to novelty, particularly the novelty that I think enlivens the theological conversation?

So I invoke the evaluation "end of doctrine" in order to invite new discussions concerning doctrinal faithfulness that are sincerely engaged with the major questions, challenges, limitations, and riches of modernity. Thus "end"—in the sense of an end to a monopoly on doctrinal faithfulness without question, paradox, or dialectic and without reality (as I argue)—is an invitation to a new fascination about why doctrine is the theological genre that bears the gift of divine reality in language and history. This position is theological; some might even say it is political, because in the history of Christianity the invocation of doctrine usually attests to power. My interest, however, is in a renewed study of doctrine on the grounds of reality. Although my work to this point has tended in the epistemological direction, I intend this beginning for doctrine to be open to novel ways of exploring reality and thus showing that doctrine has a contribution to make to contemporary theology, as well as to the study and practice of religion.

This book came into the present form with the generous support of a EURIAS (European Institutes for Advanced Study) fellowship at the Helsinki Collegium for Advanced Study during the 2012–13 academic year. I was honored to hold the title "Marie Curie EURIAS Fellow" during my tenure at the Collegium. Marie Curie was a pioneer in a field that, like the theological discipline attending to doctrine, is underrepresented by women's contributions (except perhaps as muses). I thank both the EURIAS foundation and the Collegium for providing me with "a room of my own" and a vibrant academic community in downtown Helsinki, including the Department of Theology of the University of Helsinki. I also thank Northwestern University for research leave support.

Robert A. Orsi has been my conversation partner through every stage of this book's production. Many of the ideas presented here bear the imprint of our ongoing domestic seminar on theology and the study of religion. The book also owes its prose presentation to his careful and patient work. I dedicate this book to him with deep gratitude for his love that recognizes and understands, for his thinking and writing that have shaped my own, and for his presence that makes my quotidian reality joyful. Our nine-year-old son, Anthony, spent the year with me in Helsinki, and his joyful and infectious enthusiasm for, well, for everything, managed to brighten even the dark Nordic winter. During this process I was reminded of how a rigorous and sympathetic reader can coax a manuscript to greater precision. I thank Marilyn McCord Adams for her generous gift of the most careful and engaged reading, for substantive discussion of the book's argument and its historical/conceptual moves, and for her thinking with me to imagine new ways to articulate better arguments. My thanks also goes to Dan Braden, my editor at Westminster John Knox Press, for his support of this project and for betting against the odds that this manuscript would be finished before the birth of the royal baby in July 2013.

The path I have taken toward this book is documented in a prior publication. I began thinking about the material that I have worked out in chapter 2, "From Ritschl to Brunner: Neither Mysticism nor Metaphysics, but the Problem with Schleiermacher," in the article, "Mysticism and Metaphysics: Schleiermacher and a Historical-Theological Trajectory," *The Journal of Religion* 83, no. 4 (October 2003): 517–38.

Source Abbreviations

BC   *The Book of Concord: The Confessions of the Evangelical Lutheran Church*. Translated by Charles Arand et al. Edited by Robert Kolb and Timothy J. Wengert. Minneapolis: Fortress Press, 2000.

BO   Friedrich Schleiermacher. *Brief Outline of Theology as a Field of Study (1811 and 1830)*. Translated by Terrence N. Tice. 3rd ed. Louisville, KY: Westminster John Knox Press, 2011.

CD I/1   Karl Barth. *The Doctrine of the Word of God: Prolegomena*. Vol. I/1 of *Church Dogmatics*. Translated by Geoffrey W. Bromiley. Edinburgh: T&T Clark, 1975.

CD I/2   Karl Barth. *The Doctrine of the Word of God: Prolegomena*. Vol. I/2 of *Church Dogmatics*. Translated by G. T. Thomson and Harold Knight. Edinburgh: T&T Clark, 1956.

CF   Friedrich Schleiermacher. *The Christian Faith (1830/31)*. Translated by D. M. Baillie et al. Edited by H. R. McKintosh and J. S. Stewart. Edinburgh: T&T Clark, 1999.

EBR   *Encyclopedia of the Bible and Its Reception*. 8 vols. (thus far). Edited by Dale C. Allison Jr., Volker Leppin, Choon-Leong Seow, Hermann Spieckermann, Barry Dov Walfish, and Eric Ziolkowski. Berlin: de Gruyter, 2009–.

KGA   Friedrich Schleiermacher. *Kritische Gesamtausgabe*. 5 parts,
                36 vols. (thus far). Edited by Günter Meckenstock, Andreas
                Arndt, Ulrich Barth, Lutz Käppel, and Notger Slenczka.
                Berlin: de Gruyter, 1983–.

LW   *Luther's Works: American Edition*. 55 vols. Edited by Jaro-
                slav Pelikan and Helmut T. Lehmann. St. Louis and Min-
                neapolis: Concordia Publishing House and Fortress Press,
                1958–86.

RGG   *Religion in Geschichte und Gegenwart*. 3rd ed. 6 vols. Edited
                by Kurt Galling. Tübingen: J. C. B. Mohr (Paul Siebeck),
                1956–65.

Speeches   Friedrich Schleiermacher. *On Religion: Speeches to Its Cul-
                tured Despisers*. Translated from Über die Religion (1st ed.,
                1799), edited, and introduced by Richard Crouter. Cam-
                bridge Texts in the History of Philosophy. Cambridge:
                Cambridge University Press, 1996.

SW   Friedrich Schleiermacher. *Sämmtliche Werke*. Edited by
                Ludwig Jonas et al. 3 parts, 31 vols. Berlin: G. Reimer,
                1834–64.

TDNT   *Theological Dictionary of the New Testament*. Edited by G.
                Kittel and G. Friedrich. Translated by G. W. Bromiley. 10
                vols. Grand Rapids: Eerdmans. 1964–76.

WA   Weimarer Ausgabe. *D. Martin Luthers Werke: Kritische
                Gesamtausgabe*. 120 vols. Edited by J. K. F. Knaake et al.
                Weimar: H. Böhlau, 1883–2009.

WA TR   *D. Martin Luthers Werke: Kritische Gesamtausgabe. Tischre-
                den*. 6 vols. Edited by K. Drescher et al. Weimar: H.
                Böhlau, 1912–21.

1

Theology and Doctrine

I. THEOLOGY BETWEEN CHURCH AND ACADEMY

Theology has to do with the study of doctrine; and in particular times and places, doctrine has to do with human beings' experience with divine reality that comes to but also transcends those temporal and spatial specificities. That is the argument of this book. My primary constructive aim is to inspire a revitalized interest in doctrine after decades of contentious dispute that, among other things, has served to isolate doctrine from serious engagement beyond a small circle of theologians and to render the term virtually a synonym for ecclesiastical authority that is inattentive to or even dismissive of human experience. How particular theologies define doctrine and the methods proposed for studying it vary widely among theologians and in different historical eras. But the one constant is the fact that commitments to particular accounts of the relationship between language and reality are entailed in theology's work of appropriating doctrine from previous generations and in conversation with contemporaries, in developing new doctrinal understandings, and in bringing doctrine into relationship with today's vital questions.

Personal biography, political context, and relationship with the church and the Christian community all contribute to the shape of the questions a theologian asks. His or her ideas may take a lifetime to develop; often it feels that more than a single lifetime is needed. As a theologian grows and changes, her ideas over time are continuously inflected by her personal, religious, and cultural circumstances. But then sometimes there is disruption. What has been taken for granted gives way, and the theologian is brought up short. There is a particular urgency to such moments. The theologian is impelled to seek out a language commensurate to the reality she sees emerging and to bring her

1

ideas into conversation with other thinkers of her time, within and beyond
the academy and the church. In these circumstances theology's course might
be changed forever.

Here are three paradigmatic moments of such profound reorientation
in the history of Western theology. (1) Martin Luther (1483–1546), the
sixteenth-century Protestant Reformer, endured sleepless devil-haunted
nights until he found relief in the Christ who died for sinners. Luther's religious breakthrough, prepared for by years of biblical study, resulted in his
coming to understand the human person as freed by the gospel. This discovery—which was both existential and theological, as are the others to be
described—introduced into Christian discourse the intimate address of God's
pronouncement of justification *pro te* (for you). (2) As an eighteen-year-old
seminarian at Barby, Friedrich Schleiermacher (1768–1834), who would
later be hailed the "father of modern Protestant theology," experienced a
crisis of faith. He struggled with the theology of Christ's vicarious atone-
ment and with a God who would condemn humans to eternal punishment
for failing to attain the perfection this God had intended for them. Schleiermacher was standing at the confluence of three intellectual movements—
Pietism, the German Enlightenment, and Romanticism—and he drew on all
of them as he fashioned a way out of crisis by developing a new vocabulary
of immediate self-consciousness to explain Christ's person and redemptive
work.[1] (3) When Swiss theologian Karl Barth (1886–1968) confronted the
racial politics of National Socialism in Germany in 1934, he pointed with
unprecedented theological urgency to the word of God that spoke judgment
on human politics, culture, and religion. The word of God, a phrase with
roots in the language of the biblical prophets, found decisive identification as
Jesus Christ in Barth's thought and led him to deeper engagement with the
doctrine of the Trinity.

These three brief snapshots of theologians at work in times of personal and
social upheaval vividly illustrate the perspective that orients this book. Theology, an age-old inquiry, makes its way toward new perspectives on truth by
means of theologians' critical and constructive engagement with the contin-
gencies and exigencies of their times and in conversation with their interlocutors in the university and in the churches. Theology is a discipline that is at
once oriented to the transcendent and thoroughly located in a particular time
and place. It arises out of personal needs and social crises but looks beyond

---

1. References to Schleiermacher's famous letter of January 21, 1787, to his father, in
The Life of Schleiermacher as Unfolded in His Autobiography and Letters, vol. 1, trans. Frederica
Rowan (London: Smith, Elder & Co., 1860), 46–47; cited in Friedrich Schleiermacher, *On
Religion: Speeches to Its Cultural Despisers*, ed. and trans. Richard Crouter, Cambridge Texts
in the History of Philosophy, 2nd ed. (Cambridge: Cambridge University Press, 1996), xii.

them to truth. The theologian's study is always and necessarily open to the surrounding world, heaven and earth.

When we look to how theology fares in North America today, then, we see that its historical and social surround has significant repercussions for the work of the discipline. Multiple factors shape the situation of contemporary theology. Theology has as one of its locations the denominational seminary, which today finds itself confronted with unprecedented financial pressures as it contends with the question of how to train the next generation of religious leaders for the churches they will be called to serve. Traditional models of full-time clerical leadership appear to be increasingly unviable, and this leads to a creative but also daunting search for new ways of educating pastors who themselves will be living and working in a radically changed world. Online courses, compact courses, and weekend seminars held at a distance from brick-and-mortar seminaries seem to be the wave of the future (although because the future is always unknowable, one is right to be skeptical of these successively and confidently identified waves). Educational models are being developed that prioritize both professional training and preparation for alternative careers, anticipating a time when clergy may not be able to support themselves on income derived solely from their ministry. This is not a new problem—think only of Jonathan Edwards's constant struggles over remuneration with his vestry—but it takes on particular urgency in the context of the permanent crisis of neoliberal economies. The challenge of conserving church membership also presses both on the mainline churches and, since the 1990s, on the new evangelical churches that were once heralded as the thriving alternative to the mainline denominations. Churches in turn insist that "our" seminaries—"our" in scare quotes because levels of financial support are not always commensurate with a sense of proprietorship—do their part to adapt traditional seminary education to make church attendance attractive again. This model serves the church that changes through time.

Some denominationally governed seminaries take a different tack. They continue to be dedicated to the traditional foundations of theological education. In these academic environments, history and systematic theology are regarded as indispensable for theological formation, along with biblical studies, liturgical studies, and practical theology. Since the church has as its goal the maintenance of a living institution with a distinct mission to the world, it will want to cultivate its leaders in the particular traditions that have characterized its distinctiveness for centuries. The church in this perspective requires its theologians to uphold doctrines that inform the church's identity through the ages. Theology is for the church. This model serves the church's unique and enduring identity.

These two visions of theology in the seminary do not exist in an academic vacuum. Whether theology is intended to guide the church toward relevance in the contemporary world or to serve the church's distinctive identity, both models of theological mission are developed in relation to the broader pursuit of knowledge as it takes place in the modern academy. Theology is an academic pursuit, whether it takes place in a church seminary, university divinity school, or in the theology department of a denominationally affiliated college or university. The next generation of theologians already has in hand undergraduate degrees from the nation's colleges and universities by the time they begin their postgraduate professional training, and they will be taught by professors trained in graduate schools. Thus the assumptions and methodologies informing theological inquiry are always contextualized by the cultural and intellectual commitments of the day. The academic context within which theologians learn and work informs the self-understanding of the discipline, even if the explicit relationship of theology to the broader university context may not be at the forefront of theology's public rhetoric today. Like other academic disciplines, theology is oriented to the pursuit of knowledge and understanding. Sometimes all of them are oriented to truth. However critical theology is of its relationship to the academy, however constructively it construes this relationship, theology's status as an academic discipline stands—or falls—with its openness to being in conversation with other endeavors dedicated to the pursuit of knowledge in the contemporary academy.

At the same time it must be acknowledged that theology's status as a viable intellectual discipline in the university, in particular in the secular university, is currently contested and fraught with struggle. A sometimes quite crude polemic has arisen in the past three decades that poses a particular challenge for theology, as I see it from my location as an academic theologian working in a department of religious studies in a secular North American university. The rhetoric goes like this: modern thought has developed as a free and rational enterprise, not only independent from but also sharply critical of authoritative and normative discourses. Within the frame of this historical achievement, theology is suspected of being a disempowering dogmatic discipline. More bluntly, religious studies scholar Tomoko Masuzawa calls theologians "petty criminals" whose primary interest is to keep hold of the financial benefits that come with university appointments.[2] The intellectual legacy of the German theological commitment to Christian universalism, Masuzawa argues, has so tainted the modern study of world religions that religious studies as an academic discipline must be abandoned. Its association with theology damns religious studies. Using a sporting metaphor, another critic writes that theologians

---

2. See this term in Tomoko Masuzawa, *The Invention of World Religions: Or, How European Universalism Was Preserved in the Language of Pluralism* (Chicago: University of Chicago Press, 2005), 328n15.

are "fair game" to religious theorists.[3] The only way to avoid being hunted down like a deer in season, evidently, is for theology to abandon its dogmatic doctrines—as critics state the issue—and to remake itself as intellectual history or as cultural studies or to foreground its political dimension in the new field of political theology. Only by fundamentally changing what is understood to be its core métier will theology satisfactorily conform in the eyes of its contemporary despisers to the spirit of free intellectual inquiry. In other words theology must stop being theology in order to obtain its visa into the academy.

And the worst of it is doctrine. Theology is a problem, and doctrine is the issue with the problem. Doctrine is the crime that theology must be prevented from committing upon the university. Meanwhile, to shift focus from the academy to the perspective of the churches, doctrine is purported to secure Christian belief in authoritative formulations. Within Christian churches, doctrine has to do with the unity of Christian identity across time and space. So the whole question of doctrine as it is currently set up functions as a firewall between the academy and the churches.

The rub is that theology is necessarily concerned with doctrine. But if doctrine is defined in exclusive terms as the authoritative linchpin of Christian identity, then theology's concern with it will only deepen theology's alienation from the university. On the other hand, can theology contribute to academic discussion when it inquires into the historical genesis and development of doctrine? Or when it asks how particular theologians in specific times and places interpreted doctrine in relation to their personal, social, and political circumstances? Or when it goes further to inquire into the relationship of doctrine to contemporary circumstances? This leaves us with a key question: how may theology investigate doctrine in a way that acknowledges its responsibility to church and academy while not falling into the abyss that in recent years has opened between church interests and academic inquiry, between sacred and secular, between the normative and the putatively nonnormative?

II. THEOLOGY'S CONCERN WITH DOCTRINE

Theology's relegation to distinct and multiple locations that have different agendas and interests affects how doctrine is understood. Is doctrine an outdated norm and thus irrelevant to today's Christians? Is doctrine capable of conveying what is common to Christianity through the ages, its core beliefs

---

3. Russell T. McCutcheon, "The Study of Religion as an Anthropology of Credibility," in *Religious Studies, Theology, and the University: Conflicting Maps, Changing Terrain*, ed. Linell E. Cady and Delwin Brown (Albany: State University of New York Press, 2002), 14.

and foundational identity, and if so, by which formulation and whose interpretation? Is doctrine a viable subject matter in the secular academy that now regards it as a dogmatic intrusion? The nature of doctrine inevitably changes as church and academy work out their respective aims and interests in interpreting and formulating doctrine. But given such competing interests, is it possible to work out the double task of considering (1) doctrine as a good of the church and (2) doctrine as the object of critical inquiry in contribution to the work of the university? In turn, can the academic study of doctrine connect the robust intellectual legacy of Christian theology with new generations of Christians in church and society?

Theology and the End of Doctrine examines the issue of theology's viability as an intellectual investigation into the content of Christian belief, doing so by critically considering the question of doctrine. I am interested both in doctrine as an intellectual practice relevant to the contemporary church and in doctrine as a question for theology in its relationship to the humanities broadly. It is a good moment to undertake such an examination: in the church, theology vacillates between doctrinal deconstruction and doctrinal preservation; in the university, theology is not quite sure what to do with doctrine as it engages its conversation partners in other disciplines. This work is an exploration, then, of doctrine and theology between church and academy.

Doctrine is theology's task as an intellectual enterprise, specifically as it is concerned with the way language and reality are construed theologically in the formulation of doctrine. This book may hold the promise of suggesting new areas and methods of theological inquiry as it invites a rethinking of theology's understanding of doctrine. That is my larger aim. In the meantime *Theology and the End of Doctrine* considers how the present situation of much Christian theology developed out of particular political and intellectual circumstances in the relatively recent past. The point of the book's historical excursuses is to establish what I consider to be the necessary framework for examining the constitutive elements of contemporary theology, all done with the hope that once parsed they may be recombined in new ways for the future.

Has doctrine's end already come? The end of doctrine has often been announced in recent years. Proponents of Christian orthodoxy have argued that the liberal Enlightenment and the long modern era—the period stretching from the seventeenth to the twentieth century, which witnessed the ascendancy of secular reason and the diminishment of the domain of faith (according to one familiar account of the era)—are responsible for eviscerating doctrine. The defenders of orthodox faith characterized the liberal strategy to place doctrine before the tribunal of reason, with the result that doctrine was given the poor choice of either accommodating itself to the alien standards of modern reason or being rejected by rational consensus.

Following the Enlightenment's assault on faith, according to these same proponents of Christian orthodoxy, doctrinal evocations of the supernatural and the miraculous became unintelligible, unsupported as they were by science; hence faith's mysteries could (so onlookers allege) be enforced only on those who unknowingly assented to propositions that the church imposed on them. By the standards of naturalist reason, the ontology presupposed by a doctrinal worldview that includes angels and devils, saints and spiritual forces, transcends sense perception. Naturalist reason saw this ontology as an obsolete relic of medieval Christianity; the worldview had only to be demythologized by reason. This was the fate of the idea of doctrine in modernity. So doctrine has been in crisis for a while, according to the story told by some of its contemporary defenders.

This is not the story of doctrine's end that I will tell. Rather, I will argue that those who sought to protect doctrine from what they deemed modernity's assaults have brought doctrine to its present-day challenge. This is a crisis made by doctrine's defenders, not by its revilers. I am especially concerned to probe how it came to be that theology assigned doctrine a normative function within the Christian worldview cut off from connection with the living reality of God. This is what I mean by the end of doctrine: it has come to an end when it cannot by definition say anything new and when the sole measurement of doctrine's significance is its contribution as the authoritative enforcer of the church's identity.

I proceed to this point via a historical review of theology's development in modernity. I am interested in how debates among certain leading theologians mapped out and then went down particular paths that led to where we are today. I will look specifically at the German theological legacy, in particular the inheritances of Martin Luther and Friedrich Schleiermacher, and at how interpretations of these theologians over time propelled twentieth-century theology forward. Debates over the theologies of Luther and Schleiermacher, often fiercely contested, were the engine of modern Protestant theology. The two figures continue to shape the current theological landscape in ways that are distinctly contemporary. This foray into the history of theology sets the stage for my proposing a new direction for doctrine.

To anticipate my argument aphoristically: a theology that views doctrine in relation to the reality that doctrine aims to articulate is a theology that relates experience to the production of knowledge. When doctrine speaks its truth, it speaks of experience. For this is what is at stake in this work and in the fate of doctrine. How do we understand the relationship between experience and knowledge? In particular, how do we understand the relationship between the human experience of God and human knowledge of God? Once doctrine is reconnected to divine reality and human experience—only then will theology be inspired to approach doctrine with intellectual curiosity, academic rigor, and a deep sympathy for the church's witness to God in this world.

But first there is the question of why theology ought to be concerned with doctrine in the first place. Accordingly, this chapter begins with theology's unique contribution to discerning life at its deepest and most exigent core. The eternal is what ultimately compels theology. Theology relishes the challenge of expressing the truth of God in language that can sustain Christian confidence. Theology's gaze is inward, into the eternal essence of things, and outward, into places where God dwells among humans. When modern historicism jolted theology out of heaven and down to earth in the eighteenth and nineteenth centuries, it delivered a shock to doctrine. How profound a shock can only be appreciated against the background of eternity's gravitational pull on theology.

III. THE LURE OF ETERNITY

Luther's crisis of faith, which came to be so pivotal for the making of the modern West, hinged on the burning question "Where do I find a gracious God?"[4] Luther was possessed of a terrified conscience. He was tormented by the devil; he bent his own body beneath the blows of the whip and the rigors of the fast, and his spiritual torment brought him sickness and pain. But Luther was no ordinary friar. He had the experience of his night terrors, specifically his fear of eternal salvation lost. Luther's fear arose at the point where his personal history and psychological distress converged with the manifold crises of his times: corruption and war. In the course of his days, Luther frequently encountered the sculpture of Christ as Judge, possibly located in the cemetery surrounding St. Mary's Church in Wittenberg,[5] and his fears drove him to the gates of eternity. "Here I felt," Luther wrote as an old man looking back at his momentous breakthrough, "that I was altogether born again and

---

4. For this question, see Theodor Dieter, "Why Does Luther's Doctrine of Justification Matter Today?" in *The Global Luther: A Theologian for Modern Times*, ed. Christine Helmer (Minneapolis: Fortress Press, 2009), 199: "Thus Luther's question—the Luther of the Reformation—is not, 'How do I find a gracious God?,' but 'Where do I find a gracious God?' The answer can only be 'by faith in the gospel.'"

5. In his sermons, Luther frequently alludes to the image of Christ as Judge, although the historical question of where in Wittenberg he encountered the image remains open. It would not have been on the lintel of the town church because this was decorated with a scene from the coronation of St. Mary. The sculpture may have been placed in the cemetery, although this too is uncertain since there are no images of the cemetery in the early sixteenth century. Personal correspondence with Dr. Martin Treu (July 2, 2013).

had entered paradise itself through open gates. . . . Thus that place in Paul [Rom. 1:17] was for me truly the gate to paradise."[6]

Luther's crisis of conscience was brought on by the actuality of eternal damnation in the Christian imagination as he powerfully experienced it. The terrible question "What if I have not done enough?" was the cause of his trials and *Anfechtungen* (spiritual terror). Luther was not the only theologian to be compelled by the quest to see the eternal outcome of life. Thomas Aquinas, it is reported, was so moved in his old age by the vision of eternity that he never wrote another sentence. As a young man the modern theologian Friedrich Schleiermacher was fascinated by the infinite ways that the universe revealed itself to religious feeling and intuition (later in life he tempered his theological positions with recourse to Kant's critical philosophy). There is a speculative desire and existential urgency among theologians to look beyond the limits of what reason may know, and this looking beyond often precipitates crisis.

Theologians have the benefit of an intellectual partner willing to assist them with the task of orienting thinking to eternity. Philosophy has offered theology the tools to conceptualize in "clear and distinct ideas" and to speak with finely crafted concepts. If thinking about eternity is to acquire a scientific value, it requires rigorous logic and good arguments. Plato directed reason to knowledge's unwavering stability. Knowledge transcends both opinion and faith because it is oriented to the eternal forms that are without temporality. Philosophy offered theology the epistemological means to attain stability in contemplation, that is, by ascending past the ephemera of transient appearances and elevating spirit to the eternal forms. Christian theology claimed this epistemology of ascent as its own. Yet theology's subject matter challenged theologians to refashion philosophy's instruments to suit a God who transcended the apex of the ascent.

So theology's attraction to eternity is shared with philosophy, but there comes a point when theology must go it alone. The history of the Western theological tradition may be written as the story of theologians coming to the fork in the road at which they must part ways with philosophers. The parting does not imply rejection: Luther, like the late medieval theologians William of Ockham and Pierre d'Ailly, made philosophical distinctions, created terms, defined concepts, and so on. But Luther refashioned these instruments exclusively for theology's subject matter. At stake was the preservation of God's eternal identity. Theology, in other words, was concerned with something greater than logic. The semantics of its verb tenses were made to convey

---

6. *LW* 34:337, in "Preface to the Complete Edition of Luther's Latin Writings [1545]."

eternity. God is the truth about eternity. Theology's unique position among the sciences is predicated on its compulsion to study the eternal reality.

Theologians occupy a precarious position in providing evidence for their claims out of their own lives and experience. Perhaps this is what accounts for theology's often acerbic, sometimes even brutal, quality. Theology can be a mean enterprise. Aligned with power and in the service of ecclesiastical hegemony, theological polemics have consigned dissenters to flames and dissenting colleagues to scathing reviews. Theology's obsession with binary oppositions as the key device of theological reasoning has at times reached for the power to exclude even to the point of violence. Theology's preoccupation with the eternal gives the discipline a sense of its high stakes that makes the philosopher's learned play between possibilities or her willingness to entertain counterfactuals seem less urgent and pressing. Or even trivially playful: Is the reality of omnipotence approached by musing on the question of God's capacity to grow the largest ears in the universe, as I once heard a philosopher of religion suggest in a seminar on God?

But we must say today, at this time in history, that too many heretics were burned, diversity was too fiercely condemned, and too much living reality has been ossified into the hard forms of orthodoxy. The theological commitment to truth must be more than intellectual. It is radically personal, and at the same time it aspires to the universal. Truth is not about the play of possibilities. Truth is anchored to the actuality of subjectivity together with all of creation. "I believe that God has created me together with all that exists," Luther explains in his interpretation of the first article of the Apostles' Creed in the Small Catechism of 1529.[7] The determination of all of reality is inscribed into the theologian's commitment to the object of belief. The aim of doctrine is to compress it all into an abbreviated formula accessible to humans.

That doctrine speaks of eternity is the lure of the human enterprise of theology. Much is at stake in guarding doctrine. Political and ecclesiastical battles raged over terminology, sometimes over single letters, as in the controversy in the early church about the first *i* in *homoiousios*, which erupted as theologians and church leaders struggled for precision in determining the Son's likeness to (with that *i*) or identity with (sans that *i*) the Father. Much later in time, the Protestant Reformers insisted on the church's responsibility to preserve doctrine in its purity. Throughout Christian history excommunications have been issued and anathemas have thundered forth from the church. The history of doctrine bears the marks of this contentious and violent history that is also the story of personality clashes, worldly power, and a fierce loyalty to the truth of doctrine as one party or another understood that

7. *BC* 354.2.

truth. But although it is certainly true that the development of doctrinal language was implicated in struggles for power, this is not the whole story. Such contention also gives evidence of theology's pursuit of a truth that derives its content from eternity. Doctrines point to eternal mysteries to be enjoyed and contemplated but never exhausted.

Sometimes at the core of this unedifying history of the search for doctrinal precision is the paradox that theology is a discipline existing in time as it makes claims about the eternal. Distinctions between time and eternity, creation and eternal destiny, God and the world—theology's pivotal polarities—are made with the confidence that God will not let the world fail at its own project and that God has woven the world itself into God's own project. Theology aims at this truth. It strives to develop a nomenclature and conceptuality that comprehends this truth and points to it, and theology adheres to an epistemology that maintains the paradox between its own claims, articulated in time, and its referent in eternity. Theology's lure is eternal truth, while time is its crisis.

IV. HISTORICIST SHOCK

Time perennially challenges Christian theology. Time has been theology's nemesis, from the early church's struggles to comprehend Christ's death in relation to the mid-Platonist concept of divinity's eternality and changelessness onward to Karl Barth's early metaphorical account of Christ's incarnation as a "tangent . . . touch[ing] a circle, that is, without touching it."[8] The question is, Can theology do justice to the heart of the Christian religion, its central mystery and paradox, "the Word [that] became flesh and lived among us" (John 1:14a)? Can abstract theology speak clearly of the lived reality of Christianity? Over centuries, Christian theology has been occupied with quarantining speculative axioms inherited from the Greeks, such as the view that God can neither suffer nor change. Such realities of the Christian faith and the questions that they raised have required theology to formulate the apposite terms of philosophical speculation. God's eternal being united with human nature and "was born from the Virgin Mary . . . and crucified under Pontius Pilate"—that reality has compelled Christian theology to think about God in relation to time, as well as in relation to pain and death.

The conceptual challenge of time became most pressing in academic discussions following the advent of historicism in eighteenth- and early

8. Karl Barth, *The Epistle to the Romans*, trans. of 6th ed. by Edwyn C. Hoskyns (London: Oxford University Press, 1968), 30 (on Rom. 1:4).

nineteenth-century German theology. This modern theological tradition was unique among the theologies produced in other European contexts for making the study of history the dominant academic model for the humanities.[9] The influence of German theology's preoccupation with history was far-reaching. Biblical studies, the philosophy of history, and the emerging discipline of religious studies were irrevocably shaped by a view of history that integrated an appreciation for the uniqueness of historical events with the effort to determine their causes. History is a human science. It is produced as reflection on questions of human agency and its limits, and it adheres to the rules governing historical causality.

Consider only this single strand of the trajectory of modern German theology. Martin Luther limned the mystery of time capable of the infinite (*finitum capax infiniti*), for example, in his Christmas hymn ("Whom all the world could not enwrap, Lieth he in Mary's lap"),[10] and three hundred years later German theologian Friedrich Schleiermacher set out to construct a secure historical footing for theology. Schleiermacher opened the way for modern theology by taking up the challenge that the new historical science posed to theology's eternal doctrines. But no good intellectual effort goes unpunished: Schleiermacher's name inevitably circulates in contemporary discussions of theology's capitulation to modern historicism's paradigm. The problem of Schleiermacher—the problem that much of my analysis of modern and contemporary pivots on—is the problem of history and eternity.

Friedrich Schleiermacher is widely considered the father of modern theology. One important aspect of his portfolio at the turn of the nineteenth century was to conceptualize the academic disciplines and their relations to the pursuit of knowledge on behalf of the newly founded University of Berlin.[11] This included envisioning a place for theology in the university and devising a curriculum for theology that would serve the church as an institution outside the university while at the same time ensuring that theology maintained its necessary role within the university and in conversation with other academic partners. Schleiermacher had a foot in both worlds: among his other responsibilities in Berlin, Schleiermacher served as Reformed pastor of the ecumenical

9. See Sheila Greeve Davaney, *Historicism: The Once and Future Challenge for Theology*, Guides to Theological Inquiry (Minneapolis: Fortress Press, 2006), 9–13; Frederick C. Beiser, *The German Historicist Tradition* (New York: Oxford University Press, 2011).

10. *LW* 53:241, v. 3 of "All Praise to Thee, O Jesus Christ [1523?]."

11. See the historical account in Appendix A, "Theology in the University," specifically "The Case of Berlin, 1810," in Hans W. Frei, *Types of Theology*, ed. George Hunsinger and William C. Placher (New Haven: Yale University Press, 1992), 95–115; and Thomas Albert Howard, *Protestant Theology and the Making of the Modern German University* (Oxford: Oxford University Press, 2006), 267–302.

Reformed-Lutheran Trinity Church. Theology as a "positive science" located within the university was assigned the task of coming up with theories that church leaders might utilize to correct false practices within their communities and to foster healthy piety. In this way theology would have as part of its mission the "care of souls" in support of the church's vitality.[12]

Successful fulfillment of this ecclesiastical mandate for theology required that Schleiermacher understand the present situation of the church and its relationship to the past. To this end, Schleiermacher made productive use of the emerging academic interest in the historical disciplines, calling on them to aid theology in its mission for the church. The historicist turn drew theology's gaze from eternity to time. Henceforth theology would be preoccupied with the ideas and practices of religious communities as these ideas and practices changed over time in the evolving life of communities, from their origins to their present-day manifestations.

This new envisioning of theology as a historical discipline had implications for the study of doctrine. Schleiermacher defined dogmatic theology[13] as "the knowledge of doctrine that now has currency in the Evangelical church."[14] Doctrines were the normative faith statements of the contemporary church. Their normativity had to do both with doctrine's capacity for articulating a lively faith and with the manner in which faith statements are organized within systems of dogmatic theology. Doctrines offered a focused glimpse of the present-day consensus of belief among Christians, informed by the recognition that this contemporary moment was shaped by doctrinal developments in the past. In other words, doctrine is always seen in its dynamic and dialectical relationship with the lived experience of Christians over time. Its inner dynamism—its motor force—was the questions and controversies that had arisen in specific Christian communities in different times and places. Doctrine was about faith lived in history rather than about truth fixed for all time.

The problem of Schleiermacher, as it was defined and addressed by the theologians who appear in the pages of this book, was related to the unease

---

12. Luther too regarded consolation as one aspect of doctrine. On this topic, see the insightful articles by Bo Kristian Holm: "Der Trost kommt vom Sehen—zu Katechismussystematik und Lehrbergiff," in *Denkraum Katechismus: Festgabe für Oswald Bayer zum 70. Geburtstag*, ed. Johannes von Lüpke and Edgar Thaidigsmann (Tübingen: Mohr Siebeck, 2009), 109–24; idem, "Zur Funktion der Lehre bei Luther: Die Lehre als rettendes Gedankenbild gegen Sünde, Tod und Teufel," *Kerygma und Dogma* 51, no. 1 (2005): 17–32.

13. It is significant that Schleiermacher rejects the term "systematic theology" in favor of "dogmatic theology." He favors "dogmatic theology" because it connotes the historical approach of the discipline. Theology is descriptive even when it studies the doctrines that are valid in the present context of the church.

14. *BO* 72 (§195).

provoked by this historical rendering of doctrine. Within the limits of historical reason, a theology that purports to represent God's eternal truths on earth is no longer a viable account of theology's identity and mission. The question then becomes how doctrine may make claims concerning divine truth in time. This is a classic conundrum written right into the New Testament. American theologian George Lindbeck formulated the problem this way: "How can religion claim to preserve 'the faith which was once for all delivered to the saints' (Jude 3), as all religions in some sense do, when it takes so many forms in both the past and the present?"[15] Schleiermacher's theological program paved the way for the contemporary theological (and sociological) preoccupation with religious communities and congregations as venues in which doctrine is produced to promote their flourishing. Yet the academic commitments that Schleiermacher prescribed for theology have been challenged for ostensibly compromising theology by deriving its principles from sources other than the Christian faith. This critique acquired sharp and precise focus in 1924 when Swiss theologian Emil Brunner identified the heart of the problem of Schleiermacher's approach to doctrine to be not his historicism, but an appeal to experience and metaphysics that allegedly falsified the objective truth of the word of God.

V. LINGUISTIC TURN

The linguistic turn is understood primarily as the direction taken in philosophy following the publication of Ludwig Wittgenstein's *Tractatus logico-philosophicus*. But language has also been of recent interest to theologians. Two theologians in particular, working within the broad Lutheran inheritance, have emerged as proponents of a word-oriented theology, deepening Luther's insights into the power of God's word to forgive sins but recontextualizing this insight with resources drawn from contemporary theological, philosophical, and anthropological theories of language.[16] Writing in Germany, Oswald Bayer has elaborated Luther's understanding of the *promissio*, that is, God's promise of forgiveness, which is identical to its fulfillment in

15. George A. Lindbeck, *The Nature of Doctrine: Religion and Theology in a Postliberal Age* (Philadelphia: Westminster Press, 1984), 78; cf. the 25th anniversary ed. (Louisville, KY: Westminster John Knox Press, 2009). (Unless otherwise noted, I cite pages from the original, 1984.)

16. Reinhard Hütter analyzes the theology of both Oswald Bayer and George Lindbeck as leading contemporary examples of how theology can be a church practice. See his *Suffering Divine Things: Theology as Church Practice* (Grand Rapids: Eerdmans, 1999).

the spoken declaration "*Ego te absolvo* [I forgive you]." Luther's theological innovation, according to Bayer, was to draw attention to the "speech act," uttered by God and rendered concrete for hearers in the words of institution ritually spoken by the priest during the worship service.[17] Bayer borrowed the terminology of "speech act" from philosopher of language J. L. Austin. In the United States, meanwhile, another Lutheran theologian, George A. Lindbeck, made constructive theological use of the hermeneutical model of culture proposed by American anthropologist Clifford Geertz.[18] In *The Nature of Doctrine: Religion and Theology in a Postliberal Age* (1984), published just slightly more than a decade after Geertz's game-changing *The Interpretation of Cultures* (1973), Lindbeck proposed a cultural-linguistic model for understanding religion, and by extension for understanding Christian faith as a worldview constituted by particular usages of language. Lindbeck was writing in the context of multiple commitments: a professor both at Yale Divinity School and in the Department of Religious Studies at Yale University, he was also deeply dedicated to ecumenical dialogue between Roman Catholics and Lutherans. He was one of several Protestant "delegated observers" at the Second Vatican Council. Lindbeck's constructive proposal for theology and doctrine found wide-reaching acceptance in Protestant and Catholic theology alike for offering a way past constructions of doctrine that served only to underscore what it identified as ineluctable differences among Christian communions. Theologians concerned with connecting theological reflection to church identity read Lindbeck with special avidity.

The linguistic turn in theology inspired a generation of theologians working in the inheritance of Bayer and Lindbeck to view the church as the necessary context for theological work.[19] They came to see the linguistic-literary idioms of the church at worship as a discursive practice by means of which believers are initiated into the life and language of the community and become capable of interpreting various life circumstances in terms of the faith.[20] Belief is a matter of disciplined fluency. The believer is a competent

17. See Hütter's description of Bayer's concept of *promissio* in ibid., 77–88; as well as my "The Subject of Theology in the Thought of Oswald Bayer," *Lutheran Quarterly* 14, no. 1 (Spring 2000): 21–52.

18. On the reception of Geertz by Lindbeck, see my "Luther, History, and the Concept of Religion," in *Lutherrenaissance: Past and Present*, ed. Christine Helmer and Bo Kristian Holm, Forschungen zur Kirchen- und Dogmengeschichte (Göttingen: Vandenhoeck & Ruprecht, forthcoming).

19. See Hütter's book that corrects for, as he argues, "a thoroughgoing fundamental pneumatological as well as ecclesiological deficit" in both Bayer's and Lindbeck's proposals (*Suffering Divine Things*, 26).

20. Hütter articulates this distinction as follows: "As 'catechetical theology,' it is concerned with gradually accommodating a person to the faith praxis (catechetical

"speaker" of Christian discourse, which in Geertz's terms becomes a model of and model for the world as it is found, and in this way believers inhabit this world of particular meaning as their own. As Lindbeck puts it, "To become a Christian involves learning the story of Israel and of Jesus well enough to interpret and experience oneself and one's world in its terms."[21] The believer is the "hearer" of the gospel.[22] The believer's competence in speaking the language of the faith, which is equivalent to living the faith, is exhibited in language conforming to the underlying "grammar" of Christian discourse.[23] It is this notion of doctrine as "grammar of the faith" that has been attractive to theologians.

The phrase may be traced back at least to Luther, who appealed to the Holy Spirit as having "his own grammar."[24] But in its contemporary iteration it evokes the idea of church identity as significant for an understanding of doctrine. Theology as church practice (to allude to the title of Hütter's book) has as its task to identify the rules governing the structures and usage of Christian discourse. On the one hand, theology guides and orients hearers to competent speaking; on the other hand, theology investigates the doctrines responsible for the normative grammar of the church.

This emphasis on language as the nature of doctrine in a Christian worldview evokes Luther's reformation idea of the *verbum externum*. Luther used the term to identify God's word of forgiveness as external to human reality. As Luther understood it, only God, not humans, forgives sins, and God's word of forgiveness spoken to the sinner, *"Ego te absolvo,"* is God's action that effects true forgiveness. But while Luther emphasized reception of *God's word* as the human posture in this encounter with the Divine, contemporary theologians aligned with the cultural-linguistic approach to theology stress the reception of *doctrine.* Doctrine is identified, in Hütter's words, as "the rules that are decisive for the identity, welfare, and cohesion of a certain group and distinguish that group from others."[25] Precisely as rules informing an identity said to be continuous through time, doctrines must be protected from innovation that might conceivably falsify their truth.

---

learning): as 'intratextual theology,' it is concerned with maintaining the praxis of Christian faith in the most varied life situations and with interpreting these situations within the context of faith praxis (peregrinational learning)" (ibid., 50–51).

21. Lindbeck, *Nature of Doctrine*, 34.

22. Lindbeck explicitly alludes to Luther's idea of the *verbum externum* (external word) in order to explain what he means by religion: "A religion is above all an external word, a *verbum externum*, that molds and shapes the self and its world" (ibid.).

23. Lindbeck, ibid., 81: "In any case, it is not the lexicon but rather the grammar of the religion which church doctrines chiefly reflect."

24. WA 39/II:104.24: "Spiritus sanctus habet suam grammaticam."

25. Hütter, *Suffering Divine Things*, 57.

So *reception* is a concept of common interest in theological accounts of doctrine's function in the church. But as even these few sentences above suggest, the term is multivalent. "Reception" may include studying how the Christian canon is real as a unity by applying to it a specific rule of faith or creed.[26] "Reception"—when it means receiving the "practical wisdom of the church, expressed in doctrine and normed by the canon"—may be understood as enabling practitioners "to participate in the *same* theo-dramatic action to which the Scripture attests."[27] Or the "reception" of specific doctrines from the past that are taken theologically as normative articulations of the central elements of the Christian faith may be understood to possess epistemic primacy in a Christian worldview. (This understanding of reception and doctrine will occupy me in chap. 3.) So there are various theological proposals that claim for doctrine as linguistic-literary construction a normative status vis-à-vis the church's identity—all share a common emphasis on reception as the appropriate human posture.

But while the appropriation of Luther's theology of the word is central for this emphasis on the reception of doctrine in the cultural-linguistic school of contemporary theology, it comes at the expense of another equally crucial aspect of Luther's understanding: his stress on *experience* as necessary to theology.[28] This omission first dawned on me when I began to notice the unified and consistent criticism of Schleiermacher that has taken shape in modern and contemporary theology. It occurred to me that this view of Schleiermacher was, strictly speaking, not "about" Schleiermacher at all. On closer inspection, it became apparent that "Schleiermacher" was being deployed to name and to secure a theoretical gap—really a theoretical abyss—between language and experience. Flogging Schleiermacher contributed to the taken-for-granted, once-and-for-all nature of this gap in modern theological conversation.

---

26. Robert W. Jenson, *Canon and Creed*, Interpretation: Resources for the Use of Scripture in the Church (Louisville, KY: Westminster John Knox Press, 2010), 41: "Canon and creed fitted together, and only canon and creed fitted together, could make and can now make one whole and integral guardian of the church's temporal self-identity."

27. Kevin J. Vanhoozer, *The Drama of Doctrine: A Canonical-Linguistic Approach to Christian Theology* (Louisville, KY: Westminster John Knox Press, 2005), 350, 354, italics original. Olli-Pekka Vainio characterizes Lindbeck's theory of truth as "performative." See his *Beyond Fideism: Negotiable Religious Identities*, Transcending Boundaries in Philosophy and Theology Series (Surrey, UK: Ashgate, 2010), 72.

28. Luther famously makes experience necessary to becoming a theologian. See "Quae faciant theologum: 1. gratia Spiritus; 2. tentatio; 3. experientia; 4. occasio; 5. sedula lectio; 6. bonarum artium cognition," in WA TR 3:312.11–13 (no. 3425); cited in Oswald Bayer, *Theologie*, Handbuch systematischer Theologie 1 (Gütersloh: Gütersloher Verlagshaus, 1994), 57n107.

In Lindbeck's *Nature of Doctrine*, for example, "Schleiermacher" represents a theological position that "locate[s] ultimately significant contact with whatever is finally important to religion in the prereflective experiential depths of the self and regard[s] the public or outer features of religion as expressive and evocative objectifications (i.e., nondiscursive symbols) of internal experience."[29] Lindbeck interprets Schleiermacher's understanding of immediate self-consciousness as "prereflective experiential depths of the self," identified with a generic religious experience that would only at a later phase of religious differentiation be identified with a discourse specific to a particular religion. At stake here was Schleiermacher's ostensible failure to grant doctrine a preferred status as the expression of Christian truth that secured the church's identity across time. Schleiermacher's emphasis on psychology was said to be responsible for separating interiority and human experience from exteriority and the word of God.

The "problem of Schleiermacher," as I will refer in the pages ahead to the instrumentalization of a particular reading of Schleiermacher in contemporary discussions of theology and doctrine, orients the historical investigation of this book. What are the origins and what is the legacy of this reading of Schleiermacher? To answer this question, I turn to German theology as the starting point for twentieth-century theological reflection. The history of German theology cannot be told without situating it in its necessary relationship with German history and politics over the century, with the world crises of the two World Wars, the Shoah, and by the horrific destruction of life and landscape throughout Europe and Russia. So while my primary interlocutors are theologians writing in the North American context, I begin with issues that were at the forefront of European theology more than a century ago.

First and foremost, this means Luther. His role in the history of German theology, specifically his development of the notion of the "word" in theology, cannot be overestimated. The evolving theological conceptualization of the "word" had significant implications for the understanding of doctrine. The trajectory of this theological strand eventually extends into the early twentieth century, where it is contextualized and recontextualized several times over by the philosophy, theology, and politics of successive eras. The aim of my intellectual history is to probe these braidings of "word" with various conceptual approaches in different historical circumstances in order to better discern how assumptions about the relationship between doctrine and language have arisen and taken hold. We will see how, by the time we arrive at contemporary North American theology's conceptualization of word and doctrine, the semantic field of "doctrine" has come to be ruled by linguistic

29. Lindbeck, *Nature of Doctrine*, 21.

and epistemic interests. The telos of my argument is here: that as doctrine has moved away from reality into language, a development that reaches its apotheosis in the late twentieth century, doctrine loses its inner power.

While it may seem that the story ends with this, my argument is that this is the end of a chapter of a history; the end of doctrine so conceptualized opens the space for a new chapter in the evolving story of Christian doctrine. So the end of doctrine heralded in the title of this book also signals a beginning. What about doctrine reconceived as an invitation to consider and engage the living God, doctrine as a guide to discerning God's actions in individual lives, within communities, and in history? If this becomes the end of doctrine, "end" in the sense of its purpose and project, then there is no end to doctrine. The experience of surprise will become important in the closing pages of this book, for it is my avowed aim to reconceptualize doctrine in such a way that doctrine may acknowledge what is unexpected and surprising about the actions of the living God in history and personal experience. Hence the constructive portion of this book emphasizes the production rather than the reception of doctrine. Clearly these are not mutually exclusive: just as it is a reality of human life that we are always both subjects of our worlds and subject to them, so doctrine is always both received and produced, inherited and innovated.

Yet my focus at the end will be on doctrine as production. Again, while production presupposes and is intimately related to reception, it is production that discloses most clearly and strikingly how doctrine is (1) articulated by human beings in (2) the available light and language of their times, in order to address (3) a living and multifarious audience (4) and in relation to the circumstances of particular times and places, while at the same time always (5) aiming and yearning for transcendence. The making of doctrine is where and when terms are disputed, clarified, and defined; verbal formulas become caught up in the crossfire of ecclesiastical, political, and academic controversy; and there is wrangling over Greek and Latin conceptuality.[30] As we will see, an investigation into doctrine inevitably entails epistemological questions. Doctrines aim to have the status of knowledge about God, self, and world, in the sense of knowledge as making truth claims, and so the epistemological assumptions that inform theologians' conceptualization and articulation of doctrines must be identified and analyzed. Likewise the determination of content, which is also a dimension of doctrinal production, will make the

---

30. The classic study on the particular type of development that characterizes doctrine is by Cardinal John Henry Newman, *An Essay on the Development of Christian Doctrine* (1878; repr., Westminster, MD: Christian Classics, 1968); see also Maurice Wiles, *The Making of Christian Doctrine: A Study in the Principles of Early Doctrinal Development* (Cambridge: Cambridge University Press, 1967).

point that the production of doctrine's content is a process of negotiation among conceptual-intellectual, spiritual-mystical, and linguistic-literary resources. That theologians return over and over to the doctrines of Christ and Trinity is evidence that these doctrines represent endless fascination with the Christian God and the reality of this God in people's lives. As an academic discipline, theology's contribution to the production of these doctrines is a concern of this book.

Theology will be better able to negotiate a healthy—an intellectually productive and existentially compelling—relationship between academic commitments and the interests of Christians in the churches once it is able to recognize that its doctrines require creative and faithful attention to see that they partake of and contribute to the life-giving and life-sustaining effects of the gospel. If theology's goal is, as it ought to be, to "take every thought captive to obey Christ" (2 Cor. 10:5), then theology as the practice of disciplined and attentive thought helps prepare the way for God's truth (cf. Ps. 23:3) to come into church and world. What the all-too-human, all-too-fallible, and highly contested work of doctrine is about, in the last analysis, is how to refer to a God who is experienced and known by humans.

VI. A LOOK AHEAD

This book is constructed in two parts. The first, which is historical and diagnostic, is framed by the question Emil Brunner posed in 1924 in a scathing critique of Schleiermacher. To make Brunner's question my own, I ask: Why is Schleiermacher criticized for conflating a (naturalist) philosophy of identity with mysticism, and then for appropriating this conflation as the philosophical ground to his theology? Brunner charged that Schleiermacher betrayed Christian theology to an alien philosophy and that he translated the goods and graces of theology into the cultural idioms of the early nineteenth century. The critical terms in play here are rather perplexing when compared to Schleiermacher's actual understanding of theology and religious experience. Still, the issue of reality and language became a problem for contemporary theology with Brunner, as discussed in chapter 2, "From Ritschl to Brunner: Neither Mysticism nor Metaphysics, but the Problem with Schleiermacher," and more so in the theology of the twentieth century, as traced from Karl Barth to contemporary theology in chapter 3, "From Trinitarian Representation to the Epistemic-Advantage Model: Word, Doctrine, Theology."

Throughout the discussion I pay close attention to the role of reality and language in theology and its implication for doctrine. I argue that doctrine has been increasingly understood in its affinity to language. Setting the terms for this developing view was the philosophical framework dominant at the turn of the twentieth century, neo-Kantianism. Later in the twentieth century, doctrine was increasingly conceptualized in terms of its function within a worldview. This part ends by pointing the way ahead to a new conception of the relationship of word and reality, which will orient the constructive section in the second part of the book.

Chapter 4, "Language and Reality: A Theological Epistemology with Some Help from Schleiermacher," proposes a methodology for connecting word to reality. Here I proceed in conversation with Schleiermacher, an old interlocutor of mine. I am at special pains to reconstruct the theological epistemology that I think informs Schleiermacher's understanding of the New Testament. My aim is to show how, in Schleiermacher's view, the earliest layers of the New Testament are related to specific popular experiences of Jesus of Nazareth and then subsequently how these early acclamations serve as parameters for the development of Christian doctrine. The production of doctrine emerges from this account as that which witnesses to Christ's transformative effect as the living reality of Christianity while remaining open to individual meaning-making and intersubjective discussion. Doctrinal production is not coopted on a single level of experience or thought.

The final chapter, "Acknowledging Social Construction and Moving beyond Deconstruction: Doctrine for Theology and Religious Studies," extends the epistemological and biblical focus of chapter 4 by situating the production of doctrine between theology and religious studies. If doctrine is inevitably social construction, then the relevant questions should concern the ways in which doctrine is articulated in such a way as to be adequate both to the divine reality it seeks to attest and to the historical reality that shapes its formulations. The focus of this last chapter, in other words, concerns the recovery of divine and human reality as constitutive aspects of doctrinal production. In this regard, theology can align itself with new currents in religious studies that likewise evidence concern with the reality of human experience's religious dimension. As religious studies seeks to move beyond the reductionism of the discipline, it may be viewed as a resource for theology's attempts to address religious experience as that experience witnesses to the reality of God. Theology does not need to constrict reason by holding doctrine captive to an epistemically primary proposition; it can set reason free to recover the reality of doctrine's content from history, metaphysics, and experience. When doctrine is opened to the particular reality of God and God's engagement with humanity in the world, its articulation bears witness to a living Christian faith. It is thus to the life of doctrine that this book intends to point.

2

From Ritschl to Brunner

Neither Mysticism nor Metaphysics,
but the Problem with Schleiermacher

I. WHAT DOES DOCTRINE MEAN?

The word "doctrine" in Christian theological discourse and popular usage connotes stability. Political empires rise and fall, but doctrine endures. Doctrines secure the identity of the church. So Lutherans, for example, assert justification as the article "by which the church stands or falls."[1] In this chapter I thus begin with a key question: what gives doctrine this reputation for stability across time and space? Doctrine is said to be concerned with the truth of the eternal God as exhibited by the unique and indispensable adjectives that have accrued to the word "doctrine" over time. "True doctrine" (*vera doctrina*) marked doctrine's function as a norm of truth, the standard by which all church preaching and teaching is measured. Doctrine is sacred (*sacra doctrina*). It recognizes God as its source; and like Sacred Scripture, doctrine contains the knowledge that God has revealed about divine nature and about the divine perspective on self and world. In the sixteenth century, the Lutheran Reformers held that doctrine is also pure[2] and sound.[3] Stripped of the accretions that human traditions and interpretations have added to it, doctrine is synonymous with the truth of the gospel.

These connotations—truth, sacredness, and purity—focus our attention on a term that is remarkably flexible in its meanings, usages, and associations.

---

1. See Theodor Mahlmann, "Articulus stantis et (vel) cadentis ecclesiae," in *RGG* 1:799–800.

2. Article 7 in the Augsburg Confession (1530), in *BC* 177.20, refers to the pure doctrine of the gospel (*pura doctrina evangelii*).

3. *LW* 12:407, from *Commentary on Psalm 51* (1532/1538): "Therefore prayer is necessary to keep sound doctrine among the people against such men."

As the editors of an anthology on the history of the term "doctrine" write, "What does one do with an expression that is not defined, [is] ambiguous, and [is] omnipresent, and that over-represents a content deemed essential by all those who use the term?"[4] Derived from the Latin root verb *docere*, doctrine may be defined simply as "teaching" (in Latin *doctrina*, in German *Lehre*). This opens out to further implications and meanings. "Teaching" is related to the one who teaches. "Teachers" are "doctors," whether physicians or doctors of the church (*doctores ecclesiae*). When speaking of sacred doctrine, Christ may be referred to as "divine teacher" and God as "revealer." Teachers impart knowledge. *Doctrina* is also translated into German as *Wissen*, the root of the academic designation *Wissenschaft*, or science. Knowledge considered from this perspective, *Wissenschaft*, has to do with both content and pedagogy, the ways in which knowledge is communicated. In relation to Christian pedagogy, communication occurs in the genres of catechism and confession. The personal confession "I believe" and the ecclesial declaration "We believe," for example, are oral communications of the knowledge of Christian faith. These words are repeated again and again in order to cultivate belief. Confession as a communicative practice arose from the catechetical genre of question and answer that was used in early Christian communities as they initiated neophytes into the basics of the faith. The cultivation of doctrine as an ecclesial activity is thus essentially related to the way in which doctrine is learned and confessed.

Doctrine is also a content that may be studied with the research tools of theology—*must* be studied, indeed, if the church is to understand its doctrinal identity. This is one of theology's tasks, to study doctrine. Theology is responsible for examining the historical origins under which doctrine(s) arose and to interpret the truth of doctrine(s) for a living church in its contemporary contexts. Theology approaches doctrine as a body of knowledge. The theological study of doctrine selects and organizes its disparate content into a whole. The medieval *summa*, the early modern *loci communes* (commonplaces), and modern systematics—all are theological genres that exhibit the aim of imparting a coherent and comprehensive unity among individual doctrines. This theological effort does not eliminate internal divergence or disagreement. Rather, it is a way, born of the compelling desire for the unity of truth and knowledge, of organizing multiplicity.

For all its challenging complexity, until recently doctrine has not been the subject of meta-reflection, as German historian Theodor Mahlmann writes.

---

4. Philippe Büttgen, Ruedi Imbach, Ulrich Johannes Schneider, and Herman J. Selderhuis, "Einleitung/Introduction," in *Vera Doctrina: Zur Begriffsgeschichte der Lehre von Augustinus bis Descartes / L'idée de doctrine d'Augustin à Descartes*, ed. Philippe Büttgen et al., Wolfenbütteler Forschungen 123 (Wiesbaden: Harrassowitz Verlag, 2009), 19, my ET.

This fact of Christian intellectual history was one reason for the great impact of American theologian George Lindbeck's *The Nature of Doctrine* in the English-speaking world (from 1984) and beyond, following its 1994 translation into German.[5] Especially important, as Mahlmann rightly says, was Lindbeck's aim of relating doctrine to ancillary concepts of theology and church within the framework of a particular understanding of religion as a cultural system, an understanding derived from anthropologist Clifford Geertz.[6] With this move, Lindbeck hoped to resolve the ecumenical impasse between Lutherans and Roman Catholics by opening up the possibility for engaging difference in terms of conceptual frameworks rather than isolated propositions, while at the same time preserving the goal of a "visible Christian unity" in terms of allegiance to common "historic doctrines."[7]

The work's ecumenical purposes opened up further questions in the conceptualization of doctrine so that *The Nature of Doctrine* initiated a wider discussion about doctrine's role in establishing the central commitments of the Christian community as linguistic-literary articulations. Doctrines are significant, Lindbeck argued, for establishing church identity, for determining the truth-criteria by which Scripture is to be read, and for demonstrating the common allegiances of the one church.[8] Lindbeck's cultural-linguistic approach to Christianity situated doctrine in a discourse that embraced church, truth,

---

5. George A. Lindbeck, *Christliche Lehre als Grammatik des Glaubens: Religion und Theologie im postliberalen Zeitalter*, trans. Markus Müller, intro. Hans G. Ulrich and Reinhard Hütter, Theologische Bücherei 90 (Gütersloh: Gütersloher Verlagshaus, 1994). Bruce D. Marshall notes that Lindbeck's book has also been translated into Chinese, Japanese, French, and Italian. See his "Introduction: *The Nature of Doctrine* after 25 Years," in George A. Lindbeck, *The Nature of Doctrine*, 25th anniversary ed. (Louisville, KY: Westminster John Knox Press, 2009), vii.

6. Theodor Mahlmann, "*Doctrina* im Verständnis nachreformatorischer lutherischer Theologen," in Philippe Büttgen et al., *Vera Doctrina*, 200.

7. George A. Lindbeck, "Foreword to the German Edition of *The Nature of Doctrine*," in *The Nature of Doctrine* (2009), xxx: "The purpose is not to legislate doctrinally, but to explore the mutual immanence of the changeability and unchangeability of Christian doctrine in order to make it conceptually easier to combine commitments to the search for Church unity with faithfulness to historic creeds and confessions. . . . The book, to repeat, is pretheological, and I naïvely supposed it would be interesting chiefly to doctrinally committed ecumenists."

8. Bruce Marshall states the reason for the impact of Lindbeck's book in more polemical terms, emphasizing the intellectual viability of traditional Christian theology against what is assumed to be the position of "theological liberalism" ("Introduction," in Lindbeck, *Nature of Doctrine* [2009], xii): "Perhaps the deepest attraction of *The Nature of Doctrine* has lain in the provocative conviction that communities committed to traditional Christian doctrine and identity need not be intellectually retrograde but can be entirely up-to-date—indeed, that theological liberalism's flight from traditional Christian teaching is itself intellectually out-of-date."

identity, and language. As a result these terms have become so thoroughly bound up with the discourse of doctrine that they have come to be identified with its meanings.

But today's discussions of doctrine are accompanied by an unease articulated in polemics, much of it focused on nineteenth-century German theologian Friedrich Schleiermacher, or on "Schleiermacher" as the name for a problem. That Schleiermacher has become the fall guy for a certain strain of contemporary Christian theology is intriguing. Why does a polemic against Schleiermacher's "experiential expressivism"—or as theologian Bruce Marshall writes, his "interiority thesis, . . . [which means that] Christian beliefs may be justified by appeal to inner experiences, upon which depend the contents of the beliefs and the meaning of the sentences which express them"—invariably accompany discussions of doctrine?[9]

I use what I call "the problem of Schleiermacher" as an entry point into the recent history of theology. My purpose in doing so is to figure out why doctrine has come to have the meanings it has today and why the various terms in the discourse on doctrine must construct Schleiermacher as necessary opponent, the stone on which the discourse of doctrine is ground. This chapter, then, looks at a particularly influential piece of the history of Western Protestant theology to determine the fate of doctrine as it becomes more and more associated with language and communal identity. The overarching question is *why* certain associations have come to accrue to doctrine. As we will see, (1) the term "word," widely prevalent in Protestant theology, only emerges as significant within the time frame I will identify; and (2) by the time it emerges, "word" has come to be associated with particular concepts, "spirit" and "objectivity," which in turn appeared around the turn of the twentieth century in discussions of the reality of God and of human nature.

A common place to begin a review of the topic of "word of God" is with the thought of Karl Barth, who from his earliest publications is the best-known critic of Schleiermacher.[10] Barth's polemic presupposed a theological position that set the word of God in opposition to human culture, politics, and history. In constructing this argument, Barth made constructive-theological use of a

---

9. Lindbeck, *Nature of Doctrine* (1984), 20–21; Bruce D. Marshall, *Trinity and Truth*, Cambridge Studies in Christian Doctrine (Cambridge: Cambridge University Press, 2000), 54.

10. Barth makes this respectful yet devastating criticism in 1917: "Our grandfathers were certainly right when they fought so fiercely for the Bible as revelation and not just religion, particularly when they did not let this truth be turned upside-down, even by so pious and astute a man as Schleiermacher" (Karl Barth, "The New Word in the Bible (1917)," in *The Word of God and Theology*, trans. Amy Marga [London: T&T Clark, 2011], 25).

dichotomy that was already evident in the theological currents of the 1910s, long after Schleiermacher had introduced his understanding of the relation of language and experience in his own system of theology, *The Christian Faith* of 1830/31. So rather than beginning with Barth, I will look at some figures before and around Barth, who discuss the theological question of reality in relation to word, with the aim of seeing how this discussion ends up casting Schleiermacher in terms of the dichotomy between word and experience.

The story begins with a period in German theology's history at the turn of the twentieth century, before the First World War, when theologians were preoccupied again with the doctrine of justification. Albrecht Ritschl (1822–89), a Lutheran theologian writing during the Bismarck era of German politics and influential for future generations of German theology, made justification, the central doctrine of Lutheranism, into the cornerstone of his constructive theology. His inquiries into the doctrine of justification brought him to a profound engagement with its history and then to a serious revision of the doctrine's metaphysical aspects. The result was a reconsideration of the *mediation* of justification to the sinner. To contemporary theologians, this may seem an obvious point about the doctrine of justification, especially as it concerns the word of God. But when one looks back at Ritschl, it becomes evident that the question of mediating justification to the sinner is not obvious at all. Ritschl critically appropriated the doctrine as it had been formalized in Protestant orthodoxy and reconceptualized it according to the terms of a theological discussion dominated by the neo-Kantian categories of nature and spirit. The introduction of these categories into the discourse of justification was consequential for instituting a debate among Ritschl's followers concerning the question of mediation. This turned on the relation of the word "justification" to mystical experience. Was justification available in experience, specifically as a mystical relationship with Christ? Or was it mediated by the word? In the generation after Ritschl, two important theologians, Max Reischle (1858–1905) and Cajus Fabricius (1884–1950), took up this question. As we will see, the particular polemic against mysticism and metaphysics with which Ritschl framed his constructive theology complicated the debate over justification. Standing at the end of the trajectory that concerns me is the Swiss Reformed theologian Emil Brunner (1889–1966), an early proponent of dialectical theology. Brunner framed his entire attack against Schleiermacher in terms of the word of God, which Brunner understood as being in exclusive and decisive opposition both to human mystical experience and to the metaphysics of German Idealism. Brunner's position demonstrates how far he traveled theologically from Ritschl. The nature/spirit relation that informed Ritschl's theology is torn asunder when Brunner puts the word of God in opposition to nature. Spirit comes to be associated with the word, which is the divine reality that stands against human reality. Justification and judgment are mediated by the word.

This history begins with Ritschl's new understanding of the doctrine of justification in neo-Kantian terms, which is to say, with Ritschl's contribution to the increasing attention that would be paid to the word of God.

II. RITSCHL AND THE DOCTRINE OF JUSTIFICATION

Scholarship on Ritschl has changed significantly since I first became interested in his thought a decade ago. Although a few of the older studies remain relevant, more recent discussions of his historical and constructive achievements shed new light on the profound innovativeness of his thought.[11] This reevaluation occurs as scholarship in the history of theology begins to rethink the polemical stances taken against the liberal (as they came to be called) German Protestant theologians of the nineteenth century. It has become clearer that the theologians working in this period were ingenious in creating paths forward for a theology that would exert a powerful and enduring intellectual influence even over its most vocal critics. Especially productive in this period was the theological adaptation and appropriation of two areas of discussion: first, the turn to history, namely, to Christian origins and to the history of dogma (a field of inquiry of which Ritschl was a leading and brilliant practitioner); second, the emergence of a set of questions surrounding a return to the (German Lutheran) philosopher Immanuel Kant. This latter development had broad implications for understanding claims to knowledge in the sciences, for the emergence of the concept of culture in philosophical and theological discussion, and for the reworking of Kant's ideas on ethics and religion. Neo-Kantianism had a wide impact on the sciences and humanities. It also deeply shaped the way theologians conceptualized and discussed their subject matter. I want to situate the concern with knowledge and reality, placing it in the context of these particular discussions, specifically as Ritschl opened them up for Protestant theology.

Ritschl wrote in the period before the First World War. The long monarchy of Wilhelm I, King of Prussia, was the setting for Otto von Bismarck's campaigns to consolidate German power in Prussia.[12] Ritschl began his career in this

---

11. For an introduction to Ritschl's biography and academic achievements, including a survey of the most important literature written about Ritschl over the past decade, see Christophe Chalamet, "Reassessing Albrecht Ritschl's Theology: A Survey of Recent Literature," *Religion Compass* 2, no. 4 (2008): 620–41. Chalamet cites the studies of Philip Hefner, Darrell Jodock, and Helga Kuhlmann as important foundations for contemporary work on Ritschl.

12. See the recent biography by Jonathan Steinberg, *Bismarck: A Life* (New York:

turbulent environment as a New Testament scholar before becoming professor of dogmatic theology at the University of Göttingen in 1864. His thought, as it developed, staked out a position in the robust intellectual and ecclesial debates of the time among theological liberals, orthodox confessional Lutherans, and Pietists, and with the theologians that sought to mediate among these viewpoints. Ritschl publicly articulated his theological agenda on the quadricentennial of Luther's birthday, November 10, 1883. As was expected on such an occasion, Ritschl outlined his program by attaching it to the reformer's vision, announcing rather ambitiously that he would "complete" Luther's reformation.[13] Ritschl set about to fulfill this promise by writing, among other texts, a study of the doctrine long identified as the heart of Lutheran theology: justification. Scholars today regard the three volumes of Ritschl's *The Christian Doctrine of Justification and Reconciliation*[14] as the work that defines Ritschl's theological legacy.

But Ritschl's constructive contributions had perforce to contend with the various theological controversies swirling around him. After 1880 his effort to "complete" the Reformation proceeded via a polemical engagement with both Pietists and confessional Lutherans. In this debate, Ritschl's stance is captured by the famous dictum "No metaphysics, no mysticism" in theology.[15] The polemic may sound hyperbolic to contemporary ears, but it captures the critical and even metaphysical dimension of Ritschl's explanation of the doctrine of justification in new terms.

II.1. Righteousness and Justification

Justification as the central Lutheran doctrine has to do with a divine attribute, the righteousness of God (Rom 1:17), which the apostle Paul argues is given

---

Oxford University Press, 2011); and the review by David Blackbourn from March 19, 2011, in *The Guardian*, http://www.theguardian.com/books/2011/mar/19/bismarck-life-jonathan-steinberg-review.

13. Albrecht Ritschl, "Festrede am vierten Seculartage der Geburt Martin Luthers," in *Kleine Schriften*, ed. Frank Hofmann, Theologische Studien-Texte 4 (Waltrop: Hartmut Spenner, 1999), 173.

14. Albrecht Ritschl, *Die christliche Lehre von der Rechtfertigung und Versöhnung* (1870–), 3rd ed., 3 vols. (Bonn: Adolph Marcus, 1889). Only vols. 1 and 3 have appeared in ET: vol. 1 as *A Critical History of the Christian Doctrine of Justification and Reconciliation*, trans. J. S. Black (Edinburgh: Edmonston & Douglas, 1872); vol. 3 as *The Christian Doctrine of Justification and Reconciliation: The Positive Development of the Doctrine*, trans. H. R. Mackintosh and A. B. Macaulay (Edinburgh: T&T Clark, 1900).

15. "'Keine Metaphysik in der Theologie!' und 'keine Mystik in der Theologie!'": Max Reischle's paraphrase of Ritschl's programmatic statement appears in his *Ein Wort zur Controverse über die Mystik in der Theologie* (Freiburg im Breisgau: J. C. B. Mohr [Paul Siebeck], 1886), 5. (In this chapter all ETs of German text are mine unless otherwise indicated.)

to the believer in Christ (cf. Rom. 4:5), who receives this new reality in faith, thus inheriting the forgiveness of sins and a change of heart. The "righteousness of Christ, or of faith" is the topic of article 3 in the Solid Declaration of the Formula of Concord, the confessional text for Lutherans that was signed in 1577, first published in 1580.[16] "Righteousness" is significant for the doctrine of justification because it is the divine attribute that God gives to the sinner. The gift effects the sinner's forgiveness; the sinner is made righteous through Christ's righteousness. Because righteousness is a divine attribute and *as such* is the cause of the forgiveness of sins, it is termed the sinner's "alien" righteousness. By faith, this alien righteousness becomes the believer's righteousness, yet it remains God's attribute. The question left open concerns the way in which God's righteousness is given to the sinner. The Solid Declaration mentions two senses of the term "righteousness" that seem to be in tension with each other. This tension, between a "forensic" notion and an "essential" righteousness, would affect the way in which Ritschl came to revise the doctrine of justification at the turn of the twentieth century.

The Solid Declaration actually follows the Lutheran Reformers in outlining these two senses of the term righteousness. The first, the *forensic* view, was associated with Philipp Melanchthon's theology of justification, which has it created by God through faith and imputed to the sinner, rendering the sinner righteous before God. This righteousness, by which sinners are "justified by faith," is "conveyed to us by the Holy Spirit through the gospel and in the sacraments."[17] In this sense righteousness is *performative*, as modern theologian Oswald Bayer insists.[18] The word does what it says. It is a pronouncement of the freedom from sin that is mediated through the proclamation of the gospel and in the sacraments of baptism and the Lord's Supper.

But the doctrine of justification includes righteousness in a second sense, which Theodor Dieter has shown is part of Luther's own view. For Luther, the second aspect of justification is the gift of the Holy Spirit, which "produces new movements of the soul, new desires and affections, in the believer." This adds to the concept of justification a transformation in the "substance of the believer's will, her desires, and actions."[19] The Solid Declaration terms this "the righteousness of new obedience or good works," or more clearly, "essential righteousness."[20] The appearance of a metaphysical term (the adjective "essential") might seem strange to contemporary Lutherans socialized

---

16. "Formula of Concord, Solid Declaration, Art. III," in *BC* 562–73.

17. *BC* 564.12, 17.

18. Oswald Bayer, *Martin Luther's Theology: A Contemporary Interpretation*, trans. Thomas H. Trapp (Grand Rapids: Eerdmans, 2008), 102.

19. Dieter, "Luther's Doctrine of Justification," 199.

20. *BC* 567.32; 571.54.

into thinking that forensic justification forbids a notion of righteousness that connotes a transformation of human desires and behaviors. But as Luther and his early interpreters understood it, the metaphysical designation refers only to the beginning of a process of renewal. Regarded as the gift of the Holy Spirit, righteousness contributes to a lifelong process of personal and social transformation.

The problem of the relationship between the two senses of "righteousness" is already implicit in the Solid Declaration's insistence on the distinction between them. Only when the sinner is imputed the righteousness of Christ's obedience in the forensic sense, only then "can [one] stand before God's tribunal."[21] Yet the righteousness by which the sinner is declared just before God must not be confused with the notion of essential righteousness as the Spirit's indwelling.[22] A question arises at this juncture: if the first sense of righteousness, the forensic, counts for the sinner's justification, what is the role of essential righteousness in justification?

In the late seventeenth and eighteenth centuries, Lutheran orthodox dogmatic theologians resolved this dilemma by separating the two senses of righteousness. This becomes evident at the points where the biblical language of indwelling originally used to explicate essential righteousness resurfaces. The orthodox theologians took the terminology of Trinitarian indwelling from a number of New Testament passages (e.g., John 14:23; 1 Cor. 6:15, 17; Gal. 3:27; 2:19, 20; Eph. 5:30; 2 Pet. 1:4) to mean essential righteousness. They then moved the concept of essential righteousness from its original location in the Formula of Concord—the section on justification—and relocated it to a new section, the "order of salvation" (*ordo salutis*). The passages on Trinitarian indwelling are specifically cited in the section on the mystical union toward the end of the *ordo salutis*.[23] The Lutheran orthodox theologians had devoted an entire additional doctrinal section to the process of renewal begun with justification. The *ordo salutis* stipulates a sequence of effects of justification that would much later come to be identified as the doctrine of sanctification.

The revised ordering can be seen in editor Heinrich Schmid's reconstruction of the dogmatic systems of Lutheran orthodoxy. Schmid integrated a diverse group of seventeenth- and eighteenth-century Lutheran dogmatic systems and reconstructed the ordering of doctrinal loci. His section 43 follows the section on justification (identified as §42) and introduces the *ordo salutis* with the heading "Concomitants and consequences of justifying

---

21. *BC* 567.32.

22. *BC* 571–72.54.

23. These passages are found in §47 (on the mystical union) in Heinrich Schmid, ed., *The Doctrinal Theology of the Evangelical Lutheran Church*, trans. Charles A. Hay and Henry E. Jacobs, 3rd ed. (Minneapolis: Augsburg, 1961), 480.

faith." He summarized the intention of the following section in these terms:
"Having discussed *faith* as the means by which we partake of salvation, and
justification as the effect of faith, there remain to be described the internal
conditions and the moral change which occur in man at the same time with
and after justification."[24] The five steps of the *ordo salutis* are understood as
the effects of justifying faith and are described in sections 43–48 as follows:
44 is on vocation (*vocatio*), 45 on illumination (*illuminatio*), 46 on regeneration and conversion (*regeneratio et conversio*), 47 on the mystical union
(*unio mystica*), and 48 on renovation (*renovatio*).[25] The Trinitarian indwelling
is assigned to the mystical union, directly before renovation. The mystical
union consists of the "peculiar union of God" with the "justified or regener-
ate" that constitutes "the direct operation of both these acts of divine grace
[justification and regeneration.]"[26] So rather than occurring as the second
aspect of justification, the Trinitarian indwelling is relocated from its connection to justification and moved down the line, so to speak, to the next
doctrinal section, the order of salvation.

The repositioning of indwelling with the concomitant loss of its connection to justification would emerge as the chief object of Ritschl's theological
revisions. When he announced his aim of completing Luther's reformation,
Ritschl had in mind specifically the ethical as a necessary implication of justification. It would be the Lutheran philosopher Immanuel Kant who would
aid in moving theology beyond Lutheran orthodoxy into a new period of
fertile discussion. Connecting justification to reconciliation would complete
the doctrine of justification.

II.2. A New Take on Justification

The next question crucial for this story concerns the fate of the mystical union
in Ritschl's updating of Lutheran theology, specifically, the doctrine of justification amid the intellectual and political ferment of the turn of the twentieth
century. This is important because it raises the issue of how Ritschl reconfigures justification against the backdrop of the polemic against accounts of mystical union while at the same time connecting justification to changes in the

24. Schmid, *Doctrinal Theology*, 441, italics original. Schmid's reconstruction was
criticized by Carl Heinz Ratschow, who proposed another order to the doctrinal loci.
Unfortunately Ratschow died before completing his research on these dogmatic systems and was only able to work on the first two volumes: Prolegomena and Book I
(doctrine of God). See his *Lutherische Dogmatik zwischen Reformation und Aufklärung*, 2
vols. (Gütersloh: Gütersloher Verlagshaus Gerd Mohn, 1964, 1966).

25. Schmid, *Doctrinal Theology*, 442–91.

26. Ibid., 480.

Christian life intended by the *ordo salutis* according to Protestant orthodoxy. Justification continues to be related to the effects it promotes in the justified sinner's life. But, as we will see, the specific conceptual framework that Ritschl uses to articulate justification in close relation to its effects initiates a new way of couching the reality created by justification. This section of the historical trajectory I am tracing asks how early twentieth-century neo-Kantianism was significant for Ritschl. To anticipate what is to follow here, Ritschl appropriates the neo-Kantian distinction between nature and spirit as the key category for framing the doctrine of justification. "Nature" and "spirit" will prove to be crucial terms for showing how theologians after Ritschl understand the reality of God meeting the reality of the human person in the event of justification.

There was great interest among scholars in the second half of the nineteenth century in recovering Kant's critical theory, in particular his epistemology and logic, for the purpose of articulating new theories of *Wissenschaft* (science). The question at issue for science in this period had to do with how the empirical sciences might be grounded in a transcendental structure that would unify the sciences as it provided them with a coherent metatheory of science. There was also interest in identifying the distinctive ground of the knowledge produced in the cultural sciences or humanities to avoid reducing all knowledge to the natural sciences. Theologians became concerned with theology's claims to knowledge, with its status as *Wissenschaft*, in relation to the sciences. Yet as it developed, the problem was Kant's reduction of religion to a ground in ethics. This was the intellectual context within which Ritschl worked.[27]

Ritschl's response was to reverse the order: ethics requires the doctrine of justification as its ground. As contemporary theologian Alexander Heit has recently argued, by reconstructing the doctrine of justification as the ground of ethics, Ritschl showed that justification was significant for Kant's thoughts on religion.[28] Furthermore, Ritschl's engagement with Kant was crucial for bringing ethics into systematic-theological relation with justification. The key text for analysis here is Ritschl's *Theology and Metaphysics: Towards Comprehension and Resistance*, a short treatise he wrote near the end of his life. It was

27. Andrew Chignell writes on the significance of neo-Kantianism for German intellectual history: "Still, by the turn of the [twentieth] century Neo-Kantianism had become a powerful philosophical movement, and by the early teens it was the dominant *Schulphilosophie* in much of the German academy" ("Introduction: On Going Back to Kant," *The Philosophical Forum* 39, no. 2 [June 2008]: 118).

28. See the excellent study of justification as organizing principle of Kant's theory of religion in Alexander Heit, *Versöhnte Vernunft: Eine Studie zur systematischen Bedeutung des Rechtfertigungsgedankens für Kants Religionsphilosophie*, Forschungen zur systematischen und ökumenischen Theologie 115 (Göttingen: Vandenhoeck & Ruprecht, 2006).

first published in 1881 and reissued in relatively unchanged form in 1887.[29] In this work Ritschl provides an account of the conceptual shift he is promoting in the doctrine of justification.

Ritschl composed *Theology and Metaphysics* during a break from writing his multivolume study of Pietism, a ten-year project that set the largely unsympathetic terms within which Pietism would be approached for the next century. The contemporaneity of these two projects draws attention to Ritschl's polemic against mysticism in Pietism and Lutheran orthodoxy. In the constructive contribution of *Theology and Metaphysics*, Ritschl couched his polemic in terms of the goal or end of religion. He defined the problem of goal as having to do with understanding the "task of Christianity." Kant had understood religion generally as an orientation to the "highest good." If this is religion's task, to define the highest good, then Christianity has a special place among the religions in determining this highest good from the perspective of revelation in Jesus Christ.[30] The highest good revealed in Christ is the purpose for which God created the world: transformation of the world into the kingdom of God. While the revelation of the highest good includes a supernatural dimension—the establishing of the highest good is ultimately God's action—the revelation invites Christian participation in ethical action that is oriented to the transformation of the world. Ritschl's constructive contribution to theology was to explain how justification establishes this new outlook and thereby orients justified sinners "as members of the kingdom of God to [be] subjects of the will of love," in short, to engage in ethical action.

Ritschl's complaint against mysticism is that it compromises the goal of Christianity. Discussing the eighteenth-century Protestant mystic Gottfried Arnold, Ritschl explains that Arnold's narrative of progression from "ethics" to "physics," which Arnold posited as two moments on a mystical path to the knowledge of God, ends up denying that an orientation to the "above-natural and above-worldly" "kingdom of God" determines the goal of human life.[31] On Ritschl's construal, Arnold makes the goal of Christianity the knowledge of God rather than participation in the ethical action that contributes to the transformation of the world. Thus Arnold becomes the foil for Ritschl's

29. Albrecht Ritschl, *Theologie und Metaphysik: Zur Verständigung und Abwehr*, 2nd ed. (Bonn: Adolph Marcus, 1887); repr., idem, *Kleine Schriften*, ed. Frank Hofmann, Theologische Studien-Texte 4 (Waltrop: Hartmut Spenner, 1999), 68–142; citations of this work below are to the reprint edition. For the ET by Philip Hefner, see Albrecht Ritschl, *Theology and Metaphysics*, in *Three Essays* (Philadelphia: Fortress Press, 1972), 149–217.

30. Ritschl, *Theologie und Metaphysik*, 81–83; see also Heit, *Versöhnte Vernunft*, 244.

31. Ritschl, *Theologie und Metaphysik*, 96–97.

argument that orienting Christians to God's kingdom is precisely the role of justification in human life.[32]

In discussing Lutheran orthodoxy, Ritschl adds another reason why mysticism presents a problem for the doctrine of justification. He argues that the Formula of Concord, in taking the notion of Trinitarian indwelling as the explanation for good works via the mystical union, adds a new doctrine in addition to justification. In Ritschl's view, the doctrine of justification itself must include the ethical dimension rather than allocating ethics to a separate doctrine. Ritschl thinks that the addition of a new doctrine ends up denying the active, practical effects of justification as the ground of good works.[33] He understood his own work on justification as doing justice to what he conceived as the original intention of the Formula of Concord—justification as the ground of ethical action—thus orienting Lutheran theology to a goal determined from the perspective of its practical end.

Ritschl's concern in packing an ethical orientation into the doctrine of justification reveals his shift to a neo-Kantian perspective. Here his polemic against what he has construed as the problematic view of mysticism in terms of a contemplative goal for religion is correlated with a polemic against metaphysics. Both mysticism and metaphysics resort to a problematic view of justification that has to do with the "*Ding-an-sich* [thing-in-itself]." The problem with Kant's *Ding-an-sich* was of central concern to the neo-Kantians, who were typically trying to get rid of the noumenal realm as a collection of mind-independent things, instead regarding our "natural" and "spiritual" categories as mapping different ways of apprehending the world that is given to us.[34] Thus Ritschl's polemic against the *Ding-an-sich* as a substance that has an occult reality, behind the way the substance appears to human perception, is concurrent with the neo-Kantian consensus that knowledge derives from reality as it is given to human understanding.[35] In this way the turn to the empirical sciences informs Ritschl's explicit polemic against Hegel's

32. Ritschl distinguishes between "natural morality" or the culturally specific moral norms and ethics: *Sittlichkeit*. By ethics Ritschl means a theological-anthropological determination of the human person that can explain human thought and action.

33. For the detailed critique against proponents of Protestant orthodoxy, see Ritschl, *Theologie und Metaphysik*, 124–25.

34. My thanks for helping me on this point go to Professor Andrew Chignell (personal correspondence, May 16, 2013).

35. Ritschl writes, "There is such a close affinity between mysticism and this metaphysics that it is the same thing whether one attributes to particular statements a mysticism or a false metaphysic" (Ritschl, *Theologie und Metaphysik*, 94). The polemic is quite intense, as here: "Mysticism is the practice of Neoplatonic metaphysics. It is the theoretical norm of the alleged mystical delight in God. Hence the universal being viewed as God with whom the mystic longs to be united is a cheat" (95).

terminology of God as absolute substance. On his reading of Hegel, Ritschl seems to imply that Hegel's God is a *Ding-an-sich*, and therefore God cannot be known as the carrier of metaphysical attributes apart from the way the attributes are given to human beings, specifically in Christian revelation as love. [36] Thus on Ritschl's understanding, God's revelation is the only way in which the divine attributes can be apprehended. Likewise, Ritschl understands the soul as a function of capacities that can be perceived, such as thinking, feeling, and willing.[37] Apart from its functions, the soul cannot be known.

With this shift from substance to a subject that is given to be known, Ritschl introduces a metaphysic faithful to the neo-Kantian commitment to an empirical outlook. The neo-Kantian approach to metaphysics had to do with inquiry into the fundamental categories of human knowing (*Erkenntis*). These categories disclose how self, God, and the world are given to human knowing in terms of their functions and actions. It is on this basis that Ritschl frames his theological approach to justification in terms of its effects on the human functions of thinking, feeling, and willing, as well his understanding of the orientation of justification to the goal of human action. The neo-Kantian metaphysic helps connect justification with the kingdom of God. When Christians are transformed by God's justifying action, their human functions are the empirical sites where justification has an effect. The transformation through justification is empirically given in thinking, feeling, and willing. Yet transformation is oriented toward the distinct goal—the kingdom of God. Thus neo-Kantian thought helps Ritschl rewrite the doctrine of justification in intimate relation to an ethical goal.

Another category significant for understanding how Ritschl conceives of justification in relation to the new reality of the kingdom of God is that of "spiritual mastery over the world," the sovereignty of spirit over nature.[38] This category is crucial to the trajectory I will trace in later sections of this chapter. While the terms "spirit" and "nature" appear in a specific hierarchy in the doctrine of justification, they are actually the building blocks of neo-Kantian metaphysics, associated with its southwestern German school.[39]

---

36. Ibid., 85.

37. Ibid., 118–19.

38. Ibid., 98.

39. Neo-Kantianism is identified by two distinct schools: the Marburg school, dealing with empirical and natural sciences; and the southwestern Baden school, interested in the humanities. This latter school employed the categories of nature and spirit and discussed spirit's function in culture, religion, and philosophy. Philosophical research on neo-Kantianism is only now beginning to take shape, although there is much work that still needs to be done. See two recent contributions: Andrew Chignell, Terence Irwin, and Thomas Teufel, eds., special edition on Neo-Kantianism, *Philosophical*

Ritschl introduces the terms "spirit" and "nature" at the beginning of *Theology and Metaphysics,* showing how, in consensus with neo-Kantianism, the categories inform the epistemological structure that grasps the world as it is given to human knowing. Nature and spirit are the a priori concepts that organize two kinds of reality in one world.[40] Nature (*Natur*) has to do with the objects of the natural sciences, those things that cause effects. It is the realm of human experience and social relations that is organized by the categories of cause and effect. Spirit (*Geist*), on the other hand, refers to functions of the mind, such as the capacity for self-reflection, which includes the inquiry into the possibility of empirical knowledge. Spirit has the capacity to distinguish itself from nature and to grasp nature as a whole through the category of nature's "purposiveness" (*Endzweck*).[41] These latter two functions of spirit are essential to Ritschl's concept of religion. His concept of religion has to do with a specific hierarchical arrangement between spirit and nature in which spirit is both distinguished from nature and also related to it in a relation of sovereignty over nature. Religion is a specific way of knowing that presupposes spirit's freedom from nature; this is what enables spirit to make a "value judgment" with respect to nature's goal. Spirit is free from the causality and dependence that characterize nature, and it knows nature to be determined by a final end, which for Ritschl, in theological terms, is the kingdom of God.[42]

We are in a better position now to understand the doctrine of justification in Ritschl's thought. Ritschl used the concept of religion to construe the two moments of justification: forgiveness, which is the beginning of the new reality of justification; and the orientation of the community to the telos of the new reality, which is the kingdom of God. The two—forgiveness and response—are taken together because in Ritschl's view God's justification "takes the form of a synthetic judgment."[43] From God's perspective, God makes an assertion about the sinner that attributes the divine righteousness to the sinner. Yet this assertion does not take place without the knowledge and participation of the sinner. The "synthetic judgment" of

---

Forum 39, no. 2 (June 2008); and Rudolf A. Makkreel and Sebastian Luft, eds., *Neo-Kantianism in Contemporary Philosophy,* Studies in Continental Thought (Bloomington, IN: Indiana University Press, 2009).

40. Ritschl, *Theologie und Metaphysik,* 73–74.

41. See ibid., 73–74; Ralf Geisler, *Kants moralischer Gottesbeweis im protestantischen Positivismus,* Göttinger theologische Arbeiten 51 (Göttingen: Vandenhoeck & Ruprecht, 1992), 126–27, 131, 134–37, 141.

42. See Ritschl, *Theologie und Metaphysik,* 75; Geisler, *Kants moralischer Gottesbeweis,* 144–49.

43. The citation that justification is a "synthetic judgment" is taken from Ritschl's book *Rechtfertigung und Versöhnung,* 3rd ed. (Bonn: Adolph Marcus, 1889), 3:78, as found in Heit, *Versöhnte Vernunft,* 139.

God's assertion takes the assertion of righteousness together with the sinner's participation in the righteousness communicated to this new believer. As such, God's synthetic judgment of justification results in the transformed hierarchy between spirit and nature. Spirit is free to see nature's goal as the kingdom of God.

To sum up: The first moment of justification is the communication of God's will to the human will. When righteousness is predicated of the sinner, the sinner's spirit is liberated from its entanglements with nature. Justification is a change in the orientation of the will: the new reality of faith is spirit's freedom over nature. The second moment of justification, which Ritschl calls "reconciliation," extends justification beyond the individual will to incorporate the individual will in the purpose that God reveals for nature. The content of this revelation is the kingdom of God as the highest good. Although Ritschl depicts this as a transcendental reality, justification connects the individual to a social community that may advance toward this purpose by means of ethical activity. Spirit perceives nature's goal in an entirely different matrix of interconnections than those to which nature is subject as the consequence of sin. When spirit is set free by God's love, spirit orients its actions in concert with the community toward the highest good of love.

There is, however, one aspect to Ritschl's view of justification that will emerge as significant for shaping the way Ritschl's followers accept the communication of justification and take it in the direction of historical mediation. According to Ritschl, justification includes the revelation of God's will in Christ. The communication of God's righteous will to the sinner's will takes place "through the specific memory of Christ." "The personal relationship of God or Christ to us," Ritschl writes, "is mediated through the specific memory of the word, namely, God's law and God's divine promise, and God works on us through one or the other of these revelations."[44] Ritschl mentions that the believer's relationship with Christ is crucial for justification. The historical revelation of God's will takes place in Christ. In a relationship with Christ, the sinner's "memory of the word" is the way God communicates the righteous divine will to the sinner's will. Justification by faith in Christ is taken as memory of the historical mediation of God's righteous will in Christ to the sinner. The issue concerning the historical mediation of justification in a relationship with Christ will emerge as significant in the following section. This question will concern the way "historical relationship with Christ" is mapped by the spirit/nature categories. If spirit and nature are two ways of knowing two aspects of reality, then to which category is historical mediation assigned?

44. Ritschl, *Theologie und Metaphysik*, 121.

Ritschl's formulation of the Lutheran doctrine of justification effects a powerful shift in the intellectual legacy of Protestant theology. While justification of the individual and the establishment of the kingdom of God remain God's work, both take place with human knowledge and participation. Spirit's freedom over nature and spirit's capacity, once free, to shape nature toward a specific goal allow Ritschl to conceptualize human participation as both individual at the moment of forgiveness and social in the process of reconciliation. With this move, theology acquires the task of conceptualizing reality. Ritschl took the neo-Kantian way of understanding the specific structures of mind and reality to conceptualize the reality instantiated by the doctrine of justification. He introduces the terminology of will rather than soul, of relationship rather than mystical union, and of synthetic judgment rather than essential righteousness. The goal was to connect the two moments of justification that Lutheran orthodoxy had separated. From this project, Ritschl came to understand divine and human realities meeting in a transformative encounter that came about through God's justification of the sinner.

Ritschl's followers would set about clarifying the terms he used—and with their efforts to do so the problem of Schleiermacher would begin to take shape, as we will see next. The impact of this problem on the story I am tracing is profound and lasting.

II.3. Justification and the Problem with Schleiermacher

The task of investigating doctrine introduced an epistemology and a complementary metaphysics into the legacy of Protestant theology. Ritschl opened up the doctrine of justification to a discussion concerning the way in which theology can describe different aspects of reality as they converge in justification: the reality of God for us, the reality of the human sinner, and the transformative effects of divine action on the human reality in faith. The constructive aspect of the shift was the nature/spirit category that Ritschl used to describe the two dimensions of reality in a specific hierarchy, marking out the difference between the prior stage of justification and then the new reality effected by justification. But this hierarchy of spirit over nature presupposed a tension that will become increasingly unsustainable.

The problem had to do with how the two, nature and spirit, are related. In Ritschl's language of "mediation," there is a premonition of this problem for the way the divine will is connected to the human will in justification. If the categories of nature and spirit are used to map reality, then how will they situate the different aspects of reality that are relevant to the doctrine of justification? Are there two distinct realities that "meet" in justification? How is the moment of mediation to be categorized—as nature or as spirit? As we will see, Brunner's answer to this conundrum was to disconnect the talk of reality from the talk of justification and to propose instead that God's word is a reality over and against nature, which is to say over and against human reality. The story I am tracing now becomes one of how spirit becomes separated from nature. With this separation, Schleiermacher's understanding of mysticism is cast as a falsification of divine reality by its supposed restriction of that reality to the category of "nature." Schleiermacher himself becomes the problem when the categories of nature and spirit introduced into theology by Ritschl via the doctrine of justification end up in juxtaposition: God's reality as spirit stands over and against human reality as nature. As it emerges from the doctrine of justification, the question of mediation aids in the separation of nature and spirit into the dichotomy between human and divine reality. In the process, God's word is mapped exclusively as spirit.

Ritschl's polemic against metaphysics and mysticism was the foil for his own constructive theological rewriting of the doctrine of justification. While this polemic does not diminish the legacy of Ritschl's project, Brunner will take the terms "metaphysics" and "mysticism" and use them to discredit Schleiermacher. Both terms end up on the "nature" side of the nature/spirit dichotomization that Ritschl had introduced. Schleiermacher's metaphysics and mysticism are discredited for the reason that they are accounted for exclusively by the category of nature. God's reality stands in judgment over against human reality, the "nature" that Brunner assigns to Schleiermacher's metaphysic and mysticism. But in between Ritschl and Brunner stand two relatively unknown theologians (unknown at least today), Max Reischle and Cajus Fabricius, who took up the question of mysticism in order to defend Ritschl against his critics. It is with their work that the terms of the discussion of justification shift in such a way as to set up Brunner's critique.

III. MYSTICISM TO MEDIATION

Ritschl polemicized against metaphysics and mysticism, but in his work at the same time he promoted a revision of a metaphysics in the doctrines of justification and reconciliation. Wrestling with a legacy that aligned justification with mysticism, Ritschl left open the question whether his polemic against mysticism might have led to a revisionist understanding. But he so thoroughly identified mysticism with the neo-Platonist metaphysics he was struggling to overcome that mysticism became at best a problem for the next generation of theologians. Controversy soon arose over Ritschl's brusque rejection of mysticism. Could a place be found (again) for mysticism in the doctrine of justification?

This controversy is crucial for the story of how the nature/spirit hierarchy used to explicate the doctrine of justification became more and more of a problem for the discussion of mysticism. Reischle and Fabricius appealed to the nature/spirit category as they grappled with the problem of mysticism in Ritschl. The meanings of nature and spirit became ever more reified in their reference to two different aspects of reality, the divine and the human. When Brunner arrives on the theological scene, the bifurcation will be complete. Spirit will be conceived in terms of the divine reality that stands definitively over and against nature as human reality.

III.1. Mediation in Relationship: Spirit

The controversy around Ritschl's denigration of mysticism surfaced during his lifetime, as might be expected given the emphasis in traditional Lutheran theology on mysticism as a key dimension in the order of salvation. Did Ritschl's rethinking of justification require the denial of mysticism? The problem arose as a result of the assumption that mysticism was a distraction from ethical action. Max Reischle was a Lutheran theologian who had studied with Ritschl in Göttingen. In 1886 Reischle published an important book, *Ein Wort zur Controverse über die Mystik in der Theologie* (A word concerning the controversy about mysticism in theology), in which he set out to clarify the various meanings of the term "mysticism" in order to show how mysticism could, in fact, be integrated into Ritschl's ethical orientation to justification. It was in this work that Reischle coined the motto to capture Ritschl's polemic, "No metaphysics, no mysticism in theology."[45] Reischle sought to defend mysticism in the specific sense of a key moment in justification.

His aim was to demonstrate how Ritschl's theology, primarily as articulated in the first edition of *Christian Doctrine of Justification and Reconciliation* from 1870, faithfully retained the Lutheran article on the mystical union. The answer led to the introduction of the term "mediation" into the post-Ritschlian discussion. Reischle began with the claim that Ritschl's polemic was in fact directed against mysticism, understood broadly as the erasure of difference between human consciousness and divine nature. He quotes from Ritschl's *Justification* where Ritschl defines mysticism: "Mysticism is . . . the transcending of all mediation until individual consciousness dissolves into the undifferentiated divine nature. This goal is deemed to be realizable in this present earthly existence."[46] Such an understanding of mysticism as

---

45. See footnote 15 above.
46. Quotation (from Ritschl, *Die christliche Lehre*, 1st ed., 1:113) in Reischle, *Ein Wort*, 6.

dissolution into the divine nature seems to have been common to German theologians at the time. Danish theologian Else Marie Wiberg Pedersen has recently written that it is a caricature of the common understanding of mysticism in the Christian tradition, which in fact safeguards the ontological distinction between Creator and creature.[47] Reischle clearly sees the misunderstanding in Ritschl's discrediting of mysticism. In a passage outlining various understandings of mysticism, Reischle explicitly agrees with Ritschl that any notion of the solitary soul resting in union with God at the culmination of a mystical path would not offer the soul motivation to return to the world in ethical activity.[48] But Reischle argues that there are other possible meanings of mysticism that include an ethical impulse.

The specific issue at stake in Reischle's argument is the historical dimension of personal faith. As we have seen, Ritschl understood Christianity as a historical religion that at its origins has the revelation of God in Christ. So Reischle wants to show that mysticism includes such a historical element. Yet he perceives a problem with Ritschl's understanding of justification: the lack of a personal piety that would ground ethical activity in the unity of the soul's capacities. If the soul is understood in terms of its "spiritual" capacities, in Ritschl's sense of willing, thinking, and feeling, then, as Reischle argues, these capacities must first be gathered together ("die innere Sammlung") so that together they might be directed to ethical work in the world.[49] The gathering together of the soul's functions cannot be the result of the self's activity. It is, as Reischle argues, God's work in Christ. Specifically, justification is God's work that fixes the soul's functions onto an object. But this object cannot be in the world, because the soul is already a part of the world, related to the world in reciprocal dependence. For the soul to be oriented to an object that would elevate its functions above the world—in other words, to liberate the inner human from any relation of obligation to the world—the soul's functions must be oriented to God's will in Christ.[50] The freedom of the Christian, in Luther's terminology, is for Reischle the mystical orientation of the soul's functions to the revelation of God's will in Christ. This is the religious

---

47. Else Marie Wiberg Pedersen, "Mysticism in the *Lutherrenaissance*," in *Luther-Renaissance: Past and Present*, ed. Christine Helmer and Bo Kristian Holm, Forschungen zur Kirchen- und Dogmengeschichte (Göttingen: Vandenhoeck & Ruprecht, forthcoming). Pedersen complicates the negative view of mysticism during this period by referring to Ernst Troeltsch (1865–1923), who "would save mysticism for Protestantism as a sociologically embedded element—as one of three social forms along with the church type and the sect type" (in his *Social Teaching of the Christian Churches* [1912]; quotation in Pedersen, "Mysticism," forthcoming).

48. Reischle, *Ein Wort*, 8–12.

49. Ibid., 40.

50. Ibid., 41.

aspect to be distinguished, but not separated, from the ethical dimension that characterizes Ritschl's emphasis in his discussion of justification.

Then the issue is how God's will in Christ is mediated to the sinner. Reischle's answer to this basic question of justification introduces a new element into the doctrine. The way in which God in Christ becomes the object of the soul's functions is through the mediation of the historical Christ to the historically situated human person. Reischle explicitly uses the German term *Vermittlung* (mediation). Emphasis on the historical Christ is a key aspect of Reischle's development of the concept of mediation. He first rejects the notion that the ascended Christ mediates God's will. Here Reischle's argument proceeds via criticism of Bernard of Clairvaux, as Reischle reads him. Mystical union with the ascended Christ is not historical, Reischle charges. It is not there in the historical words of the gospel. But he is not arguing here for the mediation of God's will in the word of proclamation—we must be careful not to read the word too quickly into the concept of mediation at this juncture in the term's development. At this point it suffices to say that Reischle insists on the mediation of the historical Christ—the one "who lived, suffered, and died for us"—to the sinner.[51]

In this sense mediation is available in a personal relationship with Christ. Reischle maintains that such a personal relationship is how mysticism may be rehabilitated as the crucial aspect of justification missing from Ritschl's ethical outlook. A personal relationship of love (*Liebesgemeinschaft*) is for Reischle the primary analogy for understanding how the mystical union with Christ orients the soul's functions to God's will. He describes how a personal relationship involves the spiritual dimension of the human person: "I orient my love to that personality that is conscious of its spiritual content, by valuing its worth (particularly its ethical worth), in order that it may enrich my own spiritual life."[52] Evoking the proclamation of the "images of Christ" documented in the Bible as the way in which God's will is communicated, Reischle insists that these are only the means to the end, which is a personal relationship with the *Christus praesens* (Christ present).[53]

Significant for our purposes is the fact that mysticism is rehabilitated in terms of historical mediation in a personal relationship. The effort to correct for Ritschl's lack of personal piety invokes mysticism of a particular sort, not the Lutheran orthodox idea of indwelling in a soul's ground (*Seelengrund*), but the orientation of the human soul's faculties to an object, the divine will, that is mediated by the historical Christ. The soul orients its functions to God's

51. Ibid., 12–15; the reference to Bernard of Clairvaux is on 12, quote on 14.
52. Ibid., 47.
53. Ibid., 48.

will in pious worship, not in activity, and in this relationship the soul is freed from its obligations to the world by being directed to the will that is above "natural worldly conditions."[54] Once free, the soul's functions direct its ethical activities to the realization of God's will in the world, attuned to the will that is the otherworldly purpose of ethical striving.

So it was that in the process of rehabilitating mysticism, the terms of historical mediation emerge in modern Protestant theology. Of special note here is the adaptation of the neo-Kantian category of spirit, so crucial to Ritschl, for the notion of a historical relationship to Christ. While relationship is understood in terms of "one spirit speaking to another spirit," as Reischle claims,[55] spirit is the category that orients the soul to historical mediation of Christ. The category of spirit in mediation is crucial because it is the medium in which the soul communicates with Christ. It is the reality of the historical soul's relationship to the historical Christ.

One more piece needs to be in place before getting to Brunner's identification of spirit as word of God. In the next section I turn to the second of Ritschl's major interpreters to show how he set out to rehabilitate mysticism by bringing the category of nature into the discussion.

III.2. Mysticism in Relationship: Nature

Cajus Fabricius is regarded as a faithful expositor of Ritschl's thought. He published the first critical edition of Ritschl's compendium of theology, *Die christliche Vollkommenheit (Christian Perfection)*, in 1924 and edited it with a commentary.[56] Fabricius joined the debate concerning Ritschl's problematic view of mysticism in a journal article published in 1910.[57] Fabricius, like Reischle, wanted to restore mysticism's place at the center of Lutheran Christianity. But he moved beyond Reischle by insisting that mysticism understood as the central power of Christianity was the ground for establishing the universal validity of Christianity. To make this argument, Fabricius needed to reformulate Ritschl's position on mysticism; in the process of doing so, he appealed to the nature/spirit metaphysic. But Fabricius's use of this category, as I will argue, was marked by bifurcation: nature is gradually separated from spirit, in

---

54. Ibid., 50.

55. Ibid., 47.

56. Albrecht Ritschl, *Die christliche Vollkommenheit: Ein Vortrag; Unterricht in der christlichen Religion*, ed. Cajus Fabricius (Leipzig: J. C. Hinrichs'sche Buchhandlung, 1924).

57. D. Cajus Fabricius, "Albrecht Ritschl und die Theologie der Zukunft," *Preußische Jahrbücher* 140 (1910): 16–31.

his account, and spirit eventually comes to occupy a distinctly metaphysical status that is over and against nature.

Before going further here, it must be recognized that two decades after Fabricius introduced his argument about mysticism and Christian universalism, he became actively involved in National Socialist politics. As professor of theology in Berlin, in 1935 he published a book defending the Christian religion as compatible with National Socialist ideology. It was simultaneously published in English (under the title *Positive Christianity*) and in Japanese.[58] This was all still in the future when Fabricius published his important 1910 essay on mysticism and justification, but in the story I am telling, this is the first hint of the darkness that would eventually overtake the world, darkness that Barth would so courageously address in his theology.

The 1910 article demonstrates Fabricius's conviction that the central power of Christianity resides in the mystical relationship of the believer with God. In his words, this relationship is "the way in which the whole human person is completely oriented and attuned to God."[59] This is the goal of all religions, and so Christianity has the potential to extend over all of humanity, he says.[60] Christianity introduced a new principle into history, which Fabricius identifies as the "mystical" and which drives toward the goal of history. With other theologians in the German intellectual tradition, Fabricius thus shares the idea that the telos of the historical development of Christianity is to become the universal religion.

Fabricius appreciated Ritschl's theological system for keeping both aspects of Christian life in view, the forgiveness of the sins of the individual (characteristic of the early Ritschl) and the Christian universal telos (in Ritschl's later view). But Fabricius was aware of the tension between the two, and he maintained that Ritschl did not stay true to his early interest in individual experience, instead giving up on the individual, said Fabricius, in order to emphasize the universal idea of the kingdom of God.[61] It was Fabricius's aim to correct Ritschl's increasingly singular focus by reframing the individual aspect by means of a concept of mysticism.

58. D. Cajus Fabricius, *Positives Christentum im neuen Staat* (Dresden: Hermann Püschel, 1935); ET as *Positive Christianity in the Third Reich*, trans. from original (Dresden: Hermann Püschel, 1937)]. For details concerning Fabricius's activities and writings in Nazi Germany, see the classic text on this topic by Kurt Meier, *Die theologischen Fakultäten im Dritten Reich*, De Gruyter Studienbuch (Berlin: de Gruyter, 1996).

59. Fabricius, "Ritschl und die Theologie," 22.

60. Ibid., 22, 23.

61. Fabricius writes that Ritschl "did not exhaust the riches of the Christian religion; he did not only underestimate the intuitive, the legal and the mystical forms of Christian piety according to their meanings, but also excised them entirely from Christian theology" (ibid., 22).

What was at stake in such a project? Both Ritschl and Fabricius understood Christianity to have been founded by Christ, and at its origins, both argue, "Christ reveals God by grounding the community of the kingdom of God."[62] Revelation's content is God's love, which frees sinners to promote the love that characterizes the kingdom of God. The revelation of God's love in Christ thus establishes Christianity's historical origins and continues to inspire its historical development. By means of the "immediate personal relation to Christ,"[63] the individual is integrated into the ethical orientation of the kingdom of God. Thus mysticism, which is the medium by which the individual aspect is extended in the communal and universal, is assigned a particular Christian content. God's love reveals to the Christian's "mystical consciousness," Fabricius writes, "God's self as the eternal one." Three additional aspects of God's identity are revealed to human consciousness: "God as loving father," God as "the righteous one," and God as "the almighty one." In short, mysticism as the "revelation of God in Christ," according to Fabricius, "is the redemption of the human."[64] The mystical relation with Christ entails both revelation and redemption. It orients the individual to the universal divine will as it restores the moment of piety that is the driving force of history and anchors this universality in history. Mysticism is the "seed of religion."[65] By possessing this treasure, Christianity is the universal religion.

This reframing of religion in terms of the move from the individual to the universal is of particular importance to the history I am developing. Fabricius insists that the universal cannot lose its connection with the individual, as it tended to do in Ritschl's thought. Why this is so, says Fabricius, "lies in human nature. The human is constituted simultaneously by the senses and by spirit." Children, "like their fathers, are creatures of nature, anchored in one body on earth, and retain this sensory side of their nature throughout their entire lives."[66] So Fabricius seeks to correct what he sees as mysticism's tendency to shed the body. By defining mysticism in terms of the individual's immediate relationship with Christ, which presupposes the human person as spirit and body, Fabricius secures the individual element as necessary to the mystical. However free the individual is in spirit, the human being is necessarily anchored to the world by the body.

The efforts to rehabilitate Ritschl's view of mysticism have added two key developments to the history of the bifurcation of spirit and nature. For both Reischle and Fabricius, mysticism is the problem to be solved in order to rescue

62. Ibid., 23.
63. Ibid., 20.
64. Ibid., 30.
65. Ibid., 29.
66. Ibid., 28.

Ritschl's system for a robust sense of Christianity. But what is curious about the different solutions the two propose are the terms of mediation between Christ and the believer. Reischle, who is concerned with historical mediation, insists that this relationship effects a shift in the orientation of spirit. Fabricius, who is concerned with relationship, insists that nature captures the aspect of the relationship with Christ that ties it to individuality by means of the body. Nature is part of the relationship with Christ. What is becoming clearer now is the way in which spirit and nature—even as they come into relationship with each other in the history of modern German theology—are being gradually separated in order to capture two distinct realities. An odd dynamic of attraction and repulsion has developed. The divine aspect of the relationship is coming to be associated with spirit, and the human aspect with nature.

One more step—and the two come apart. This is what Emil Brunner accomplished. In doing so, he connected spirit and word *against* nature.

IV. BRUNNER AND THE WORD
AGAINST SCHLEIERMACHER

In 1924 the Swiss Reformed pastor Emil Brunner published a sustained attack against Schleiermacher: *Die Mystik und das Wort* (Mysticism and the word). (A revised edition came out in 1928.)[67] The book had two effects that make it an apposite end of the trajectory I am following. The first is that in Brunner's hands, Schleiermacher becomes the articulatory pivot for revisiting theological questions in terms that had been cycling through theology for decades, specifically the issues of theological commitment to an alien ground and of experience in opposition to word. The critique of Schleiermacher comes to a fine point in Brunner: the commitment to the word of God as external reality. But this commitment did not come out of the blue. It was the result of the nature/spirit tension, terms that, as we have seen, Ritschl introduced to explain divine and human reality in relation to each other within the categories of the Kantian inheritance. Brunner's book finally severed them, culminating and in this sense bringing to an end the story of the deepening tension between the terms. Spirit comes to be associated with the word of God; nature is the descriptor of human reality.

Brunner shared with Barth this focus on the word of God as a reality distinct from human reality. (Barth is the subject of the next chapter.) Brunner

---

67. Emil Brunner, *Die Mystik und das Wort: Der Gegensatz zwischen moderner Religionsauffassung und christlichem Glauben dargestellt an der Theologie Schleiermachers*, 2nd ed. (Tübingen: J. C. B. Mohr [Paul Siebeck], 1928). On Brunner, please see the recent biography by Alister E. McGrath, *Emil Brunner: A Reappraisal* (West Sussex, UK: Wiley-Blackwell, 2014).

was aware of Barth's critical engagement with Schleiermacher. (In 1924 Barth was teaching theology at the University of Göttingen in Germany.) But Brunner did not anticipate Barth's review of *Die Mystik und das Wort*, which appeared in the journal *Zwischen den Zeiten* (Between the times), associated with the movement of dialectical theology with which both Barth and Brunner were aligned.[68] In the review Barth distanced himself from Brunner's position on Schleiermacher; this was round one of an argument that would recur a decade later, in 1934, the same year Barth helped formulate the Barmen Declaration. The relationship between Brunner and Barth was further marred by their (in)famous dispute over the question of the "formal or material use of the *imago dei* [image of God]" in the reception of grace.[69] While Barth said a strong "Nein!" to the issue of a human contribution when receiving divine grace, Brunner was less dismissive. In the intervening years, Brunner had worked out his position on the divine-human encounter as the basis of the articulation-of-faith statements in his 1928 book on the philosophy of religion.[70] Brunner would go on to be appointed as Professor of Systematic and Practical Theology at the University of Zurich, teaching there until his retirement in 1953.

But in 1924 Brunner made an extreme case against Schleiermacher by invoking the category of nature/spirit I have been tracking in this chapter. It is to this book that I now turn in order to show how Brunner splits nature and spirit apart when discussing the question of the reality of God and the human.

68. Karl Barth, "Brunners Schleiermacherbuch," *Zwischen den Zeiten* 8 (1924): 49–64. At the end of his life, Barth grudgingly acknowledged his deep respect for Schleiermacher in the afterword to the *Siebenstern* publication of an anthology of Schleiermacher's works (1968). See the ET in Karl Barth, "Concluding Unscientific Postscript on Schleiermacher," in *The Theology of Schleiermacher: Lectures at Göttingen, Winter Semester of 1923/24*, ed. Dietrich Ritschl, trans. Geoffrey Bromiley (Grand Rapids: Eerdmans, 1982), 261–79.

69. John McDowell convincingly argues that the debate between Brunner and Barth is truncated by casting it solely as a methodological issue on the human capacity for God, in short, as a natural theology. McDowell shows that for Brunner, the issue is the theological distinction between a formal and material construal of the *imago dei*. See John C. McDowell, "Karl Barth, Emil Brunner and the Subjectivity of the Object of Christian Hope," *International Journal of Systematic Theology* 8, no. 1 (January 2006): 27–28. A book on this exchange is John W. Hart, *Karl Barth vs. Emil Brunner: The Formation and Dissolution of a Theological Alliance, 1916–1936*, Issues in Systematic Theology 6 (New York: Peter Lang, 2001); see also the correspondence in ET: David Andrew Gilland, trans. and ed., *Karl Barth–Emil Brunner Correspondence* (Edinburgh: T&T Clark, 2013).

70. On the distinction between theology and a philosophy of religion concerned with the "foundational coherence of faith statements" (*Begründungszusammenhang der Glaubensaussagen*), see Emil Brunner, *Religionsphilosophie evangelischer Theologie* (1927; repr., Munich: Leibniz, 1948), 7.

The word of God is shown to be the key category for viewing divine reality, and Brunner ends up casting this reality in terms of "spirit."

IV.1. The Problem of "Ground": Metaphysics

Brunner's most significant charge concerned Schleiermacher's indebtedness to nineteenth-century German Idealist philosophy. Brunner identified this metaphysic with mysticism.[71] I will turn to this issue in the next section. For now, Brunner's critique of this metaphysic introduces the problem of modern religion as it was associated with Schleiermacher. What does Brunner understand by Schleiermacher's metaphysical commitment, and why does he see it as a problem?

Brunner uses the frame of Schleiermacher's systematic theology as the hermeneutical key for interpreting the latter's thought, in particular in examining the question of how Schleiermacher conceived of theology in relation to the concept of knowledge and its concretization in different academic disciplines. Brunner focuses on Schleiermacher's *Lectures on Dialectic.* This is arguably Schleiermacher's most obscure work, rarely read in relation to his other works,[72] but Brunner claims that every knowledgeable reader of Schleiermacher must know the *Dialektik*.[73] These lectures, which Schleiermacher delivered six times at the University of Berlin (1811, 1814, 1818, 1822, 1828, 1831), represent his contribution to the discussion of dialectic taking place in the early nineteenth century, motivated by Wilhelm von Humboldt's creation of the new University of Berlin in 1809.[74] As Brunner correctly notes, some key insights of the *Dialektik* were used to frame Schleiermacher's system of theology, his *Christian Faith* from 1830–31.[75] The "Introduction" (§§1–31) to *The Christian Faith* exhibits the methodological procedures informing Schleiermacher's theology while also demonstrating how theology "borrows" insights from other academic disciplines in order to make theological claims to knowledge.

---

71. Brunner, *Die Mystik,* 11: "Immanence philosophy (namely, mysticism)."

72. For a new direction in interpreting the *Dialektik* in relation to other works by Schleiermacher, see Christine Helmer, Christiane Kranich, and Birgit Rehme-Iffert, eds., *Schleiermachers Dialektik: Die Liebe zum Wissen in Philosophie und Theologie,* Religion in Philosophy and Theology 6 (Tübingen: Mohr Siebeck, 2003).

73. Brunner, *Die Mystik,* 110: "Every naive reader—and everyone is vis-à-vis Schleiermacher a naive reader who does not know the *Dialektik*."

74. Brunner had available to him the Jonas edition, published by Reimer in 1839, five years after Schleiermacher's death. See Friedrich Schleiermacher's *Sämmtliche Werke,* III/4.2 (Berlin: G. Reimer, 1839). The critical edition edited by Andreas Arndt was published in 2002 by de Gruyter in a 2-volume edition in the *KGA* (II/10.1–2), titled *Vorlesungen über die Dialektik.*

75. Brunner, *Die Mystik,* 111.

It is when Brunner attempts to describe the content of Schleiermacher's philosophical framework that he begins to cast Schleiermacher as a problem for theology. The issue at stake is the metaphysical question at the center of early nineteenth-century German Idealism. Schleiermacher, Brunner writes, "discerned that the idealism of mind [*Geist*] or of 'the I' had trespassed beyond the critical border of Kant's philosophy; Schleiermacher knew that reality, as irrational facticity, came up too short [in speculative Idealism]." But Schleiermacher did not go far enough, according to Brunner, in freeing philosophy from its speculative orientation, and so Schleiermacher, still in Brunner's account, comes to share a "metaphysic of identity" with his German Idealist colleagues, according to which "spirit" is joined with reality as two "appearances of an (unknown) unity."[76] Spirit (*Geist*) is correlated with the real as the two aspects of a metaphysic that determines reality as appearances of both aspects, yet the "ground" for these appearances is hidden. The Idealists maintained that the ground might be accessed through an action of the mind; Schleiermacher differed by taking the ground as a hidden identity between ideal and real. Where Brunner then goes astray is in his discussion of the relation of the hidden ground to a theory of consciousness in Schleiermacher's metaphysic.

The philosophical frame of Schleiermacher's system, according to Brunner, is a "reflection theory."[77] The problem, as Brunner understood it, had to do with the subjective reduction in Schleiermacher's theory of consciousness. It is clear today that Schleiermacher's theory has specific epistemological interests and makes distinct ontological claims.[78] But Brunner reduces Schleiermacher's philosophical orientation to a subjectivist position, charging that Schleiermacher's philosophical commitments reflect the subjectivism that underwrites modern religion in contrast to the objectivity of biblical Christianity.[79] Thus what surfaces in Brunner's account of Schleiermacher's position on metaphysics is the dichotomy between subjectivity and objectivity.

How did Brunner understand Schleiermacher's "subjectivist" position? Here the distinction between spirit and nature comes explicitly to the fore.

---

76. Ibid., 171.

77. Ibid., 109.

78. On this point see the articles on Schleiermacher's *Dialektik* by Manfred Frank, "Metaphysical Foundations: A Look at Schleiermacher's *Dialektik*," trans. Jacqueline Mariña and Christine Helmer, in *The Cambridge Companion to Schleiermacher*, ed. Jacqueline Mariña, Cambridge Companions to Religion (Cambridge: Cambridge University Press, 2005), 15–34; and on Schleiermacher's philosophical ethics as frame to his system, see Eilert Herms, "Schleiermacher's *Christian Ethics*," trans. Jacqueline Mariña and Christine Helmer, also in *The Cambridge Companion to Schleiermacher*, 209–28.

79. Brunner, *Die Mystik*, 120–46.

Brunner introduces and develops his concept of "spirit [*Geist*]" in relation to the concept of "word," which he defines in opposition to Schleiermacher's alleged subjectivism. Word is related to "spirit," Brunner argues, because word has primacy in human existence. "The word is the foundation of human existence, . . . not reason." To this claim Brunner adds an understanding of "word" as the origin of humanity, a direct allusion to the eighteenth-century German Lutheran philosopher Johann Georg Hamann's philosophy of "word." Word creates the sense (*Sinn*) of the "interconnections, or the spiritual unity, of the manifold."[80] The word makes sense out of a manifold, not in a discursive or logical way, but aesthetically, binding connections into an aesthetic whole. In this way word is identified with a creative action together with an aesthetic value, which Brunner attributes to "spirit."

"Spirit is only there where the word is," Brunner claims.[81] The word's creative capacity to make beautiful sense of the whole denotes freedom that is attributed to spirit. Spirit is not determined by dependencies on nature; rather, spirit is free actively to create sense in nature's manifold.[82] In this sense both God and humans have the word that is free to determine sense. But Brunner makes a distinction: God's word has the priority to speak the truth of human existence and thereby to make sense of the human condition of sin and of the grace that comes to humans from the objectivity of God's word. "The word of God," Brunner writes, "is the sense that is given by God and received by humans; the word is not discovered by humans, but is revealed to them. This is the sense that is God's alone, and that through God's initiative comes to us."[83] Any human capacity to make sense of the manifold comes from God. God's reality, furthermore, is external to human reality. The value of objectivity is assigned to spirit and word in their primacy in God. "Spirit is there where one inquires into objective validity. . . . [Spirit] is objectively necessary."[84] The word resides in the divine objectivity and remains objective, even when humans receive it.

The contrast of spirit to nature comes into the argument most forcefully via the contrast between divine objectivity and human reality. If spirit is characterized by freedom, then nature is determined according to causality.[85] Brunner follows Ritschl in seeing nature in the causal terms of natural laws and reciprocal social dependencies, not in freedom. Spirit is also an aspect of

80. Ibid., 88, 89.
81. Ibid., 89.
82. Ibid., 88–92.
83. Ibid., 95.
84. Ibid., 92.
85. Ibid., 85.

human existence. It is, says Brunner, the *imago dei* in human nature.[86] Yet the human spirit's freedom is derivative. It is predicated on the condition that God, as creator of all sense, creates for humans. In this way human reality is bound to the reality of natural causality. The human subject cannot gain objective truth because its subjectivity is caught up in the world's causal nexus. The human subject reaches for objectivity when it acknowledges God's word as source and condition of existence. It can even "think after [*nachdenken*]" God's word.[87] Yet the human cannot claim divine objectivity for its own; objectivity is the prerogative of God's word as freedom alone.

Here, then, is the bifurcation between (on the one hand) word, with valences of spirit and objectivity, and (on the other hand) human existence, as derived and created. Brunner preserves the notion of spirit as an aspect of human reality, precisely as the image of God. But the invocation of the distinction between divine objectivity and the human spirit pulls nature and spirit apart.

In Brunner's understanding, what Schleiermacher has done is to confuse objectivity with human subjectivism. Schleiermacher believed he had framed his theology from the perspective of divine objectivity, whereas in fact he grounded his system in a subjectivist paradigm that placed human "spirit" as primary in making sense of God. As Brunner saw it, Schleiermacher's enterprise was not theology, but philosophy, grounded in the effort of human spirit as this spirit is bound up in the reality of causal relations. The human spirit is not free. Its freedom can only be spoken to it in an encounter with God's word. In its lack of freedom, the human spirit deceives itself into thinking it makes objective claims about God. But these claims result from the efforts of human thought; in framing claims about God, they end up capturing God in the nineteenth-century philosophical idiom of the Absolute.[88]

IV.2. The Problem of Immediate Self-Consciousness: Mysticism

Brunner also identifies a problem with Schleiermacher's understanding of religion. Just as Schleiermacher's metaphysics mistook human reflection for objective truth, according to Brunner, Schleiermacher's view of religion had to do with human subjectivity: the way in which God is posited in human consciousness.

Ethics for Schleiermacher is the study of human agency in history. When the human spirit acts on nature and in specific relations with nature, it produces

86. Ibid., 92.
87. Ibid., 92–93: "The human spirit, specifically as a 'creative,' extraordinary thinking, is an after-thinking, a tracing of lines after they have already been drawn."
88. Ibid., 113.

cultural institutions that contextualize human activity.[89] Schleiermacher distinguished action within four different institutional contexts: religion, the state, the academy, and free sociability. Religion has its own "province," as Brunner argues from Schleiermacher's *Speeches*.[90] Yet because this province is determined by a parameter, its terms are already surrendered to the terms of the parameter. Brunner frames this problem again in relation to spirit. He argues that the philosophical scheme of Schleiermacher's ethics subordinates (human) spirit to "reason [*Vernunft*]," the particular category that Schleiermacher begins with in his philosophical ethics in order to establish the four domains of human activity. This, says Brunner, creates a view of religion that confuses the human with God.

Next Brunner turns to the issue of the self's capacity for religion in Schleiermacher's thought. Brunner takes Schleiermacher to task for the famous proposition in paragraph 4 of *The Christian Faith*, which defines religion in psychological terms as a distinct feeling that is located in "immediate self-consciousness." The proposition articulates the relation of self to the external cause of both self and world as the "consciousness of being absolutely dependent." Schleiermacher added an additional definitional clause to this in the second edition (1830): "which is the same thing, of being in relation with God."[91] This was intended to alleviate possible misunderstandings of the formulation of the first edition (1820) that the feeling of absolute dependence is referred to an external cause. But it did not prevent Brunner from interpreting Schleiermacher's psychologically couched concept of religion in terms of immanent subjectivity. Religion is allocated a distinct place in human self-consciousness. In immediate self-consciousness, religious feeling registers a relation of the self with itself as the condition for any of its actions and for thinking (including philosophical thinking). This self-relation at the ground of the self is, for Brunner's interpretation of Schleiermacher, "the relation of the human to its own ground of the soul [*Seelengrund*]. . . . It finally is self-relation," having to do with the immanence of God in the soul.[92] Schleiermacher's religion, in short, is the mysticism of a self-relation at the ground of the soul. If the soul is the place in which divinity dwells, then the religion of consciousness has to do with the divine immanence in the "depths of spirit."[93] Immediate self-consciousness, a function of human nature, holds God captive in its interiority.

89. For the best description of Schleiermacher's philosophical ethics and the grid representing spirit's action in nature in four ways, see Hans-Joachim Birkner's *Habilitationsschrift* from 1964, published as *Schleiermachers christliche Sittenlehre: Im Zusammenhang seines philosophisch-theologischen Systems*, Theologische Bibliothek Töpelmann 8 (1964; repr., Berlin: Alfred Töpelmann, 2012), 30–50.

90. Brunner, *Die Mystik*, 181.

91. *CF* 12 (§4, proposition).

92. Brunner, *Die Mystik*, 186.

93. Ibid., 172.

Brunner's criticism of Schleiermacher's mysticism arises from the opposition between mysticism and word. The lines are clearly drawn: "Either mysticism or the word."[94] Mysticism characterizes modern religion in terms of its interiority, in contrast with the objective status of the word. In a passage laced with sarcasm, Brunner writes of Schleiermacher's account of mysticism in speech 2 of the *Speeches on Religion*: "The word is not any more word in the sense of truth, but is form, expression for inner stimulation. It is expressionistic artistic medium; it is merely expression, relief of tension, ejaculation, glossolalia."[95] The word is trapped in the interiority of human consciousness and is the expression of the inner states of that consciousness produced when the affections are stimulated.[96] Word cannot free itself from human nature. The contrast between human word and divine word could not be sharper. The word of God is the word that sets free, writes Brunner in reference to John 8:32.[97] Because the word of God is outside of human reality, it occupies a status of reality that is self-determined. It is "spirit" that is not subject to any dependencies in nature. Word is free to confront the human, to speak to the human from a position external to it, and to speak in a way that frees the human without itself surrendering to the reality of human nature.

The opposition that Brunner constructs is the one between modern religion and the faith world of both apostles and the Reformers. He argues that there is "the inner impossibility of an alliance between every type of mystical immanence philosophy and the Christianity of the Bible."[98] The modern religion of mysticism has nothing to with the Christian faith as attested in Scripture and by the Protestant Reformers. This opposition between word and nature, objectivity and human interiority, signals that the separation between spirit and nature has been achieved. The twentieth century's problem with Schleiermacher is initiated in terms of opposition between word of God and human nature.

IV.3. Theology of the Word

But the conditions for holding up the objectivity of the divine word had changed since the Protestant Reformation. While Luther had argued for the certainty of the external word on the basis of God's speech in Scripture, Brunner identifies word by means of the neo-Kantian distinction between

94. Ibid., 88.
95. Ibid., 117.
96. See also ibid., 30.
97. Ibid., 96.
98. Ibid., 10.

nature and spirit. What Brunner achieves at the culmination of this trajectory initiated by Ritschl is the opposition between nature and spirit. In fact, as I have argued, Brunner is an exemplary figure in the critique of Schleiermacher because he crystallizes the terms of the word of God in opposition to human nature. When Brunner argues on behalf of the word as divine objective truth framed in the language of spirit, he separates God's word from human nature. He goes further, moreover, to say that if it were left undetermined by God's word, human nature would falsify the ground for its intellectual operation, including theology, converting theology into philosophical idioms. A theory of self-consciousness implies a mystical account of religion that is determined by nature, whereas the truth of spirit is distinct from nature. Nature has confused God with human consciousness. By the time Brunner has turned Schleiermacher into modern theology's necessary object of attack, word's ontological difference from nature has been secured.

Brunner's polemic crucially shaped the way Schleiermacher's understanding of religion and theology was viewed in the twentieth century. Although Ritschl's overt polemic against a distinct kind of metaphysic and mysticism accompanied his construction of the doctrine of justification, Brunner mapped this polemic explicitly onto Schleiermacher. With this move a paradigmatic discourse emerges that has powerfully shaped the theology of the word in the twentieth century. The word alone mediates God to humans, yet in such a way that it commands obedience.[99] When the word encounters the human, God encounters the human as Lord.

The discourse of encounter and obedience adds specific aspects to Brunner's framing spirit as objective word. The divine address becomes the major trope of the divine-human encounter. The word of God is free to address the human from a position external to human reality. The objectivity of the word is secured by its freedom from human nature; it is free to encounter the human in its radical "Otherness." Once the theology of the word is renewed for the twentieth century by the fundamental opposition between spirit and nature, its terms can then be determined. It is to this determination of the word, both as address and as doctrine, that we turn in the next chapter.

V. THE PROBLEM WITH SCHLEIERMACHER

Thus at the dawn of the twentieth century, the seeds were sown for the subsequent century-long problem with Schleiermacher. What began as an intra-Lutheran debate on the doctrine of justification turned into the construction,

99. Ibid., 158.

within Protestantism, of a word-oriented theology that left Schleiermacher behind, relegating him to a theology of immanent subjective self-consciousness incapable of conceiving a God over and against human reality and mediated only by the reality of God in his word. Nature was the category under which mysticism and metaphysics were subsumed and with which both were cast as falsifying the truth of the clear distinction between God and human. Spirit became the category underwriting theology's truth. With "word," theology acquired a term that could point to a divine reality that was distinct from human reality. In the next chapter we investigate further the implications for the theological task that the axiology of word assigns to it. At this point, we conclude this chapter with some brief remarks on what has been lost by leaving Schleiermacher behind.

Mysticism was divorced from its connection to word over the course of the trajectory I have plotted in this chapter, and with it went the productive tension that Schleiermacher maintained between experience and its relation to both church proclamation and to academic theology. Brunner acknowledged as much. Pausing in his diatribe against Schleiermacher, he grudgingly acknowledged that the object of his wrath had "loosened the essence of religion from the husks of dogmatic and philosophical doctrine and interpreted the essence of Christianity as an issue of life and of the heart."[100]

To this we can add the evidence of Schleiermacher's biography. The vitality of Schleiermacher's religious life was formed by Moravian piety that, as he wrote to his publisher Georg Reimer in 1802, "nurtured the mystical predisposition that was an essential part of" his individuality. When the "storms of skepticism" challenged his youthful beliefs, added Schleiermacher, "this mysticism had preserved me and saved me. . . . At that time, mysticism germinated as from a seed, now it is fully developed, and I can now admit that I have become a Moravian of a higher order."[101] When Schleiermacher later used the term "mysticism" in *The Christian Faith* to describe and explain how Christ redeems the believer in the context of the Christian community, he admitted his reticence in even mentioning it.[102] The term is never evoked in the introduction to *The Christian Faith*, as we might expect from reading

---

100. Emil Brunner, *Erlebnis, Erkenntnis und Glaube*, 4th and 5th eds. (Zurich: Zwingli-Verlag, 1923), 12.

101. In German: "Hier entwickelte sich zuerst die mystische Anlage die mir so wesentlich ist, und mich unter allen Stürmen des Skepticismus erhalten und gerettet hat. Damals keimte sie auf, jetzt ist sie ausgebildet, und ich kann sagen, daß ich nach Allem wieder ein Herrnhuter geworden bin nur von einer höheren Ordnung" (Friedrich Schleiermacher, *Briefwechsel (1801–1802)*, in *KGA* V/5:393.17–21.

102. *CF* 429 (§100.3): "This expression is so extremely vague that it seems better to avoid it."

Brunner, but it appears in the theological system under specific soteriological interests. The topic of mysticism in Schleiermacher brings together issues of personal spiritual formation in a particular religious culture and specific theological discourse to elucidate a doctrine at the center of Christianity. Theology is never simply a matter of terminology. It has to do with a transformative encounter with the *Christus praesens*, to use Schleiermacher's designation, and from this angle the relation between mysticism and word must be reevaluated.

Metaphysics, analogous to mysticism, was cast in the terms of a "philosophical" ground for theology, alien to the distinct Christian appeal to the word as theology's primary reality. The original polemic has morphed into more contemporary concerns with Schleiermacher, to be sorted out in the next two chapters. Lost in the translation of Schleiermacher into the terms of opposition between metaphysics and Christian faith, however, is the tension that Schleiermacher held on to between (on one hand) his understanding of the idea of knowledge, even for theology as a discipline engaged in the pursuit of knowledge, and (on the other hand) the distinct theological task to elucidate its subject matter, or Christian faith statements. Schleiermacher held both together in his introduction to the *Christian Faith*, for the purpose of explaining how theology's pursuit of knowledge could take place in common conversation with other academic disciplines and regulated by common intellectual practices. As an academic theologian, Schleiermacher knew that theology's claims to truth were to have an impact in changing Christianity. Theology was a "positive science" whose sole task was to yield knowledge that could be applied for the flourishing of Christian churches. But as a theologian committed to the pursuit of knowledge, Schleiermacher advocated a common conversation with other academic disciplines, such as psychology, sociology, and history. Metaphysics, then, was a transcendental construct that explained why humans in the first place could be engaged in the pursuit of knowledge with distinct epistemological considerations. Its relation to theology was one of conveying these human capacities for thought to a discipline that was grounded in the experience of Christ in the community—in short, in a mystical relationship with Christ.

One hundred years after this crucial formative period in modern theology's history, the term "word" and its accompanying valences of spirit and objective truth are present today in the way word, doctrine, and theology are understood. This chapter has shown how a new framing of word as a spiritual reality was undertaken by loosening it from the matrix of mysticism and metaphysics in which it had been conceptualized in Lutheran orthodoxy. In the next chapter I continue this biography of word as it undergoes another change. Theology takes an epistemic turn, which results in an idea of doctrine even further distanced from a connection with mysticism and metaphysics. The consistent polemical focal point will remain Schleiermacher. As we continue this discussion of how changes to the conceptualization of word imply changes in the understanding of doctrine and in theology's task of elucidating doctrine, we look ahead to what really matters: theology's talk of experience and its engagement with reality.

3

From Trinitarian Representation to the Epistemic-Advantage Model

Word, Doctrine, Theology

Part 1

I. FROM WORD TO DOCTRINE

Word becomes increasingly attached to spirit in the neo-Kantian philosophical inheritance. This was the argument of the preceding chapter. In this philosophical framework, word is opposed to nature and mystical experience. This turned the tide against Schleiermacher. The polemic against Schleiermacher's alleged conflation of metaphysics and mysticism with nature is explicit in Brunner's vitriolic critique. The central issue at stake in Brunner's argument is his spiritualizing of word against its naturalization in sense experience. God is speaker of the word, Brunner argues, and God's word is spoken to humans. God addresses humans from a position over and against human reality. Brunner's claim turns on the issue of word's mediation. What is the vehicle by which word is mediated to the human? Theology's answer to this question is spiritual mediation, and as a result the relation of language to human reality became tenuous in modern Protestant thought. The spiritual valence attributed by theology to word had distinct repercussions for how doctrine would be understood in the twentieth century. This was especially so for the question of whether (or not) doctrine's linguistic formulations were to be taken as a dimension of human reality.

Now in this chapter, doctrine moves to the center of inquiry. I will consider the particular valence attributed to God's word by theologians at the beginning and then at the end of the twentieth century; this will show how the meaning of doctrine shifts with changing understandings of God's word. How can doctrine be taken as a historical reality when word is understood in terms of spirit as seen over and against human reality? How do developments in the theological understanding of God's word affect the way theology understands and analyzes doctrine? To anticipate what follows, I will argue that a crucial reorientation takes place regarding doctrine's transcendent referent. Specifically, I will trace a theological trajectory that begins by insisting that "word" can refer to the transcendent reality of God and ends by undercutting the very possibility of such reference.

In order to track this sea change in the understanding of doctrine, I have chosen two interlocutors as representative of important divergent theological positions at either end of the long twentieth century. Part 1 of this chapter addresses the first interlocutor, Swiss theologian Karl Barth. The key question for modern Protestant theology, as Barth formulated it, asked how it is possible for theologians to speak about God in human words while at the same time claiming that God is the speaker of God's own word. This paradox informed Barth's earlier views on the distinctive rhetoric that theology must deploy in order to open human words to the possibility that God might speak. The problem of God's word in relation to human words about God also guided Barth's theological reflections on the doctrine of the word of God in relation to the Trinity that he took up in the first two volumes (I/1 and I/2) of the *Church Dogmatics*. We will see that Barth's concern in retaining God's prerogative in the word is related to his understanding of theology as a human endeavor that articulates and interprets the doctrine of the Trinity in response to new social and religious circumstances. In Barth's account, Christian theology is possible as a historically located discipline uniquely dependent on the word of God for its criterion, truth, and subject matter.

The second part of this chapter focuses on another theological position that, like Barth's, takes theological assertions to be especially important human words about God that identify the subject matter of Christian theology. Theological assertions succinctly condense Christian belief into the linguistic formulas of the confession of faith, which stands firm and secure amid the confusions and chaos of human societies. "The Holy Spirit has prescribed formulas for us," Luther writes in the disputation on the divinity and humanity of Christ from 1540. "We should be walking in that cloud [Exod. 13:21]."[1] But between Barth and the second position I will discuss, a significant change occurs in the understanding of the nature of theological assertions. My interlocutor here is American theologian Bruce D. Marshall. Theological assertions have a place in Marshall's thought, but he does not share Barth's insistence on their capacity to refer to the divine word that transcends human formulations. In Marshall's view, which I take as representative of the "epistemic model" of contemporary theology, assertions lose their

---

1. WA 39/II:104.18–19 (my ET): "Praescribuntur enim ibi nobis a Spiritu sancto formulae; in illa nube ambulemus."

referential status; as linguistic abbreviations of the Christian faith, assertions are timeless norms for Christianity. Although Barth understood doctrine as comprising historical formulations that always stand in the face of the possibility of God's judgment, Marshall lifts theological assertions out of history and assigns them to the transcendent position that Protestant thought had previously reserved for God. In this view, doctrine has a normative epistemic function in a Christian worldview.

The shift in the twentieth century is from what I call theology as "Trinitarian representation" to theology as "epistemic advantage." God's word comes to be construed quite differently between Barth and Marshall, particularly as it is related to the nature of doctrine. When doctrine is enlisted as the grammar of a worldview—as it is by theologians working within the "epistemic model"—it loses its connection to the word that gives life. Instead of describing God as norm, theology and its doctrinal formulations *become* the norms of belief and practice. Doctrine assumes the position of divine transcendence and is thereby promoted to an unchanging epistemic normativity.

What troubles me about this is the loss of doctrine's connection to its subject matter. To look ahead to my conclusion, in my view such a move to elevate the linguistic doctrinal formulations to the status of norms for a Christian worldview cuts doctrine off from a living connection to the reality of God. If theology is to describe and explain divine reality in relation to persons living in their worldly environments, as I believe it ought to do, then it must be oriented to an understanding of doctrine that opens up this aspect of reality to human intellectual and existential practices. Barth's commitment to a transcendent God who can judge human formulations of doctrine reinvigorates such a position. The other is to take the theological production of doctrine seriously as embedded in human history and lived religious experience. Barth's theology points to divine judgment on human social and theological constructions in the context of Germany's major involvement in two World Wars and the rise of fascism. But if we are to move beyond Barth's claims about theology's peril at the hands of the God who judges while at the same time reclaiming for contemporary theology his insistence on doctrine's referent to the living reality of God, then we will need to consider how theology can be a lived intellectual practice of deepening doctrine with the knowledge and experience of self, world, and God.

Is doctrine a static norm, or does it orient and inform human beings for further theological discovery? I invite readers to consider the following question as they read this chapter. Does the twentieth-century trajectory I will outline mark the end of doctrine, understood as epistemic norm? Or is it possible to reconnect doctrine with word and history, experience and reality? In chapter 4 I will propose a theological epistemology that treats doctrine in terms of its production in history, diverting attention away from the epistemic model that insists on doctrine as static norm. But there is still a way to go before getting to that point. The first step is to revisit the theologian who made the doctrine of the word of God the sole focus of the first part of his theological system.

II. THEOLOGY AND
TRINITARIAN REPRESENTATION

The vision and development of Christian theology in the twentieth century is to a large extent shaped by Protestant theologian Karl Barth. He is credited with giving preeminent status to the doctrine of the Trinity and for inspiring theologians to regard the Trinity as crucial for Christian doctrine. In his multivolume system of theology, *Church Dogmatics*, Barth assigns the Trinity to the first part of the system, the "prolegomena." In eighteenth-century Protestant orthodox systems of theology, this initial section was intended to explain how the word of God in Scripture grounded theological truth claims in subsequent parts of the system. By converting the formal task of prolegomena from a treatment of Scripture to the explication of Trinitarian doctrine, Barth assigned the Trinity a new foundational role for theology.

In this chapter Barth's approach to the Trinity interests me for the specific question at stake regarding Trinity's relation to the word of God. Word had risen to theological prominence at the turn of the twentieth century, as we have seen, understood according to the spirit/nature dichotomy in Brunner. This orientation of word to spirit over against nature took on additional influence in Barth's early theology around 1920. In the political context of Germany at war, the 1919 publication of *Der Römerbrief* (written in 1918) and more importantly its revised second edition (written in 1921, published in 1922), are regarded as constituting a watershed in theology. In this work Barth insists on God's word as radically different from human reality, not only from nature as Brunner understood it, but also from human history, culture, and politics. God's word—as divine reality standing over and against human reality—has radical critical potential. God's word pronounces divine judgment on human reality. At this point Barth asks the key question that would determine the course of his theological reflection. How can human words in Scripture, doctrine, and proclamation be articulated in relation to the divine word that judges human words?

After the section on the early Barth of the *Epistle to the Romans*, I explore Barth's developing understanding of the word of God. My primary interest is in how Barth specifies the relation of human word to the reality of God and how that reality is made available in theology. I will focus on Barth's theological preoccupation with the word's revelation of the reality of God and the implication that this claim has for how theology may circumscribe the divine reality without rendering it under human control. The dialectic between word of God and human word characterizing Barth's early theology is significant in this regard; then the later work unfolds the theological presupposition of God's word in a systematic theological reflection on the doctrine of the Trinity.

My aim is not a comprehensive exposition of Barth's thought with reference to his entire corpus.[2] Rather, my exploration of Barth's theology focuses on the question of how word and doctrine are understood to relate to the reality of God. As a scholar primarily interested in Martin Luther and Friedrich Schleiermacher, I approached Barth with trepidation about his disagreements with his theological predecessors. But I have become convinced that Barth ought to be read as a critical challenge to contemporary theology, which ironically appeals to his work as its most significant ally. In my view, Barth is a powerful witness on behalf of doctrine's relation to divine reality as unpredictable and surprising, as living and existentially significant. How Barth has captured this aspect of the divine word in his Trinitarian theology while insisting on the alterity of the word beyond human control—that is the subject to which I now turn.

II.1. Word in the Aftermath of War

Christian theology of the twentieth century—with its emphases, concerns, and questions—is to a large extent the legacy of the German intellectual tradition. Even if current developments in theology in the English-speaking world are less connected to Germany than they were half a century ago due to an increasing alliance with Anglo-American analytic philosophy (the situation in biblical studies is somewhat different), the powerful inheritances from German theology must be acknowledged. Twentieth-century German thought is inextricably bound together with its political history. Ideas are always articulated in and shaped by history. In the case of Germany, this history comprises the World Wars and the Holocaust (or Shoah). German theologians, as was true of the nation's citizens broadly, participated in Germany's political

---

2. For fuller treatments of Barth's thought, see the following learned monographs: George Hunsinger, *How to Read Karl Barth: The Shape of His Theology* (New York: Oxford University Press, 1991); Eberhard Jüngel, *God's Being Is in Becoming: The Trinitarian Being of God in the Theology of Karl Barth*, trans. and intro. John Webster (Edinburgh: T&T Clark, 2001); Bruce L. McCormack, *Karl Barth's Critically Realistic Dialectical Theology: Its Genesis and Development, 1909–1936* (New York: Clarendon Press, 1995).

decisions and fate as abettors and resisters. A critical theological position forged in the aftermath of the Great War (WWI) would necessarily take seriously the devastation wrought upon Europe; by doing so, Barth set theology on an unprecedented course. Karl Barth's *Römerbrief*, or in English translation, *The Epistle to the Romans*, insisted on a new orientation for theology: God, not the human, was its sole subject.

As Germany's humiliation at Versailles (1919) spiraled into the breakdown of the fragile democracy of the Weimar Republic and led to out-of-control inflation that fueled a nascent racist fascism, Barth saw a timely ally in Paul.[3] The apostle's insistence on divine righteousness as utterly distinct from human reality, divine righteousness as judge of the totality of human existence, became for Barth the perspective from which he could discern the "signs" of his own "times."[4] Theology could not responsibly appeal to the repertoire of Barth's predecessors, such as his teacher Wilhelm Herrmann (himself a student of Albrecht Ritschl). Herrmann had interpreted the Lutheran structure of law and gospel as the religious search for authenticity that would then lead to the gospel. Barth thought that this interpretation was a problem because it diminished the priority of revelation. Herrmann had compromised revelation by inserting a preceding condition of a religious deficit, "law," and then understood "gospel" as the divine reality that could take hold of human religious reality.[5] Herrmann's view that intimately connected religious piety with God was not adequate, according to Barth, to situate the reality of God in sharp opposition to war and genocide. A responsible theology, Barth said, has the duty to join the struggle of its day. Theology, even academic theology, must become an "[emergency] sign" that "something is terribly wrong."[6] The sign is the "real question" of divine righteousness in

---

3. See the article by Paul Dafydd Jones on Barth's use of war imagery as rhetorical resource to articulate a theological anthropology in the *Epistle to the Romans*, 2nd ed.: "The Rhetoric of War in Karl Barth's *Epistle to the Romans*: A Theological Analysis," *Journal for the History of Modern Theology / Zeitschrift für neuere Theologiegeschichte* 17 (2010): 90–111.

4. The phrase is included in a response that Jesus gives to the Pharisees and Sadducees, who ask him "to show them a sign from heaven" (Matt. 16:1b). "You know how to interpret the appearance of the sky, but you cannot interpret the signs of the times" (16:3b). Jesus' claim should press upon every theological generation to responsibly address the concerns and issues of its particular day and age.

5. On Barth's "theological farewell" to Herrmann, see Christophe Chalamet, *Dialectical Theologians: Wilhelm Herrmann, Karl Barth and Rudolf Bultmann* (Zurich: Theologischer Verlag Zurich [TVZ], 2005), 106–10, esp. 177.

6. This is my ET of Barth's German original. Here is Amy Marga's ET: "Theology is a sign of need in the university, a sign that all is not well, even in the *universitas literarum*." Karl Barth, "The Word of God as the Task of Theology (1922)," in *The Word of God and Theology*, trans. Amy Marga (London: T&T Clark, 2011), 180; ET

the context of war. In a 1916 speech Barth asks, "If God were righteous, could he then simply 'allow' all that is now happening in the world?"[7] Yet is it not God's righteousness that calls into question every single aspect of "human righteousness" (*Gerechtigkeiten*, plural in the original German)?[8]

The theologian's métier is to speak of God, as denoted by the Greek original of "word of God [*logos theou*]."[9] In times of cultural and political crisis, the theologian must be compelled by the necessity of acknowledging this task.[10] In such times theologians are required to be obedient to God's word that speaks judgment on human words and human reality. But theologians inevitably speak human words as they try to be faithful to their task. This is the fundamental paradox of the theologian: to be caught in the web of human words while grasping at God's word.

For Barth, theology done by humans stands under God's judgment as an impossible task.[11] In situations grasped under the Pauline "all" (cf. Rom 1:18), the theologian cannot stand apart as sole exception. Yet theology's distinct and peculiar vocation, expressed by its very name, must point to God's reality. As its one and only task, theology must open up occasions for God to speak even if it can never circumscribe God's words in human terms. Barth identifies the Bible as the apposite tool for theology's task. The Bible is the word of God that provides the possibility for God's word to speak its reality into the contemporary situation. In his reading of Paul's Letter to the Romans, Barth's authorship is merged with Paul's. The title of Barth's text, *The Epistle to the Romans* (in German, *Der Römerbrief*), eclipses human authorship. *The Epistle* is neither Paul's nor Barth's, making the theological point that human words standing under divine judgment must press forward to God's speech.

When God speaks, however, the speech precipitates a crisis. Barth's *Epistle* upholds "crisis" as the key term in the text.[12] "Rather, it is for us to perceive

---

of "Das Wort Gottes als Aufgabe der Theologie (Elgersburg, October 1922)," in *Das Wort Gottes und die Theologie: Gesammelte Vorträge* [Munich: Chr. Kaiser, 1925], 162).

7. Karl Barth, "The Righteousness of God (Lecture in the City Church of Aarau, January 16, 1916)," in *The Word of God and Theology*, trans. Amy Marga (London: T&T Clark, 2011), 10.

8. Ibid., 6–7: "We go off and build the pitiful tower at the Babel of our human righteousness, our human self-importance, our human earnestness!"

9. "We ought to speak of God" is the first of three famous theses in Barth's lecture on "The Word of God (1922)," 177.

10. Cf. ibid., 194.

11. The second of Barth's three theses in "The Word of God (1922)" is "But we are humans and as such cannot speak of God" (184).

12. In the New Testament *krisis* means "decision of the judge," the "judgment"; in nonbiblical sources, *krisis* can cover a range of terms in English, such as "parting, estrangement, conflict, selection, decision of an umpire or judge, verdict, sentence," and even "accusation." See Friedrich Büchsel, "*Krisis*," *TDNT* 3 (1965): 941–42.

and to make clear that the whole is placed under the *krisis* [judgment] of the Spirit of Christ," Barth writes in the preface to the third edition (1922).[13] In view of Romans 1–3, Barth explicates the theme of God's righteousness as a crisis for humanity. This same Pauline passage had, as Berlin theologian Karl Holl demonstrated in 1910, been the cause of Luther's terrified conscience.[14] Yet in contrast to Holl's understanding of Luther's interpretation of Romans 1–3, Barth presses the different terms in the passage—wrath, judgment, and gospel—into a more explicit unity.

All three moments reveal God's righteousness. The wrath of God, which Barth interprets from Romans 1:18 as "apart from and without Christ," judges as godless the presumption that the human relationship with God can be secured by piety and emotion or as the reward for decent conduct.[15] The divine judgment mentioned in Romans 2:14–15 is issued against the "Gentiles," identified by Barth as his contemporaries who observe the law "by nature and in the natural order." Barth describes such people in terms directly invoking Schleiermacher's ethical and religious sentiment. They have a "religious feeling" that indicates a complacent satisfaction that the requirements of human righteousness have been met. Barth hermeneutically transfers onto "western European culture" the judgment that Paul invokes on the Gentiles. The "ethical and religious illusion" is rendered as nothing under the divine righteousness. . . . Hence emerges the incomprehensible possibility that lawless men are brought to judgment."[16] Similarly Barth identifies his contemporary culture with the Jews that Paul mentions in Romans 3:1–4. In contrast to Gentiles, Jews are the people who have been given the law. Yet Barth uses

---

13. Barth, *Epistle*, preface to 3rd ed. (1922), 17.

14. Karl Holl's study of Luther's 1517 *Lectures on Romans* precipitated the "Luther-renaissance," or new interest in Luther from historical and biographical perspective. Holl used Luther's lectures to chart a development in Luther's "religion" from the terrified conscience to the Reformation breakthrough. In his analysis of Luther, the main theological concept that Holl focused on was the doctrine of justification in relation to the question of the certainty of salvation. See Karl Holl, "Die Rechtfertigungslehre in Luthers Vorlesung über den Römerbrief mit besonderer Rücksicht auf die Frage der Heilsgewißheit," *Zeitschrift für Theologie und Kirche* 20 (1910): 245–91. On Holl's interpretation of Luther from 1910 to 1926, see the learned monograph by Heinrich Assel, *Der andere Aufbruch: Die Lutherrenaissance—Ursprünge, Aporien und Wege: Karl Holl, Emanuel Hirsch, Rudolf Hermann (1910–1935)*, Forschungen zur systematischen und ökumenischen Theologie 72 (Göttingen: Vandenhoeck & Ruprecht, 1994), esp. 89–100. Luther's *Lectures on Romans* inspired theologians to read either Paul's *Letter to the Romans* or engage in a vibrant discussion of Luther's text through the 1920s. Barth's explicit references to Luther in his *Römerbrief* point to Barth's participation in this common discussion.

15. Cf. Barth, *Epistle*, 43, 44.

16. Ibid., 66, 68, 69.

both terms from Paul's text in order to characterize his contemporaries and uses the designation "Jews" in an echo of Ritschl's theology of history. "For when we have clearly perceived that, if divinity be so concreted and humanized in a particular department of history—the history of religion or the history of salvation—God has ceased to be God." Barth continues to articulate a charge against Ritschl's key term of the kingdom of God: "Set in the midst of human life, righteous men bear witness to reliance upon God and to the advent of His Kingdom." But religion, culture, and history are negated under the divine judgment.[17] "The true God, Himself removed from all concretion, is the Origin of the *krisis* of every concrete thing, the Judge, the negation of this world in which is included also the god of human logic." God speaks. The judgment begins with complete negation.[18]

The passage in Romans 3:21–22a marks a crucial shift in Barth's *Epistle*.[19] Up to this point, Barth has hermeneutically identified Jews and Gentiles with the cultural, religious, and historical currents of his times—all under the divine judgment. From Romans 3:21 onward, however, he treats the divine righteousness that is revealed apart from the law, following Paul's text by shifting the focus onto Jesus Christ. Yet Barth chooses to approach the topic of Christ by laying out the alternative perspective marked by the phrase "apart from the law" (Rom. 3:21). Here Barth explicitly upholds his term "Word of God," which is not found in the biblical passage under consideration as the particular way by which God reveals the divine righteousness. Divine speech is correlated with the revelation of divine righteousness. At the end of a lengthy paragraph in which Barth interprets the opening phrase in Romans 3:21 ("But now") as a series of questions regarding the origin of the *krisis*, he immediately directs attention to the divine speech that comes from a place "beyond time, to space which has no locality," to "*a new heaven and a new earth*," an allusion, of course, to Revelation 21. Barth asserts: "This is the Word of God."[20] The word is God's and hence completely autonomous from human cultural, religious, and historical determinations. God speaks when God wills.

---

17. Ibid., 79.
18. Ibid., 82, on Rom. 3:5–6; see also: "We stand here before an irresistible and all-embracing dissolution of the world of time and things and men, before a penetrating and ultimate *krisis*, before the supremacy of a negation by which all existence is rolled up" (91, on Rom. 3:21–22a).
19. Ibid., 91, quoting Rom. 3:21–22a): "But now apart from the law the righteousness of God hath been manifested, being witnessed by the law and the prophets; even the righteousness of God through his faithfulness in Jesus Christ unto all them that believe."
20. Ibid., 91–92, on Rom 3:21, with emphasis added in the ET.

God's spoken word puts humans in a precarious position, but precarious does not imply chaotic. Rather, human precariousness is given a distinct determination through the word. Barth makes the move to identify the one word of God with Jesus Christ in order to show that both judgment and grace are determined exclusively by their unity in Jesus Christ. Negation and affirmation stand as distinct effects of the one word of God, united in the reality of Jesus Christ, which is external to human reality. Barth asserts that Jesus Christ is the righteousness of God precipitating the human person into the precarious situation. "Apart from the law," he writes, "the righteousness of God is that 'nevertheless' by which He associates us with Himself and declares Himself to be our God." Divine righteousness includes both moments, the moment of judgment that negates human culture, and the moment of affirmation that "pronounces us, His enemies, to be his Friends." The "creative verdict" of a "positive relation between God and man" is available together with the negation of any automatic relation between God and the human.[21]

Thus for Barth, *krisis* has a distinct content. The one word of God encloses human reality under divine judgment, and at the same time that judgment is declared, human reality is "crossed by the deeper marks of the divine forgiveness."[22] Both negation and affirmation are revealed in the gospel, which is composed of the duality of judgment and grace.

Barth is at great literary pains to avoid the suggestion that God's word comes under human control. It always remains external to human reality. He does this by using a spatial designation to refer to the paradoxical place at which the human is addressed by God's word. "The righteousness of God is our standing-place in the air—that is to say, where there is no human possibility of standing—whose foundations are laid by God Himself and supported always by Him only; the place where we are wholly in His hands for favour or disfavour."[23] The famous geometrical metaphor of a tangent "touch[ing] a circle, that is, without touching it" is another way that Barth illustrates the moment of revelation as a single point that cannot be sustained in a line.[24] Revelation takes only a moment. Jesus Christ creates the point of intersection between eternity and time, but in a way that does not surrender eternity to temporality.

---

21. Ibid., 93–94, on Rom 3:21.

22. Ibid., 95, on Rom 3:21. Earlier in *Epistle*, Barth identifies *krisis* with Christ; yet the Rom. 3 passage gives him the opportunity to explicitly address the topic of forgiveness: "Through Jesus Christ men are judged by God. This is their *krisis*, but it is both negation and affirmation, both death and life" (ibid., 69, on Rom. 2:15–16).

23. Ibid., 94, on Rom. 3:21.

24. Ibid., 30, on Rom 1:4.

Remaining is the question of how the theologian makes use of the Bible to instantiate the moment of divine speech. The *Epistle* offers insight into Barth's exegetical practice as a way of embodying the theologian's paradox. Barth claims that the exegetical task is to get to the text's subject matter, to pursue the text "until the actual meaning of it is disclosed." For Barth, the Bible's actual meaning is the word of God that is identified with Jesus Christ.[25] The interpretation of the scriptural word of God is pursued in order to hear Christ, who is the "Voice of God."[26] This is not a work of historical-critical interpretation of Romans. If it were, writes Barth, an analysis of Paul's text would be "a mere repetition in Greek or in German of what Paul says."[27] What Barth has in mind is not "a commentary *on* Paul's Epistle to the Romans," but a commentary "as far as is possible *with* him [Paul]—even to the last word."[28]

Barth's interpretational method works with Paul in trying to discern the text's matter, which Barth describes in the Trinitarian terms of either Jesus Christ or the "Spirit of Christ." By committing oneself to a posture of "utter loyalty" to Paul, the interpreter's task is to press beyond "the author's literary affinities" and "disclose the Spirit of Christ in his reading of Paul." The passages in which Paul himself is "controlled by his true subject-matter" are the passages that Paul's interpreter must identify. Barth must find the specific passages that register the expectation of an encounter in order to assume this posture with Paul. The assumption of this posture is the occasion that Paul's word might be the vehicle of contact with the Spirit of Christ. These "fragments" point to the "whole," by which Barth means that such fragments refer to their subject matter.[29] The exegetical process has as its goal "to see beyond Paul" and thereby to reach the moment of *krisis* at which the Bible "beholds . . . the figure of Jesus Christ."[30] The disclosure of the text's meaning is the encounter between interpreter and the Bible's extrabiblical referent.

The theologian's dilemma is represented in the predicament of being attuned to God's word while always being cognizant that the word is God's prerogative. When the word touches time, the theologian shares in the fate that the word of judgment issues on human religion, culture, and history. Theology's specific task is to orient hearers to a word that it cannot produce in view of a possibility that theology cannot guarantee. Given this description of its task, theology cannot be taken in the usual sense as a third-person objective

---

25. Ibid., preface to 2nd ed. (1921), 7, 10.

26. Ibid., 104, on Rom 3:24.

27. Barth distances his method of interpretation from a historical reading of Paul's text. See ibid., preface to the 2nd ed. (1921), 6–7.

28. Ibid., preface to 3rd ed. (1922), 17, with emphasis added in ET.

29. Ibid., preface to 3rd ed. (1922), 17.

30. Ibid., preface to 3rd ed. (1922), 19; preface to 2nd ed. (1921), 10.

study establishing distance between its claims and the subject matter under investigation. Rather, theology has a unique function to open the possibility of hearing God when God speaks.

The early Barth of the *Epistle* achieves this aim by the rhetorical force of the literary text. Barth's *Epistle* captured the imaginations of theologians in the 1920s with its riveting rhetoric. Rather than articulating his theological claims in propositions concerning the content of divine revelation, as he would later do in the *Church Dogmatics*, the early Barth deployed a distinctive poetics in order to prepare his hearers to expect an event of God's word while at the same time securing God's prerogative to speak. Barth chose a biblical text in order to develop his theological point to existential effect. The Bible served as the site of expectation because an author who had experienced the encounter with God's word had written its texts. Barth adopted a hermeneutical vantage point alongside the apostle Paul in order to wait for the divine speech, and yet waiting required the deployment of a distinct rhetoric that would resist a theology that treated its subject matter as an object to be analyzed. Theology for Barth was to be provocation.

What is heard? The word of God is heard, but the word of God identified with Jesus Christ. Christ is God's word. The identification between word and Christ in Barth's theology allows for a constant referral to the divine subject. God speaks God's word. God's word is Christ. Thus the word, the speech, has a speaker. As speaker of the word, God is subject of the speech, while the word reveals who God is in Christ. Barth explained that the word reveals God's identity as Redeemer and Creator. "But in Christ God speaks as he is. . . . In Christ God offers himself to be known as God beyond our trespass, beyond time and things and men; to be known as the Redeemer of the prisoners, and consequently, as the meaning of all that is—in fact, as the Creator."[31] The word that is identified with Christ is the word that refers Christ to God. It is God who consistently remains God in the word. Christ is utterly transparent to God because Christ is God's word and the word reveals God's identity as Creator and Redeemer of all of reality.

The theologian writes in expectation of an event that theology cannot determine, according to the early Barth; and yet the theologian may make some claims, albeit minimal, about the crucial identification between God's word and Jesus Christ. In his 1924–25 Göttingen lectures, Barth explicitly coins the Latin phrase *"Deus dixit* [God has spoken]" in order to refer to a subject that transcends linguistic formulation. The assertion, as a phrase that condenses Barth's theological identification with word and Christ, has a specific verbal form. Barth explains his choice of the Latin perfect tense:

31. Ibid., 40, 40–41, on Rom 1:17.

> I have chosen the Latin *Deus dixit* not least because of the Latin perfect tense (*dixit*), which expresses something that the translations do not. To be sure, we have here a remarkable and unique perfect. What is denoted is an eternal perfect. But in the first instance it takes the form of the usual perfect, and the meaning cannot be separated from this form. The contingent fact that the church finds the witness to revelation in these specific writings, and that in the witness it finds revelation, is no accident. The contingency lies in the nature of revelation. *Deus dixit* indicates a special, once-for-all, contingent event to which these specific writings rather than any possible writings bear witness.[32]

The choice of verb tense underscores the reason for expecting God's word in the Bible. The past event of God's word in Christ, narrated in the biblical stories of Jesus of Nazareth, remains the ground for any future possibility that God might speak again. On the basis of the "moment" at which eternity has already touched time without capturing Christ by temporality, Christ can again touch time and convey God's word. The "eternal perfect" of divine time encompasses both past event and future possibility. Christ is the point of intersection at which eternity has touched time. The possibility in the future captures the ground by consistently referring to Christ. God has prerogative over God's word because God issues it from the "eternal perfect" perspective; from human perspective, the eternal perfect opens the possibility that God can speak in the present. Although the actual phrase *Deus dixit* appears less often in Barth's subsequent work, where it is gradually replaced by the terminology of the "root of the Trinity" (in vol. I/1 of *Church Dogmatics*), the intention that shaped it is consistent.[33] God's word in Christ has been spoken in the Bible. If God is to speak today, theology has the task to make room for this contingency. It is this status of contingency that must be underlined here since this will be contested in the epistemic-advantage model to be discussed in the next part of the chapter.

The *Deus dixit*, as Barth articulated it in 1924, later served as the theological basis for his understanding of how the human words in Scripture, in the church's proclamation, and in dogmatic theology refer to the word of God. The later theological development concerned the dialectical relation between three kinds of theological words in relation to the one word of God as external to human words, although the possibility is anticipated that God's word will be spoken. Barth developed the anticipatory aspect of the

---

32. Karl Barth, *The Göttingen Dogmatics (1924–25): Instruction in the Christian Religion*, ed. Hannelore Reiffer, trans. Geoffrey W. Bromiley, vol. 1 (Grand Rapids: Eerdmans, 1991), 59.

33. See *CD* I/1:304–33 (§8.2).

word by connecting the earlier identity between the *Deus dixit* and Christ to the "root of the Trinity." Henceforth theology moves beyond rhetoric to the analysis of the specific Trinitarian content that is identified by the *Deus dixit*. God's word that is Christ has a Trinitarian structure. Thus anticipation of the possibility of God's word requires explication of the Trinity as prolegomena, as the doctrinal locus that is devoted to taking up the presuppositions involved when making claims about God's word. The word will become the "root of the Trinity" because the word that is Christ refers to God as its subject. Word and Christ, form and content, are united in the revelation of the triune God. Theology is then required to explicate this "root" according to a Trinitarian concept of revelation. Hence Barth muses in the final sentence of his "Word of God" essay: "The question now, is whether theology can and ought to get beyond being a prolegomena to Christology. It could also indeed be the case that with the prolegomena *everything* is already said."[34]

The two volumes (I/1 and I/2) of the prolegomena to the *Church Dogmatics* demonstrate Barth's commitment to explicating the content of the word of God as doctrine of the Trinity. At this early point in our narrative, Barth has only argued for a distinct rhetoric and for a phrase, the *Deus dixit*, to guide his understanding of theology. He will need an additional resource in order to help him figure out how the *Deus dixit* can sufficiently ground an entire theological system. In the following section, I will consider the next step in Barth's theological development, his contribution to the Barmen Declaration in 1934. The theologians, seminarians, pastors, theologians, and laity of the Confessing Church united to articulate an uncompromising and unequivocal theological rejection of the politics and Christianity of the alliance between Nazism and the *Deutsche Christen* (German Christians). The central concept that enabled the adamant rejection of any association between culture and politics was the primacy of Christ as word of God.

II.2. Word in the Crisis of National Socialism

The Barmen Declaration of May 1934 is one of the most important theological documents of the last century. The six articles that comprise it were composed during a meeting of members of the Confessing Church who represented three Protestant traditions in Germany: Lutheran, Reformed, and United. Theologians and pastors put their names to a theological refutation of the "false doctrine," coercive measures, and "insincere practices" that the German Evangelical Church was enforcing on the churches in order to create

---

34. Barth, "The Word of God (1922)," 197–98, italics in Amy Marga's ET.

a political-ecclesial unity.[35] In its mandate to secure a common stance of resistance under political and ecclesial duress, the Barmen Declaration represents a theological consensus that, in the eyes of its later interpreters, bears close affinity to Barth's theology.

Recent studies have concentrated on the first article of the Barmen Declaration, which declares Jesus Christ to be the critical norm for judging the sin of ideological commitments.[36] Christology is offered as the ground for the unambiguous condemnation of National Socialism and the false Christianity it espoused. In the words of the first article, "Jesus Christ as he is attested to us in Holy Scripture, is the one Word of God that we have to hear, and which we have to trust and obey in life and death." The christological focus is extended over the succeeding five articles and serves to elevate the rule of Christ above any compromise of religion with culture and politics. Christ exercises his lordship in the church, which mediates Christ "in word and sacrament" to a "sinful world."[37] Christ is ruler of church and world, yet he appoints the church as special witness to his sole proprietorship and to "God's mighty claim upon our whole life."[38]

In the first article the insistence on the "one Word of God" played a crucial role in inspiring Barth to develop a theology of Christ in relation to human reality. Whereas in the *Epistle* Barth had insisted on God's word as interruptive of human reality, here in the Barmen Declaration Barth uses the christological assertion of the first article to establish the unity of the word in Jesus Christ and its primacy in "life and death." Christ is identified as the sole word of God and the referent of the human words in Scripture. In addition to the Bible, which (as we have seen in the earlier Barth) has the status of human word that is endowed with a capacity to be interrupted by God's word, Barmen adds church proclamation in Word and sacrament as another theological genre that mediates Christ. But the context of Barmen stipulates

---

35. Text in ET: http://www.ekd.de/english/barmen_theological_declaration.html.

36. Bayer, *Theologie*, 336–79; Martin Heimburger, ed., *Begründete Freiheit: Die Aktualität der Barmer Theologischen Erklärung; Vortragsreihe zum 75. Jahrestag im Berliner Dom*, Evangelische Impulse 1 (Neukirchen/Vluyn: Neukirchener Verlag, 2009).

37. Articles 3 and 2 of the Barmen Declaration (see n. 35). On "word and sacrament," see art. 3's affinity to the Augsburg Confession, art. 7. Thus Barmen, art. 3: "The Christian church is the congregation of the brethren in which Jesus Christ acts presently as the Lord in word and sacrament through the Holy Spirit"; and Augsburg Confession, art. 7 (*BC* 42): "For this is enough for the true unity of the Christian church that there the gospel is preached harmoniously according to a pure understanding and the sacraments are administered in conformity with the divine Word."

38. See Michael Welker, "Rethinking Christocentric Theology," in *Transformations in Luther's Theology: Historical and Contemporary Reflections*, ed. Christine Helmer and Bo Kristian Holm, Arbeiten zur Kirchen- und Theologiegeschichte 32 (Leipzig: EVA-Verlag, 2011), 183–84.

the specific word of God that lays a claim of entire "proprietorship" on the hearer. The article declares Christ's primacy in the church and in the world and demands the obedience of faith. A similar emphasis on Christ's primacy is evident in a debate Barth had, also in 1934, with Emil Brunner on the issue of the formal use of the *imago Dei* in the reception of grace. In Barth's mind, the question was resolved by the rejection of any confusion between Christology and church politics and by the adamant assertion of a decisive "no" to any identification of Christ with "nature," by which Barth meant culture, religion, and politics.[39] Christ is sovereign over church and world, yet Christ may be identified as the divine subject in the relationship between the humans who hear and the scriptural word spoken to them. This carries with it the obligation of the hearer to listen and to obey.

Barth would go on to make productive systematic-theological use of the christological assertion in Barmen's first article. With Christ's primacy over human reality, a system could be established that simultaneously had both an external referent funding the coherence *of* the system and an axiom adjudicating and informing the truth of any theological statements made *within* the system. On the other hand, German Lutherans—who had emphasized Christ as twofold word of God, as law and gospel, following the work of Erlangen theologian Werner Elert—were unable to establish a point of unity for a theological system. Instead they turned to theological genres that clearly articulated the dualism of law and gospel (form criticism, for example, and topical essays).[40] But Jesus Christ is the one word of God for Barth, the unity of judgment and grace, and on this he grounded an entire system of theology with Christ as its key.

The significance of Barmen for Barth's systematic work rests with the consolidated link between Scripture and proclamation that attests to Christ. Critical norm and content are supplied by the attestation but are not in identity with it. The references to attestation in human words and obedience by humans—these references assign sovereignty to a reality external to the human words. While Barmen deemphasizes Barth's earlier concern with the unpredictability of God's word interrupting human life, the text's articles identify God's word exclusively as Christ, who is Lord over all of human reality. The lordship of Christ determines human reality in relation to Christ. The church has a special role in witnessing to this word. The basic building

---

39. Bayer (*Theologie*, 345) works out the historical relation between Barth and Brunner.

40. See Christine Helmer, "United and Divided: Luther and Calvin in Modern Protestant Theology," in *Calvin and Luther: The Unfinished Conversation*, ed. R. Ward Holder, Refo500 Academic Studies 12 (Göttingen: Vandenhoeck & Ruprecht, 2013), 195–211.

blocks for Barth's system are established here: the human words as they attest to Christ's primacy, the insistence on Jesus Christ as one word referred to by numerous words, and the emphasis on Christ as the term of systematic coherence. From this point forward, Barth endows "word" with the theological interest of constructing doctrine. Theology's task has moved beyond providing a rhetorical occasion for an encounter with the word of God, onward to an explicit theological elucidation of the doctrine of the word of God. The next step in Barth's theology would be to orient the word of God to the Trinity, thereby setting up prolegomena as the foundation of his theological system.

II.3. Word in the Prolegomena to Theological System

Barth's theological vision boldly frames his multivolume *Church Dogmatics*. The first two volumes (I/1 and I/2) are decisively concerned with the word of God, considered in light of the question of God's word and its relation to human words in Scripture, church proclamation, and dogmatic theology. The concern of the "prolegomena"—literally translated from the Greek neuter plural present passive participle of the verb *prolegein* as "things that are spoken before"—is the word of God that precedes human words and also grounds them so that they can fulfill the theological task of being "words of God" in a responsible way.

The prolegomena to a system of theology was classically regarded as an anticipatory review of the issues at stake in the task, subject matter, and method of theology. In eighteenth-century Protestant orthodoxy, for example, dogmatic theologies began with prolegomena that articulated a doctrine of Scripture as justification for the truth of subsequent theological claims. The word of God in Scripture grounded theology in its own truth, which was revealed to biblical authors by the Bible's divine author, the Holy Spirit. Barth follows the precedent set by his theological predecessors by concentrating his prolegomena on "the doctrine of the word of God," as the title indicates. But he does not elucidate a theology of Scripture as source and norm for theological truth. Rather, he attunes the topic of word of God to the complex issue at stake, identified in a crucial theological question: How can theology preserve the divine sovereignty of God's word while (1) explicating its conceptual and doctrinal presuppositions, (2) identifying the existential circumstances in which it becomes visible in human words, and (3) defining the requirements for a dialectic that keeps dogmatics open for inquiry.

This far-reaching question necessitated treatment of a number of key methodological and substantive dogmatic-theological issues. The result is an extensive and compressed survey of "the doctrine of the word of God," which intimately relates word to the doctrine of the Trinity.

II.3.1. Word and the Dialectics of Genre

Barth's prolegomena gave a new orientation to theology. "The prefix *pro* in prolegomena," he wrote, "is to be understood loosely to signify the first part of dogmatics rather than that which is prior to it."[41] The decisive theological move is to begin the theological system with a substantive reflection on the content of doctrine, rather than with an epistemological rationale for doctrine.

This move also sets up a direct confrontation with Schleiermacher's theological system. Schleiermacher had commenced his *Christian Faith* with an "Introduction" that came before parts 1 and 2 of the actual system. In it, Schleiermacher defines the task and method of dogmatic theology in view of a consideration of its subject matter, the faith statements articulated by historical Christian communities. Human words are the object of Schleiermacher's introduction. His analysis gives an account of the religious, cultural, and historical factors that have shaped the expression of these words. When Barth headlined his prolegomena as the "first part of dogmatics," the contrast with Schleiermacher could not have been sharper. According to Barth, theology begins with an elucidation of the "presupposition" that theology can speak of God at all.[42] What makes theology possible is "the Word of God as the criterion of dogmatics."[43] In Barth's view, theology's ground is nothing other than the revelation of the triune God; hence the prolegomena becomes the extensive treatment of the doctrine of the Trinity. "The most striking anticipation of this kind will consist in the fact that we shall treat of the whole doctrine of the Trinity and the essentials of Christology in this connexion, namely, as constituent parts of our answer to the question of the Word of God."[44]

Yet theology is a human task, as Barth acknowledges. His prolegomena are his own all-too-human words about God under the parameters he has assigned to theology's words about God. While Barth's theology aims to analyze the concept of the word of God, its status as a human enterprise must honor the fundamental assumption regarding God's word outside of human theological words. As a subjective genitive (word *of* God), word belongs to God and has primacy over all human words, even the words documenting Barth's thoughts on theological prolegomena. Barth insists on the alterity of God's word: "In both its investigations and its conclusions, it must keep in view that God is in heaven and it [dogmatics] on earth, and that God, His revelation, and faith always live their

41. *CD* I/1:42 (§2.2, with italics in ET).
42. *CD* I/1:89 (§4.1).
43. *CD* I/1:43 (§2.2): "In the prolegomena to dogmatics, therefore, we ask concerning the Word of God as the criterion of dogmatics."
44. *CD* I/1:44 (§2.2).

own free life over against all human talk, including that of the best dogmatics."[45] But God's word "in heaven" is the "presupposition" of theology on earth. With the term "presupposition," Barth underscores his key theological point regarding the utter dependence of human words, including his prolegomena, on God's word. Barth's "presupposition" has to do with reliance on the possibility of God's entrance into the time of human words, with that moment when God as source of all knowledge speaks. When this moment occurs, it is "grace being the event of personal address," "the present moment of the speaking and hearing of Jesus Christ Himself, the divine creation of light in our hearts."[46] Theology's presupposition has to do with God's reality, which is not contained in theology's concept. Prolegomena has the task to refer to the transcendent reality that is its own presupposition.

For Barth, prolegomena is not the only genre in which theology can be practiced. There are three human "words" that may refer in distinct, complementary, and mutually correcting ways to the divine reality, according to Barth. As we have seen, these are the genres of (1) Scripture, (2) proclamation, and (3) dogmatic theology. Barth gives a historical reason for identifying these particular genres. Scripture, proclamation, and dogmatics have been the ways in which the Christian community through history has shaped its orientation to God's word in faithful reliance that God's word retains divine sovereignty.[47] Barth uses the temporally tinged language of repetition—rather than the term "presupposition"—to explain that the three genres refer to God's word on the basis of an expectation grounded in the past. These words may repeat what in the past has been true, but their deployment in the present is no guarantee. It is the expectation that God might endow the human word with the truth attached to the repetition. Barth refers to this action of God's word when God speaks by using the language of grace and presence. "The presence of God is thus the grace of God, . . . and therewith fulfils the promise in a twofold sense: by making the repetition effected by men a true one, and by corresponding to the proclaimed promise by a real new coming of His Word."[48] The repetition in human words of God's word from the past opens the horizon of future expectation that God's word will grace the present again.

The goal of theology is witness. Barth defines this key term in his theology thus: "Witnessing means pointing in a specific direction beyond the self and on to another."[49] All three genres of theology participate in the task of

45. *CD* I/1: 85–86 (§3.2).
46. *CD* I/1:41 (§2.2).
47. This is the main point of *CD* I/1:88–124 (§4).
48. *CD* I/1:67 (§3.1).
49. *CD* I/1:111 (§3.3).

witnessing to the transcendent divine reality.[50] Yet each participates in this
activity by means of dialectical relations among themselves, relations whereby
each genre contributes key dimensions to the witness and is irreducible to
the other two genres. God's word in the past is recorded in Scripture and
can become the topic of proclamation that anticipates the future. "The Bible,
speaking to us and heard by us as God's Word, bears witness to past revelation. Proclamation, speaking to us and heard by us as God's Word, promises
future revelation."[51] Between past and future, Scripture and proclamation, is
an "inner connection" that requires the application of a criterion to determine
the truth of the connection. Dogmatic theology is conventionally assigned
the task of discerning theology's truth. But in this passage (in *CD* I/1, §4),
Barth underlines that the criterion is "not at our disposal. . . . It is the criterion which handles itself and is in no other hands."[52] The task of dogmatics
is critical and constructive, carried out in reciprocal relation to Scripture and
proclamation. "From this 'becoming what it is' there develops for the Church
another task alongside that of proclamation, namely, that of dogmatics, i.e.,
the task of testing, criticising and correcting the actual proclamation of the
Church at a given time."[53] The application of the criterion, like the repetition of Scripture and the proclamation of the word, takes place in the moving space of the present as this tense refers to the past and expects the future
event. The activity of witness, as it combines the efforts of all three genres
of God's word in human speech, is located in history. "This content must be
found each time in the middle space between the particular text in the context
of the whole Bible and the particular situation of the changing moment."[54] All
three work together in order to provide the occasion for a theology that does
not rely on past formulations as timeless norms but anticipates the novelty of
divine advent.

The crux of Barth's claims about human words in the three genres of
Scripture, proclamation, and dogmatic theology is that they are on *this* side
of the human/divine divide. They each contribute a distinct perspective that
refers to the transcendent word of God. Yet no single genre has a monopoly
on the word. The event of an encounter with God's word cannot be predicted

---

50. *CD* I/2:814 (§23.2): "Dogmatics cannot desire to be anything but a witness to
this transcendent point of view, just as preaching itself and Holy Scripture, and even,
on its human side, the revelation of God in Jesus Christ, can only be a witness to it."

51. *CD* I/1:111 (§3.3).

52. *CD* I/1:192–93 (§4.1).

53. *CD* I/1:288 (§7.3).

54. *CD* I/1:79 (§3.2). Barth continues: "Dogmatics can only be a guide to the right
mastery and the right adaptability, to the right boldness and the right caution, for the
given moment when this space has to be found."

with any guarantee on the basis of rehearsing a scriptural passage or doctrinal formulation. Rather, the past is part of the living tradition in the present by recollection, which has the aim of providing the occasion for the reality of God's word in the future. For Barth, the externality of the word is retained as a referent of witness. The three types of witnessing are mustered in dialectical relations among one another in order to responsibly fulfill their task. This activity, however, requires more than a formal delineation of a dialectical process. Theology must be referred to content, namely, the content of the word of God. It is to this content, introduced by Barth's identification of the criterion of dogmatic theology, that I now turn. We will see how Barth retains the contingency of his own representation of the doctrine of the Trinity while also making claims regarding its truth.

II.3.2. Word and Dogmatics

The task of dogmatic theology is to apply the criterion of the word of God to a particular relation between two *relata* (narrations). Both are related to the word of God in distinct ways: the Bible attests to the revelation of the word of God that has taken place in the past, while proclamation anticipates the word of God as event in the future. Dogmatics adds another aspect of referring to the word of God by its task of applying this criterion in order to measure the agreement between proclamation and revelation attested in the Bible.[55] Dogmatics cannot possess the criterion because, as the word of God, the criterion is the transcendent reality of God's word. But dogmatics can anticipate the criterion when it executes its task of measuring the relation between word of God in Bible and proclamation. The task of dogmatics is the dynamic assessment of both past revelation and proclamation in addition to providing a judgment about the adequacy of the relation between revelation and proclamation.

Defining doctrine's responsibility as that of assessing relations between Bible and Christian proclamation lends to the genre of doctrine a particular property that may surprise those familiar with contemporary readings of Barth. Barth insists that dogmatic theology poses a question. Dogmatic theology is open inquiry into a relation of Bible and proclamation rather than a precise formulation of it, and it remains an open inquiry throughout. Barth illustrates the triple aspect of questioning that dogmatic theology practices when assessing the word of God in the relation between Bible and proclamation.

> Thus the real results of dogmatics, even though they have the form of the most positive statements, can themselves only be new questions, questions to and fro between what the Church seems to proclaim and

55. *CD* I/1:265 (§7.1).

the Bible seems to want proclaimed, questions which can be put only with the greatest modesty and a sense of supreme vulnerability if they are perhaps serious and significant questions.[56]

None of the human formulations of the word of God—Bible, proclamation, or dogmatic theology—can be identified with any certainty or predicted as word of God. As human words and human judgments, they remain open to the reality of God's word, and in their openness, they are characterized as inquiry, not answer.[57] Barth combines the language of striving with the quest for truth. Dogmatic theology must use human language to formulate the results of its inquiry; yet even when language makes a claim of truth, it must be understood in the sense of referring to truth outside of its linguistic formulation. "These are propositions which grasp and reproduce the truth of revelation only to the extent that they strive after it."[58] There is no perfect representation of the transcendent reality of the word of God in human language, judgments, or dogmatic propositions. There is only the human task of dogmatic theology that always retains its character of open inquiry conducted in obedience to God's word.[59]

An intriguing conclusion may be drawn from Barth's understanding of dogmatic theology as inquiry that never reproduces the truth of God's word in human words. Dogmatic theology is open to novelty! Barth argues that novelty is part of dogmatic theology's critical task. "Its scientific character consists in unsettling rather than confirming Church proclamation as it meets it in its previous concretions and especially in its present-day concretion."[60] Doctrine's "scientific" or academic task, which involves historically evaluative and constructive dimensions, applies an academic theological method so that church proclamation might better prepare for the event of God's word. The method of critical inquiry binds the theologian to his location in time, to his academic context, which is historically contextualized by his methods, language, and academic consensus.[61] Barth makes clear that any reliance on past formulations results in the desiccation of doctrine. A historical repetition of the past without scientific critical inquiry is "complacent," "its critical nerve is perhaps dead," "its significance is merely that of a pleasant certification that all

56. *CD* I/1:268–69 (§7.1).
57. *CD* I/1:266 (§7.1): "Yet it is still the word of man. The Word of God is above dogma as the heavens are above the earth."
58. *CD* I/1:267 (§7.1).
59. *CD* I/1:274 (§7.1): "The question of its obedience includes that of its truth."
60. *CD* I/1:281 (§7.2).
61. *CD* I/1:283 (§7.2): "The dogmatician, too, must think and speak in a particular age and should thus be a man of his age, which also means a man of the past that constitutes his age, i.e., an educated man."

is well and can go on as it has been."[62] Open inquiry in dogmatic theology has as its goal to serve the word of God, which, as we have seen in Barth's thought since the *Epistle*, has the unsettling dimension of judgment on human culture, even upon the dogmatic theologian's words. Critical inquiry is a production of novelty because it strives to prepare church proclamation for God's truth. Yet in its very historical location and with the apposite critical edge, it might yield formulations that are open for the novelty of God's encounter.

II.3.3. Word, Trinity, and Dogmatics

Dogmatic theology open to the encounter with God's word requires historical, critical academic, and constructive dimensions. This is Barth's claim. Formal considerations of the task of dogmatic theology have not yet taken into account the content of the criterion that dogmatic theology applies, however. The question concerning content is integral to Barth's understanding of dogmatic theology. The criterion cannot be applied without some determination of its content. This criterion refers directly to the identity of the one who has spoken, and furthermore, to the content of who God is.[63] Here we get to the heart of the Trinity as the doctrine of the word of God.

The question of articulating content concerns its inevitable rendering into human speech. We are back to the question that had plagued Barth from his early years as a theologian, pondering the "impossible possibility" of the theologian's task. What is the procedure by which he can purport to make doctrinal claims about the Trinitarian content of the word of God when the word's judgment is acknowledged as a possible judgment on human formulations, even the theologian's articulations about the Trinity? The answer is an intriguing movement through distinct modalities of theological thought, which underscores Barth's recognition that he is participating in a human activity.

The *Deus dixit* emerges as the initial point for Barth's discussion of content. Barth lifts the phrase up in section 8 of *Church Dogmatics*. Since Barmen, *Deus dixit* had taken on the meaning of Jesus Christ as one word of God and lordship over culture, religion, and politics. Barth reiterates this claim by identifying speech with divine speaker. "God's own direct speech . . . is not to be distinguished from the act of speaking and therefore is not to be distinguished from God Himself."[64] The *Deus dixit* ought to be taken in terms of content that is "spoken." Barmen had explicitly stipulated "lordship" as integral to this content. Barth rehearses this stipulation in a claim concerning the divine

---

62. *CD* I/1:281–82 (§7.2).
63. Cf. *CD* I/1:297–301 (§8.1).
64. *CD* I/1:304 (§8.2).

speech that reveals divine identity. When God speaks, "God reveals Himself as the Lord."[65] What began as the minimal phrase referring to the transcendent reality of God's speech (*Deus dixit*) is now in the *Church Dogmatics* a claim about the content of revelation.

If one looks solely at the rhetoric of "revelation" here, one might assume that Barth couches his approach to the Trinity in epistemological terms, with revelation taken as an epistemological principle that awards access to the Trinity. But Barth lets us know that his approach to the Trinity via the assertion of Christ's lordship has a different purpose. The assertion "God reveals Himself as the Lord" is not found verbatim in the Bible or church creed. It is Barth's own abbreviated formulation about the "revelation itself as attested by Scripture."[66] As such, it is not to be identified with an actual revelation. The fact of revelation is a reality that cannot be captured by, but merely attested to, in the human words of Scripture. If Scripture is a direct attestation, then the assertion is a concept of revelation concerning "the reality of revelation" that "stands beyond the concept, even and precisely the concept derived from the Bible and proclamation."[67] It is an indirect reference to the fact of revelation. As such, it has a theological function as "root of the doctrine of the Trinity."[68]

The function of the abbreviated formula as "indirect" reference to revelation is crucial for understanding the status that Barth assigns to the theological task of working out the doctrine of the Trinity as a human enterprise.[69] Barth clarifies a lingering misunderstanding from the first edition of the prolegomena. "The words were obviously not meant to be proof themselves. They were simply meant to reduce a completed proof provisionally to a suitable formula which would be as perspicuous as possible."[70] As a formula in Barth's own words, the assertion has a specific function in the articulation of doctrine of the Trinity. It is an abbreviation of the fact of revelation in Scripture; on the basis of the fact of revelation, the question can be asked concerning its possibility. "The God who reveals Himself here can reveal Himself."[71] At stake is the modality of possibility. Here is the doctrine of the Trinity as "the

65. *CD* I/1:306 (§8.2).
66. *CD* I/1:307 (§8.2).
67. *CD* I/1:291 (§7.3).
68. *CD* I/1:307 (§8.2).
69. *CD* I/1:308 (§8.2): "The doctrine of the Trinity is a work of the Church, a record of its understanding of the statement or of its object, a record of its knowledge of God or of its battle against error and on behalf of the objectivity of its proclamation, a record of its theology and to that degree of its faith, and only to that extent, only *indirectly*, a record of revelation" (emphasis added).
70. *CD* I/1:296, in fine print (§8.1).
71. *CD* I/1:316 (§8.2).

inner possibility of this fact [of revelation]."[72] The Trinity is the "inner condition" in God that makes possible the reality that "the God who has revealed Himself according to the witness of Scripture, is the same in unimpaired unity and yet also the same thrice in different ways in unimpaired distinction." In the modality of possibility, the Trinity offers a consideration of God's triune identity. As Barth writes, "The doctrine of the Trinity is an analysis of this statement, i.e., of what it denotes."[73] The relation of assertion to Trinity is not deductive, but a denotation at the level of conceptual possibility.

When the doctrine of the Trinity is taken in the modality of possibility, it renders explicit the "inner condition" for the possibility of Trinitarian revelation. This status of possibility informs Barth's understanding of the truth claim of the doctrine. It is, as he writes, an *interpretation*.[74] By this he means more than the historical claim about the gap between biblical statements and Trinitarian formulations in fourth-century creeds. By using "interpretation" here, Barth makes a conceptual point concerning the possibility of revelation as attested in Scripture and proclamation. The doctrine of the Trinity is the interpretation, the making explicit, of the "inner condition" of revelation. The text of the doctrine is related to the attestations of revelation, possibly making use of biblical terms and concepts, while also "translat[ing] and exeget[ing] the text. And this means, e.g., that it makes use of other concepts besides those in the original." Interpretation is not verbatim repetition of past formulations but explanation that "sets something new over against what is there."[75] The theological work of analyzing the root of the Trinity is in this sense an interpretation that produces the doctrine of the Trinity. As interpretation, doctrine is a human endeavor that inquires into the inner possibility of God's revelation. The doctrine of the Trinity thus remains a question for theology, not its answer.

II.4. Doctrine and Ground of System?

Another question concerning the "root" of the Trinity needs to be asked here, having to do with the degree to which the linguistic-literary articulation of the doctrine of the Trinity functions as the ground of Barth's system of theology. The question of ground, as in Brunner's riposte against Schleiermacher, is the systematic-theological question of prolegomena. To recall an earlier point,

---

72. *CD* I/1:291 (§7.3).

73. *CD* I/1:307–8 (§8.2).

74. *CD* I/1:312 (§8.2): "What we do in fact gather from the doctrine of the Trinity is who the God is who reveals Himself, and this is why we present the doctrine here as an *interpretation* of revelation" (emphasis added).

75. *CD* I/1:308 (§8.2).

systems of Protestant orthodoxy appealed to a doctrine of Scripture in order to ground the truth claims of dogmatic theological propositions articulated in subsequent sections of the theological manuals. The issue of ground is especially important for Barth because of his claim concerning the distinction between human theological articulations and divine reality. In the prolegomena to his system, how does Barth negotiate the relation between his theological claims about the doctrine of the Trinity and the external reality of the word of God?

Again, dogmatic theology, as Barth has represented this discipline, has as its task the application of the criterion of the word of God to the agreement between Scripture and proclamation. The invocation of a criterion for measurement presupposes the actuality of the event of God's word in Scripture and an anticipation of this actuality in the future. A modality of actuality serves as point of entry for conceptualizing the task of dogmatic theology. Yet the articulation of the criterion in dogmatic theology, in order to apply it to the relation between Scripture and proclamation, is an exercise in another modality: not actuality, but possibility. While Scripture is witness to past revelation, and proclamation is the expectation of a future revelation, doctrine that measures the agreement between past and future is concerned with the inner possibility of God's revelation. Barth characterizes the dogmatic-theological description of the root of the Trinity in the modality of possibility. Access to the possibility, however, is through the actuality of God's revelation in the past and its anticipation in the future. The root of the Trinity is the "inner condition" or possibility of God's revelation of God's self. But in terms inquiring into theological truth, Barth presses another modality. At this point in his prolegomena, he asks how necessary the doctrine of the Trinity is. Although Barth admits that all language, even that of the Trinitarian doctrine, is on the human side, may a claim of necessity, and thereby a claim of truth, be made concerning the Trinity in a specific linguistic-literary articulation?

The conceptual move to querying "necessity" is located in the section of prolegomena to the *Church Dogmatics* heading the systematic treatments of the persons of Jesus Christ and the Holy Spirit. Having made claims about the doctrine of the Trinity as interpretation in volume 1 (*CD* I/1), Barth looks in the second volume (*CD* I/2) at the actuality of Jesus Christ and poses the question: "How far is God free for us in His revelation?" Barth proceeds by approaching the reality of revelation from the modality of possibility. The question of possibility, as posed from the human conceptual perspective, is that the human can offer no reasons for why the reality of God's word as event is at all possible. "No less than everything, i.e., no less than the whole of man's cosmos, seems to speak against this possibility taking place."[76] The avenue of

---

76. *CD* I/2:30 (§13.2).

possibility is exhausted. No concept that can be articulated in human terms can explain the reality of God.

Barth attempts another approach, this time inquiring into the divine nature for an explanation. The answer is grounded in the nature of divine freedom. "So it becomes possible in His freedom that He should be our God."[77] The reality of the divine "condescension to earth" in Jesus' incarnation gives the human theologian a clue as to how to represent in thought the divine reality of the word of God as it moves to the human. Human conceptual thinking may represent this movement in a modality that corresponds to divine freedom. Barth moves from the modality of possibility—"if He wished to impart Himself to us"—to the modality of necessity—"He had to . . ."[78] The vocabulary of necessity, as Barth deploys it with formulations such as "should" and "had to,"[79] is surprising given his qualifications concerning the relation of human speech to the truth of God's reality, even in this particular section, which speaks in the modality of necessity.[80] Does this modality of necessity prove the exception to Barth's own rule regarding the human capacity for formulating theological truths corresponding to the divine nature? Is Barth formulating a ground to his theological system on this side of the human speech/divine word distinction, thereby making a normative truth claim for his linguistic-literary formulation of the doctrine of the Trinity?

These questions concern how we are to take Barth's mention of the modality of necessity when he refers the reason for the incarnation to the divine nature. We must be careful to see that Barth mentions this particular modality in this section, which refers to a specific Trinitarian content. His claims about necessity are not to be extended beyond the particular claims he makes concerning the Word's capacity for relationship with humans. Barth attaches this capacity to a speculative claim about the Trinity in eternity: "Because already from eternity, already in Himself, before we or the world existed, He was ready and open for us, He was confederated with us in His Word or Son."[81] Barth has moved from the modality of reality in the incarnation and onward to its ground in the triune nature of God. The movement in human thought from reality to divine necessity follows a distinct logic. Barth explains:

> Or (because interpretation is involved in the question of fact, and nothing but fact is involved in the question of interpretation) we must

77. *CD* I/2:31 (§13.2).
78. *CD* I/2:32 (§13.2).
79. *CD* I/2:31–32 (§13.2).
80. *CD* I/2:31, in fine print (§13.2): "It corresponds with the greatness of God, however, not to be tied down and limited by His own nature."
81. *CD* I/2:34–35 (§13.2).

first understand the reality of Jesus Christ as such, and then by reading from the tablet of this reality, understand the possibility involved in it, the freedom of God, established and maintained in it, to reveal Himself in precisely this reality and not otherwise, and so the unique possibility which we have to respect as divine necessity.[82]

Barth understands necessity in a particular way. Having first assigned possibility to the divine nature of freedom, he goes on to locate necessity in the divine nature of the Trinity. It is Anselm of Canterbury's *Cur Deus homo?* that surfaces at this point as Barth's model for necessity.[83] The question of "why" God has become a human is an inquiry into the divine nature. This inquiry is initiated by the question concerning the possibility of the incarnation, which is located in divine freedom. On the basis of this possibility, which in Barth's conceptuality is external to any human possibility, "we take our stand not above but beneath the reality of revelation, and assign necessity to it and not to our grounds, not even to our grounds in Trinitarian theology."[84] Even the movement in thought that assigns necessity to the incarnation as it is viewed from "beneath the reality of revelation" cannot usurp the place of God's word. The doctrinal claim about divine necessity is distinct from God's reality.

What truth can be assigned to the linguistic-literary articulation of the content of the triune God as thought through in the modality of necessity? Barth provides two answers to this question. In the relevant section (13) that I have been discussing in detail, Barth advances the language of repetition. The modality of necessity is "thrice repeating what was previously told us. By such repetition we shall and must acknowledge the necessity of His actual manifest will, His *potentia ordinata* [ordered power]."[85] Barth seems to suggest that the movement in thought from reality to necessity is informed by the theologian's disposition of obedience to God's word. The theologian's task of articulating doctrine presupposes this posture of obedience to God's word. When the theologian makes doctrinal claims about the Trinity, she is connected to past revelation by virtue of her obedience to the word of God spoken in the past. Yet this stipulation is articulated, as was the case at Barmen too, in view of the content of the "manifest will," which is Christ. Necessity is invoked in view of the specific content of the word of God, Jesus Christ. It is only in view of this particular christological content that necessity, and its repetition in human speech, can be entertained as a theological claim. Barth's discourse on necessity quickly fades. Necessity is qualified by other possibilities that reside

82. *CD* I/2:7–8 (§13.1).
83. The explicit reference to Anselm occurs in the fine print immediately after the above citation; in *CD* I/2:8 (§13.1).
84. *CD* I/2:35 (§13.2).
85. *CD* I/2:37 (§13.2).

in the divine freedom.[86] Barth entertains the modality of necessity only as it is restricted by the *Deus dixit* axiom. He has, however, added a Trinitarian determination to the christological content of this axiom, as articulated in the Barmen Declaration. Does the doctrine of the Trinity then function as the ground of his system?

The second answer to the question concerning the necessity of a Trinitarian claim refers to the broader systematic-theological claims of Barth's prolegomena. One might think that the modalities he has adopted in order to make claims about the doctrine of the word of God in Trinitarian theological terms have established assurances for a normative truth. But we must remember that, for Barth, the norm is always God's reality, not human formulations. Barth brings up the issue of norm when writing about the principle informing his system. Particularly the question for the theological system comes up in the wake of the problem of Schleiermacher. In a section at the end of *CD* I/2 (§24.2), Barth explicitly addresses this issue of the basic principle that justifies constructing a dogmatic theological system. He raises the question as to whether a dogmatic system can have a "material principle" that serves as ground or axiom or principle of coherence for the system of theology. But in terms characteristic of the early Barth of the *Epistle*, the later Barth lays this idea to rest. "Rightly understood, it is the material principle of dogmatics itself which destroys at its root the very notion of a dogmatic system. Where there is no longer a secure platform for thinking and speaking, there is likewise no system." Here Barth does not disqualify academic thinking from being systematic. In fact, he considers it a feature of academic thought, including theology, to engage in the process of scientific discovery and the integration of the results of discovery into a coherence scheme. What cannot inform the system of theology is, for Barth, the unique center of the theological system. *God* is the transcendent reality to which theology witnesses. In this regard, theology's linguistic formulations cannot be said to correspond with this reality or fail to correspond with this reality. The transcendent reality must be understood as poised to judge the entire theological system. If the word of God is "understood as the centre and foundation of dogmatics and of Church proclamation," then with any "unfolding and presentation of the content of the Word of God," we must be aware that the event of the word of God can be destabilizing.[87] The theological system that is committed to referring to the externality of God's word can be a system in the sense of a coherent elucidation of a center. But this system must be open to disruption

---

86. *CD* I/2:39 (§13.2): "We acknowledge this reality to be necessary. But we cannot deny that it might have pleased God to reveal Himself in another way as well."

87. *CD* I/2:868, 869 (§24.2).

by the word of God because its center lacks the stability of corresponding (or failing to correspond) to God's reality.

In this sense, Barth can say that theology is perpetually in a state of beginning again. "There is only the investigation and teaching which take place in the act of dogmatic work and which, strictly speaking, must continually begin again at the beginning in every point." As an academic discipline, theology must strive for systematic coherence. But because it is perpetually attuned to "receive new truth," its system as grounded in God can also be judged by God.[88] Theology is cognizant of the basic paradox of its own task: rendering in human words a reality that has a prerogative in its own terms.

Barth's commitment to the radical exteriority of the word of God remained consistent from the *Epistle to the Romans* to the prolegomena in the Church *Dogmatics*. Theology maintains that its primary reality is God; God's word remains the divine prerogative to judge human words. Theology is a human activity standing under judgment, but a special understanding of its referential relation to God's word keeps it open, as an emergency sign, to the activity of articulating theological claims amid distinct dialectical relations between three genres of Scripture, proclamation, and dogmatics. Even in view of his own constructive work—as he represents the doctrine of the Trinity according to the three modalities of actuality, possibility, and necessity—Barth continues to be true to his commitments regarding the theologian's word, its historical and social situation, and its function to point to God's word as external reality. The theologian owes her word to the reality that she seeks to understand, interpret, and elucidate. But as human words, her words inevitably are historically and socially located and subject to the reality to which they refer. Faithful obedience to God's word characterizes the responsible theologian's disposition. Yet the theologian must not be surprised when God's word interrupts her words. When God speaks, God's word precipitates a crisis, even for the human words that must make way for this event.

Part 2

I. THE EPISTEMIC-ADVANTAGE MODEL OF DOCTRINE

When Barth took the doctrine of the Trinity as the theological representation of God as speaker of the word, he inspired theologians to pay attention to the material content of doctrine as they wrote prolegomena to systems of

---

88. *CD* I/2:867–68 (§24.2).

theology. The explication of the doctrine of God's word was not restricted to epistemological and methodological issues. In the wake of Barth's new direction for prolegomena, the issue of ground arose. If a doctrine having to do with the material content of Christian belief functioned as ground for a theological system, then it could be used as a material-theological source for drawing analogies and connections between doctrines. The Trinity as key doctrine proposed by Barth inspired theologians to pay attention to this doctrine and to give it new prominence in their theological system.[89] In the process of this emergent awareness of how ground provided the doctrinal content for interpreting the material-theological claims of related doctrines, the concept of doctrine would undergo a transformation.

Here the second part of this chapter considers how the issue of ground, which Barth had oriented to the reality of God, has come to be identified with the doctrine of the Trinity. We have seen how Barth persisted in distinguishing doctrine from God's reality. When one turns to contemporary theologians who claim Barth as their inspiration, however, one notices that the doctrine of the Trinity has come to be identified with a different theological purpose. I will look at a specific theologian at the beginning of the twenty-first century, one whom I take to be representative of a more widely shared contemporary understanding of doctrine, which I call the *epistemic-advantage model*. Bruce D. Marshall has articulated a view of doctrine that is premised on linguistic-literary articulations of Christian faith. His theology assigns to doctrine an epistemic function that organizes the Christian worldview according to particular "categories." By appealing to Kant's terminology in an attempt to convey what Marshall might mean by "epistemic," I see the approach to doctrine exemplified in Marshall's work as both requiring articulation in linguistic-literary formulations and functioning as categories through which the world is perceived. Doctrines, like Kant's categories of the understanding, inform the believer's perception of the world, so that the world is shaped by these particular doctrines. By the logic of this approach, doctrine may extend its normative function over an entire Christian worldview in all its many dimensions. But in the process of assigning to doctrine its epistemic status, this way of conceptualizing doctrine ends up losing its

---

89. See Kathryn Tanner's *Jesus, Humanity and the Trinity: A Brief Systematic Theology* (Minneapolis: Fortress Press, 2001), which is a condensed systematic theological treatment of the key doctrines of Christianity. The concept of gift-giving emerges as central to the immanent Trinity and is subsequently extended as coherence principle into other doctrines, such as incarnation, redemption, and ethical response. See my extended review of this book, "A Systematic Theological Theory of Truth in Kathryn Tanner's *Jesus, Humanity and the Trinity: A Brief Systematic Theology*," *Scottish Journal of Systematic Theology* 57, no. 2 (May 2004): 203–20.

referent to a transcendent reality, as I will argue. What happens to doctrine when it loses its referent? This part concludes by examining the implications of such a position, which in my opinion yields a view of Christian truth as normative social construction.

I begin with the way in which doctrine is formulated. We take up the issue, already introduced by Barth, of the theological role that a particular phrase, in Barth's case *Deus dixit*, plays in the construction of doctrine. Barth formulated this term in order to condense Christian doctrines into one root phrase that could then be unpacked in terms of distinct doctrines. Such a root phrase, or assertion, also appears as a feature of contemporary theology. My first question is how the condensation of doctrine into a root assertion is deployed in the epistemic-advantage model of doctrine, and second, how it is then applied to the Christian worldview.

I.1. Doctrine as Root Assertion

Assertion is a striking mode of speech that has captured the interest of Christian theologians. What better linguistic genre than assertion to capture the indicative force and literal meaning of a faith proposition? "The Holy Spirit is no Skeptic," Luther writes to Erasmus in the opening lines of *Bondage of the Will* (1525), "and it is not doubts or mere opinions that he has written on our hearts, but assertions more sure and certain than life itself and all experience."[90] Although in this passage Luther commends the assertion, he is specifically referring to the articulation of Christian doctrine in the literary genre of the confession of faith. For Luther, doctrinal truth and certainty are grounded in a transcendent source. The Holy Spirit reveals who God is, and doctrine represents this revelation in language, which in the context of debate is invoked in the assertive mode. As Luther writes, "For it is not the mark of a Christian mind to take no delight in assertions; on the contrary, a man must delight in assertions or he will be no Christian."[91] When the Christian is tempted by the devil, when faith's certainty is under assault, she can put her trust in the God invoked in the confession "I believe . . ." Assertion characterizes the illocutionary force of the confession of faith. When one orally professes the content of faith, certainty is grounded in the truth of God, who is the object of the confession.[92] The delight in assertions reflects the confidence that doctrine refers to the God in whom trust can be placed.

90. *LW* 33:24.
91. *LW* 33:20–21.
92. Heikki Kirjavainen discusses how, for Luther, doctrine is related to its object: "Die Spezifizierung der Glaubensgegenstände bei Luther im Licht der Spätmittelalterlichen Semantik," in *Thesaurus Lutheri: Auf der Suche nach neuen Paradigmen der*

The connection between assertion, doctrine, and God is implied in Luther's theology. It is the fate of this connection in contemporary theology that is at issue in this section. Let me illustrate what I mean here by turning to the contemporary Lutheran theologian Robert W. Jenson, who uses the *verbum externum* (external word) in order to situate the gospel as the object of theology. As a linguistic-literary object, the gospel may be rendered in a "root assertion" that, for Jenson, is the first step in grounding his study of the doctrine of the Trinity. The work of doctrine begins with the identification of its content. For Jenson, the crucial thing is that theology has to do with a specific object, the gospel, which in Lutheran terms of the *verbum externum* means the gospel that is heard.[93] The gospel is communication occurring in language; and as linguistically formulated communication, the gospel is rendered as the object of theological reflection. If it is to be the object of theological reflection, Jenson argues, it must have a specific logical form. He writes, "Thus every theologoumenon has the implicit form: 'To be saying the gospel, let us say 'F' (rather than 'G'). 'F' may be a *sample* of right gospel or it may be a *metalinguistic stipulation* about the gospel."[94] Although he offers the concrete example of such a "metalinguistic stipulation," Jenson prefers a more biblically oriented "sample" of the gospel, which he takes from 2 Corinthians 4:14: the resurrection as central event communicated in the gospel has to do with "God self-identified as the 'one who raised the Lord Jesus.'"[95] Once the key "logical form" of the gospel is identified, this root assertion may then be unpacked in order to yield a number of Christian doctrines. Theology does so by describing the particular doctrines related to the gospel's logical form. To refer again to Jenson's particular sample, the root assertion is related to the doctrine of the Trinity. He writes, "The present, here much unclarified, point to attend theologically to the Resurrection of Jesus is to attend to the triune God."[96]

Two aspects of Jenson's approach help to contextualize Marshall's work. The first concerns the selection of the root assertion. Jenson claims that the

---

Luther-Forschung, ed. Tuomo Mannermaa, Anja Ghiselli, and Simo Peura, Veröffentlichungen der Finnischen Theologischen Literaturgesellschaft 153, in Zusammenarbeit mit der Luther-Agricola-Gesellschaft A24 (Helsinki: Finnische Theologische Literaturgesellschaft, 1987), 237–57.

93. Robert W. Jenson, *Systematic Theology*, vol. 1, *The Triune God* (New York: Oxford University Press, 1997), 11: "What is first given to theology is the gospel itself as a communication occurring in fact in human history."

94. Ibid., 16–17, with original emphasis. Jenson refers to Thomas Aquinas as his example: "To be saying the gospel, let nothing be said that would imply potentiality in God" (17).

95. Ibid., 12 (also 42–45).

96. Ibid., 13. See also 17: "Statements of theology's logical form allows us to specify the indispensable churchly notions of 'doctrine' and 'dogma.'"

linguistic formulation of the logical form of the gospel can be rendered either in a "sample," meaning a paraphrase of the gospel that is close to original biblical terminology, or in a metalinguistic formulation concerning a rule for making theological truth claims. His own preference is for a biblical para- phrase (2 Cor. 14:4). This selection is similar to Marshall's, but as I discuss below, Marshall argues that the root assertion captures an agreement between Luther and Thomas Aquinas on the central content of Christian faith. In Jenson's approach, the second issue at stake concerns how the root assertion inchoately implies other doctrines. This has to do with the relation of bibli- cal material to doctrinal formulation, a relation that historically represents a process of doctrinal development in the first four centuries of the Christian church's existence. For both Jenson and Marshall, the relation between root assertion and doctrine is not one of historical development in early Christian- ity; rather, it has a sociological intention. The identity of the church is at stake in the relation of Bible to Trinity. Marshall will explicitly press this specific issue, thereby moving doctrine in a normative direction.

The work of Bruce Marshall, who studied with George A. Lindbeck at Yale in the 1970s, draws Jenson's insights into considering the relation of root assertion to doctrine. Marshall begins his 1999 essay "Faith and Rea- son Reconsidered: Aquinas and Luther on Deciding What Is True" with an attempt to find a root assertion. His goal is the possibility of ecumeni- cal agreement between Roman Catholics and Lutherans. Marshall starts with the claim "that Aquinas and Luther hold basically the same view of faith and reason."[97] In support of this, Marshall deploys two terms, "faith" and "Chris- tian belief," which he regards as equivalent. The success of an ecumenical agreement depends, in Marshall's view, on the particular definition assigned to these two terms. Rejecting any notion of faith as a "prelinguistic *Vertrauen auf Christus* [trust in Christ]" experience, with "prelinguistic" here meaning a notion of faith as *fiducia*, or heartfelt trust, Marshall aims to bring Luther deci- sively in line with his own view, which defines faith as necessarily articulated in linguistic propositions, faith as assertions held to be true.[98] Once Luther on the topic of faith is moved into the linguistic arena, Marshall presses him to say the same thing that Thomas Aquinas says. This permits him in turn to

97. Bruce D. Marshall, "Faith and Reason Reconsidered: Aquinas and Luther on Deciding What Is True," *The Thomist* 63, no. 1 (1999): 2.
98. Ibid., 30, with German from the original text. Marshall apparently does not have the historical Luther in mind but rather the Luther of early twentieth-century German theological scholarship: "We should pause briefly to observe that a long tra- dition of Luther interpretation (of which Albrecht Ritschl and Wilhelm Herrmann may be regarded as the progenitors) has maintained that 'faith' for Luther is at bottom not a matter of holding sentences true at all" (28).

identify Luther and Thomas with regard to how they "basically agree on how to decide what is true."[99] Agreement does not take place on the grounds of meaning or referent; in other words, it consists in establishing linguistic and argumentative equivalence.

Marshall is further interested in finding the root assertion that articulates the "chief matter in the teaching of Christian faith."[100] To do so, such a phrase must abbreviate a number of beliefs, distilling them into a single formulation. One might expect such distillation to result in thinning out the meanings that have accrued over time and in different places to the beliefs being abbreviated. But Marshall is more concerned with formulating a root phrase that both Luther and Aquinas may be said to have held as true. He locates the requisite statement for Aquinas in the latter's commentary on 1 Corinthians: "the salvation accomplished by the cross of Christ," focusing on this because it is prefaced explicitly by Aquinas's locution concerning its significance as "chief matter in the teaching of Christian faith."[101] I argue that this issue of the chief matter for Aquinas may be taken quite differently, in particular if one considers the order of the *Summa theologicae*, in which the topic of the cross is treated only in part III. But Marshall's choice of this sentence of Aquinas becomes clearer when viewed in light of his consideration of Luther.

As many readers of Luther before him have discovered, Marshall finds it difficult to identify an exact and consistent root phrase in Luther's work. This is because in his homiletical enthusiasm, Luther used the phrase "chief article and doctrine" for whatever doctrine he happened to be preaching on in the church calendar. He used it for the Trinity on Trinity Sunday, for instance, and for the crucifixion on Good Friday, and so on. So Marshall is able to find the evidence he is looking for: Luther asserted the gospel of Christ's resurrection in a sermon he preached on 1 Corinthians 15.[102] Then Marshall moves to the conclusion that Luther and Aquinas agreed that the central claim of Christianity is the gospel of salvation as accomplished by Christ's cross and resurrection. Whether Aquinas and Luther did, in fact, mean the same thing by similar sentences is contestable. But significant for Marshall's position on doctrine is his understanding that historical difference must be erased for the purpose of ecclesial identity, which is singular. The church has one identity. That singular identity is dictated by the sameness of the linguistic-literary formulation, which captures in a root phrase the identical content of belief. Then this root phrase will further be directly related to other Christian

99. Ibid., 3.
100. Marshall (ibid., 4) attributes this citation to Aquinas.
101. Ibid., 4.
102. Ibid., 23.

doctrines, notably the doctrines of the Trinity and Christology. It is how Marshall understands the relation among Christian beliefs that frames his theology of doctrine in epistemic terms.

I.2. Christian Beliefs, Communal Identity, God

If the root assertion concerning salvation through Christ's cross and resurrection functions as a condensation of the Christian faith, there are other statements of belief that are related to this primary claim. Marshall offers a detailed understanding of the various relations between beliefs as he unpacks the root assertion. In this section I analyze three aspects that I take to be important to Marshall's argument concerning the coherence of Christian belief. The first concerns the relation between Bible and doctrine; the second has to do with the relation of doctrine to the church's identity; and the third concerns the appeal to God's self-knowledge. Marshall's argument for his epistemic model of doctrine entails specific moves that relate belief to doctrine, church, and God.

I.2.1. Christian Beliefs and the Harmonizing Hermeneutic

Within the Christian inheritance, many statements may be taken to articulate Christian belief. In his discussion of Aquinas, Marshall claims that the fourteen articles in the Apostles' Creed are statements that "enumerate[] the leading elements in this complex of belief." These deal with a specific articulation "having to do with the hidden majesty of God and those having to do with the narrative . . . of Christ's particular humanity, by which we are inducted into the vision of God's otherwise hidden majesty—or, as Thomas elsewhere puts it, those pertaining to the Trinity and those pertaining to the incarnation." Salvation through Christ's cross, Trinity, and incarnation all contribute to the articulation of "this complex of belief."[103]

Marshall's list of statements poses certain problems, however. The fourteen articles of the Apostles' Creed do not explicitly refer to the Trinity, in comparison to the Nicene Creed, which does. Then there is the question of what is implied by the step of gathering statements about God's hidden majesty, Trinity, and incarnation. Such a move goes beyond what is contained literally in the Apostles' Creed. On what grounds does Marshall claim that the Apostles' Creed covers a full range of doctrines, including those it fails to mention? Jenson's list raises the same sorts of question.

How this latter question is answered is crucial to Marshall's epistemic model of doctrine. A concise phrase in an introductory paragraph to Marshall's essay offers a clue. The reason why the "most central Christian beliefs" may be

---

103. Ibid., 7 and 7n16, referring to Aquinas, *Summa theologicae* II–II, q. 1, a. 8.

thus gathered is that they are "drawn from Scripture in order to organize communal reading of the biblical text."[104] This claim concerns a hermeneutic that is attributed to the "Church" (or "Christian community")—and Marshall puts "Church" in the singular with a capital C. The Bible is read with the aid of an hermeneutic informed by the statements just articulated concerning cross, Trinity, and incarnation. This does not address the problem concerning the historical distance between Scripture and creed or between Scripture and dogma, matters that since at least the seventeenth century had preoccupied theologians concerned with the lack of explicit Trinitarian-dogmatic content in the Bible. Rather, Marshall disposes of the historical problem by appealing to "communal reading."

Here it becomes clearer why Marshall identifies Scripture so closely with a particular selection of doctrines. Although the "specific contents of . . . [such a list of beliefs] naturally change somewhat over time," as Marshall notes inside parentheses, the "body of beliefs" articulated in Scripture and creeds are both "generated by Scripture" and are "interpreted in the Christian community according to shared creedal rules."[105] Scripture and creed mutually inform each other when they are located in the church. The reason for this ecclesial location is the historical application of the *regula fidei* (rule of faith). This is what guides scriptural reading. The term *regula fidei* goes back to the second-century church father Irenaeus of Lyons. It was an oral tradition that may eventually have been set linguistically in the ecumenical creeds; although Irenaeus might have had a literary articulation of the hermeneutic in mind, he did not specify one for posterity. Marshall's appeal to the *regula fidei* goes beyond Irenaeus by identifying the linguistic-literary articulated form of the hermeneutic as the creedal statements. He claims that these inform "the" (singular) communal reading of Scripture. The idea of the *regula fidei* thus provides the rationale for Marshall's unification of doctrines under the rubric of the Apostles' Creed and then determines these doctrines to be the sole biblical hermeneutic for the church.

Here a question arises concerning the restriction of scriptural interpretative strategies to the creed as sole hermeneutic. Marshall sets this limit by negation. "The Church's Trinitarian and Christological confession adds nothing to Scripture," he writes. The matter of "adding" to Scripture is known as a synthetic judgment, meaning that a predicate would add to the knowledge of the subject term. In the particular example under consideration, the creed adds a Trinitarian determination to Scripture that is not already contained in it. This synthetic claim is made by theologians who insist on the historical

104. Ibid., 2, 7.
105. Ibid., 8.

discrepancy between Bible and creed and who therefore argue that there is a difference in meaning between proto-Trinitarian comments in the Bible and later Trinitarian doctrinal statements about the coequality between Father and Son. But Marshall rejects the synthetic judgment and instead holds that "the Church's Trinitarian and Christological confession . . . is drawn from Scripture in order to organize communal reading of the biblical text."[106]

This affirmation suggests a nonhistorical relation between Bible and doctrine. The creed is "drawn" from the Bible, or in other terms that Marshall uses, the creed is "generated by communal interpretation of Scripture according to creedal rules."[107] The relation between Bible and creed that Marshall affirms is one that minimizes differences in Scripture by imposing one doctrinal reading of Scripture as the church's norm. Other theological or historical possibilities for understanding the relation of Bible to hermeneutic are not considered. The hermeneutical relation suffices to make a normative claim concerning doctrine for the church's activity of interpreting Scripture. In this view, there is no difference between belief attested in New Testament and Trinitarian belief articulated centuries afterward. Marshall deploys a harmonizing hermeneutic that takes Bible and creed to mean the same thing.

I.2.2. Christian Beliefs and Communal Identity

There is a further issue, distinguished from the Bible/creed harmonizing hermeneutic, having to do with the relation among statements of belief. The Apostles' Creed contains different statements of belief, and Marshall adds more statements within the purview of belief, such as the Trinity. While the article on the Trinity describes the necessary Trinitarian being of God, the articles on the incarnation and salvation do not have the same degree of necessity. Rather, they are contingent divine policies. Thus the Trinity represents a doctrine whose truth is not dependent on the contingent doctrines related to salvation on Christ's cross. Yet when Marshall claims that Christian statements of belief include statements about the divine hidden majesty and the Trinity, he presupposes that these different beliefs are included in the body of Christian beliefs. How does Marshall argue in favor of this particular body of belief?

In *Trinity and Truth*, Marshall sets up his argument relating belief to Christian identity. "Essential beliefs are those which are necessary to a community's identity, those upon which its survival depends. . . . Beliefs, therefore, are truth claims."[108] Doctrine is relevant to the community's identity. The implication

---

106. Ibid., 7.
107. Ibid., 2.
108. Marshall, *Trinity and Truth*, 44, 45.

is that the connection between beliefs is sociological, however, not one of logical relation. The church determines which beliefs are central to its identity. Because Marshall assumes that identity conditions are true—at least for his case of Trinity and church—we are not asked to consider how these claims are true, under what conditions an identity condition can be said to be true or false, or even how true belief may be distinguished from myth as an identity condition. Rather Marshall maintains that truth has to do with how the church makes assertions as to which beliefs are essential to its identity. "This means, of course, that there is no standard for deciding to hold true 'Deus est homo' and the nest of beliefs in which it is most closely imbedded, that is, no higher or more central beliefs against which we could test their truth."[109] "The church determines that its trinitarian identification of God is true by taking that body of beliefs as the standard by coherence with which the truth of other beliefs is to be decided."[110] The concept of truth invoked here has to do with the practice of assertion as it takes place within the Christian community. The church makes its assertions as part of its practice, and by virtue of claiming specific beliefs to be essential to its identity, these beliefs are true.

It is here that the epistemic understanding of doctrine comes to the fore. Coherence emerges as the significant criterion of the community's practice of assertion in view of the question of identity. Coherence designates the relation among beliefs. When beliefs are true by virtue of their coherence with each other, however, their truth-value is measured as a function of their relations to each other rather than in terms of their relation to a transcendent reality or according to claims regarding their content. Yet coherence requires another aspect so that beliefs not necessary to communal identity can be excluded. What accounts for the coherence of beliefs? Marshall's answer is that the church's identity is defined by a specific "package deal." "Epistemically, the articles of Christian faith are for Thomas strictly a package deal. The central nexus of Christian teaching is made up of many beliefs, but they are all mutually fit for one another in such a way that the 'perception of divine truth' depends upon holding them all true together." Holding specific beliefs together in such a "package" is necessary for forming an adequate picture of God. The package of beliefs is necessary for defining the communal sense of who God is, and the relation among beliefs is coherence. If strong relations mean logical relations or mutual entailment, the weak concept of coherence is described, as Marshall does, in the aesthetic term of "mutual[] fit for one another."[111] Thus we are left with a truth-value that gathers assertions by

109. Marshall, "Faith and Reason," 45.
110. Marshall, *Trinity and Truth*, 47.
111. Marshall, "Faith and Reason," 9.

virtue of weak relations. Nevertheless, Marshall adds another value to coherence that assigns it greater normativity. He invokes God.

I.2.3. Christian Beliefs and God

Until now there has been no reference to a "transcendent reality" that might bestow divine truth on human words. But when Marshall looks to ground the coherence of human assertions about Christian faith, he calls on God, making an argument that relates coherence to the divine simplicity. Marshall acknowledges that he is appealing to a "technical device . . . of the way a simple or incomposite reality may be known," which Thomas "derived from Aristotle." With Aquinas as his interlocutor, Marshall claims that the divine simplicity is the way in which God holds things together as one. God's "own self-knowledge" is true, furthermore, because God is the "first truth." By contrast, according to Marshall, human minds can know composite reality through sense perception, but in "'simple things'. . . there are no real distinctions which correspond to the distinctions between the relevant true sentences."[112] The simplicity argument undergirds the coherence among beliefs. There is a problem in identifying the kind of simplicity that Marshall might have in mind, however. He does not make the relevant distinctions between the simplicity of God's mental act by which God knows all things, for example, or the simplicity of objects of God's thought, or even if the objects of God's thought are connected by relations of entailment.

Further down the line, Marshall must find a way of relating God's self-knowledge to human beliefs that can be deemed perceptions of divine truth. These linguistically articulated statements, as they exist in the human mind and are "conformed to . . . reality," admit no distinctions between them when they are conformed to a reality that is simple. That reality is God, and the simplicity of this reality is preserved when God reveals God's own knowing to humans. Even though these assertions are "manifold" in the human intellect, because they are conformed to the reality of God's knowing, which is simple, they yield "perception of divine truth."[113] Marshall's argument goes as follows: "Faith, in other words, clings to the incarnate and triune God who manifests himself to us as first truth by way of the scripturally normed discourse of the Christian community. Indeed the teaching and preaching of the Church are not simply this community's talk about God, nor even God's talk about himself, but God's way of giving the world a share in his own

---

112. Ibid., 9–10. My reconstruction of the argument Marshall presents for the coherence of human assertion of Christian faith is my best effort at making sense of Marshall's dense and terse text.

113. Ibid., 9–10, esp. 9n23.

self-knowledge."[114] Although this statement regarding revelation in incarnation does not quite cohere with the earlier claim about God's simplicity—because incarnation disrupts the divine simplicity—it identifies revelation as the source of belief and its truth as coherence among the articles of faith. In addition to the simplicity argument, revelation too emerges as another explanation for coherence among beliefs. When God reveals some of what God knows about God's self to us, then the divine act of revealing this body of beliefs together is what constitutes their coherence. Under the human conditions of faith, the revealed "package deal" is truly and normatively formulated. The different assertions are asserted to cohere by virtue of God's revelation.

I.3. Luther's Contribution

When Marshall turns to the question of coherence of belief in Luther's theology, he looks to the 1539 disputation on John 1:14, *Verbum caro factum est* (*The Word Became Flesh*).[115] Among Luther's later works, this is regarded in Luther scholarship as evidence of Luther's advocacy for the separation of theology from philosophy. Luther formulates the idea of the "novis linguis loqui [speaking in a new language]" in view of how linguistic use is governed in the particular areas of philosophy and theology. When one term is used by philosophy, as Luther argues, the term has a meaning that is radically different from the way the same term is used in theology. Marshall refers specifically to the two examples Luther provides in his disputation: the new significations that the term "mother" acquires when applied to Mary and the term "creature" when applied to Christ. "So, to use two of Luther's examples, 'mother' when applied in theology to Mary continues to signify a woman who gives birth, but does so in a new (viz., virginal) way; 'creature' when applied to Christ continues to signify that which God makes by an act of will, but which he now makes by uniting it absolutely to himself, rather than by separating it infinitely from himself."[116]

The sole reason why theological terms acquire new significations, to return to Luther's argument, is the new reality of Christ's incarnation. On the ground of the novelty introduced by Christ in his assumption of human nature, the theological area reconfigures terms that must reflect the new reality inaugurated by Christ. Marshall understands Luther's argument a bit differently, however, orienting Luther's text to a new truth commitment. He

114. Ibid., 8–9.
115. Ibid., 32–46.
116. Ibid., 44; see also ibid., 44n93, in which Marshall translates WA 39/2:19.33–34; and 39/2:105.4–7.

writes, "Theology is new not primarily in the meaning it gives to terms but in the way it combines them, that is, in the radically unexpected sentences it holds true."[117] The new way of speaking has to do with the arrangement of terms in statements of belief. Their arrangement, rather than referent or content, is at stake.

Here Marshall's interpretation differs significantly from the one given by Simo Knuuttila, professor of medieval philosophy, who sees Luther's position more in line with medieval logic. For Knuuttila, Luther's disputation considers the possibility of drawing logical inferences from philosophy to theology, which Luther disputes because theology must regulate inferences with reference to its own subject matter.[118] Marshall, however, takes Luther to represent a position that considers the way terms are used to form propositions without reference to the subject matter. "The scripturally and creedally formed discourse of the Christian community is, as Luther sees it, God's own way of talking in our language; as such the sentences it teaches us to hold true are shockingly novel and odd by comparison with the way we combine terms in the rest of our discourse."[119] Truth is the issue at stake, specifically the truth of the propositions that have been formed from terms arranged in a specific way. Propositions are true by virtue of a combination of the same terms that, when combined in different ways in other propositions, would be judged false.

The issue of the "new theological language" is then for Marshall an "epistemic" one. Again, by "epistemic" I take Marshall to mean a linguistically construed belief that functions like a Kantian category, informing the way in which we see and apprehend the world as well as the way we make judgments about the world. An epistemic understanding of doctrine construes doctrine in terms of a worldview. Doctrine has, in Marshall's words, an "epistemic primacy . . . across the whole range of possible belief." It serves to establish a coherence among the "range of possible belief," even "the rest of our discourse."[120] When doctrine informs one's grasp of the world, it functions to unite different aspects of the world into one world.

I.4. Christianity as a Worldview

The final question to be addressed with regard to the normative epistemic function of doctrine is its range. How far does the "epistemic primacy of the gospel and the articles of faith" extend? If epistemic primacy qualifies the

---

117. Marshall, "Faith and Reason," 44.

118. Simo Knuuttila, "Luther's View of Logic and Revelation," *Medioevo: Rivista di storia della filosofia medievale* 24 (1998): 219–34.

119. Marshall, "Faith and Reason," 45.

120. Ibid., 35, 44.

normative lens of a worldview, then over which other beliefs does it reach? Does it extend to other religious beliefs? To other spheres of human thought and action? To music theory, for example, or to natural science? The questions concern epistemic primacy in relation to a worldview. Marshall takes the issue of extension by continuing his discussion of Luther on new language. "These considerations [arrangement of terms in a proposition] may also help explain why the gospel and the articles of faith can retain their 'natural force' or plain sense *and* be held true only when they function with unrestricted epistemic primacy across the whole field of possible belief."[121] Although the creed is restricted in scope to distinct articles about the triune God, Marshall is interested in seeing if the statement of beliefs can be compatible with all dimensions of a worldview. The issue, again, is truth.

In what sense does doctrine function epistemically over a wider range of human beliefs, activities, and sciences? In his book *Trinity and Truth*, Marshall considers this question by referring to the christological hymn in Colossians 1:17b: "and in him [Christ] all things hold together." He interprets the christological focus of this verse in terms of the Trinity's work. "The work of the Trinity in making all things hold together in the one who is the Father's image has two aspects with particular epistemic significance," he writes, and he goes on to explain the "two aspects" of "epistemic significance." The first concerns the passage's verb, "to hold together." Marshall understands "to hold together" in the epistemic terms he has been developing as relations among linguistically articulated beliefs. In his words, "All true beliefs must hold together in—be logically consistent with—the narratives which identify him, and the triune God with him. He must have 'primacy in everything,' including decisions about truth."[122] Christ is thus represented as an epistemic principle that gathers together the gospel narratives about him, beliefs concerning his identity, and beliefs about the Trinity. These beliefs that cohere by virtue of their unity in Christ inform the epistemic function of doctrine. Christ determines the epistemic reach of a worldview that is shaped by Christian beliefs. By virtue of logical consistency, other beliefs, such as scientific claims, can be said to be governed by the epistemic conditions of the Christian worldview.

The second aspect of epistemic significance is related to the question of worldview. "Believing the gospel (that is, the narratives which identify Jesus and the triune God)," Marshall writes, "therefore, necessarily commits believers to a comprehensive view of the world centered epistemically on the gospel

---

121. Ibid., 43, emphasis original.
122. Marshall, *Trinity and Truth*, 112, 117. "Justification is a relation not between beliefs and the world, but between belief and beliefs" (88).

narrative itself."[123] It is here that the question concerning the degree of comprehensiveness included in this worldview demands our attention. Does Marshall think that all claims, scientific, practical, or otherwise, are somehow epistemically governed by the gospel narratives? The appeal to the concept of a worldview would lend credence to an interpretation that Christian belief affects all knowledge available within that particular worldview. Marshall does not spell out the extent to which the gospel is related to scientific and practical knowledge. But the question lingers. Suffice it to say that given the above evidence, the doctrines of Christ and Trinity are understood as they inform the epistemic conditions for a coherent set of beliefs that absorbs the world.[124]

So what has transpired? Let me review the steps of Marshall's argument. He begins by seeking an apposite assertion establishing a condensation of Christian belief that Aquinas and Luther can agree on. The assertion he offers is in English, which allows him to proceed without considering historical or linguistic differences between Aquinas and Luther. Then this assertion is granted epistemic primacy among other beliefs deemed to be coherent with it. Coherence among assertions of belief—pertaining to incarnation, Trinity, and divine majesty—is the condition of their truth. There is a shift from assertion to the notion of the "package deal" of Christian beliefs, with a view toward a harmonizing hermeneutic between Bible and creed, belief and Christian identity. This ends with an appeal to God. Marshall takes up Luther's idea of new language and uses it to consider the epistemic terms of Christian belief in view of a worldview. But Marshall does not explore—indeed, his methodology obviates any need to explore—the reasons why these assertions have come to be related historically. Rather, he argues that God reveals these assertions as a unity in the creed, and as such, it defines the church's identity. The analytic relation between church and creed excludes other possible readings of Scripture or creed.

All along, Marshall understood the assertion together with other beliefs as the product of the reception of the *regula fidei*. He invoked God's revelation as justification for its truth. The analytic relation between church and creed seemed to suggest that the *regula fidei* is so bound up with the church that

123. Ibid., 118.
124. George Lindbeck had introduced the idea of a worldview in his appropriation of cultural anthropologist Clifford Geertz's notion of culture. Lindbeck borrows from Geertz the idea that religion as "stated more technically . . . can be viewed as a kind of cultural and/or linguistic framework or medium that shapes the entirety of life and thought" (Lindbeck, *Nature of Doctrine*, 33). For Lindbeck, Scripture functions to shape a worldview. Interpretation of both Scripture and world takes place within the worldview shaped by Scripture in the first place. "A scriptural world is thus able to absorb the universe" (117).

there are no other possibilities for understanding the tradition of beliefs to be received. Marshall gives linguistic-literary articulation to the *regula fidei*, claiming that its constitutive beliefs are as the church has received them in terms of the coherence among incarnation, Trinity, and divine hidden majesty. With his appeal to the divine simplicity, however, Marshall holds that the complex of beliefs exists as such in God's own self-knowledge, which holds them together, and that God reveals them as a unity. So God is the first cause in the sense of a first cause of the linguistically defined community.

Once God has revealed these beliefs in a way that constitutes the community's identity, then the community has the norms in linguistically articulated propositions. The church no longer needs God then, for the *regula fidei* is in the church's possession, and to the *regula fidei* is assigned the epistemic function of the Christian worldview. Because for Marshall God's self-knowledge is simple, one revelation suffices to define the church's identity for all time. There is no other possible set of beliefs that God can reveal at some point to challenge or add to what has already been revealed.

What is doctrine, then? Marshall's own formulations of the set of beliefs that form Christianity's core, represented as the *regula fidei*, are a prescription for a normative understanding of doctrine in a specific literary-linguistic formulation. Normativity is secured by assigning it to the church-creed analytic that has been cut off from any divine transcendent reality. Doctrine has lost its witnessing capacity to the God who might call doctrine into question. Thus doctrine has also lost its historicity by being endowed with a normativity fixed for all time.

I.5. Conversion to a Worldview

We have come a long way from Barth. For Barth, human language in Scripture, proclamation, and doctrine pointed to the divine reality as the possibility of judgment; for Marshall, human language is a social construction that is cut off from the divine reality and fixed in literary-linguistic articulations via terminology from the past. Although Barth sees theology as interpretation invoking novelty while anticipating the word of God as an event, Marshall sees doctrine in the normative terms of its epistemic advantage in a worldview. The final question to be raised concerning the epistemic-advantage model of doctrine has to do with how one gains access to the worldview. How is one to appreciate the advantage of the epistemic model over other possible candidates? Or to put this another way: If the Christian worldview is true by virtue of the coherence of its beliefs, how can one get into a position to see this truth?

It is at this juncture that Marshall appeals to the external reality of God. Conversion is the necessary cause of a dramatic entrance into the Christian worldview. Conversion is so dramatic that it must be ascribed to God, to the third person of the Trinity, to be exact. The Holy Spirit is the divine person who accomplishes the epistemic shift involved in the conversion from one worldview, say the secular, to another. "Only the Holy Spirit," Marshall writes, "is up to the epistemic effort involved."[125] To the Spirit is assigned the epistemic role of converting a person from one worldview to the Christian worldview. Conversion enables the Christian subject to see that the church-creed analytic is true and that it is more comprehensive than other discourses. But Marshall's appeal to the external reality of the Holy Spirit belongs to the worldview that is already assumed. The Holy Spirit is the gatekeeper for his epistemic-advantage model. The activity of selective revelation is assigned to this divine person. Once the Holy Spirit decides to convert someone, that person will have the same set of beliefs as others sharing the worldview;[126] and once among the converted, a believer shares with them the epistemic advantage of this worldview. And further, the Holy Spirit continues to exert an epistemic role of "persuasion" by "creat[ing] the willingness to order the whole epistemic field around a particular set of beliefs."[127] The Spirit continues to exert an influence on the believer's actions by coaxing believers to be agents commensurate with beliefs articulated in the first place. Thus the appeal to this external reality is not an appeal for legitimating the truth of the doctrinal system, but as a conversion-producer and sustainer of the worldview. God is encased within the notion of a worldview, even if the Spirit is the transcendent reality who decides to whom the beliefs might be revealed and who might be persuaded to act in accordance with those beliefs. The Holy Spirit's transcendence is thus established on epistemic grounds.

Within the epistemic-advantage model, doctrine has lost its dialectical relation to Scripture and proclamation. Instead, it has turned into the dogmatism of a *regula fidei* by virtue of asserting its production in the analytic relation between church and creed. There is no other church, no other interpretation. There is only the one Scripture, read through the *regula fidei* that the church has produced. This is what grounds the church's identity as a Bible-reading community with a distinct doctrinal hermeneutic. Once the church has garnered the prerogative of the truth of a worldview, however, it is cut off from the living possibility of being open to God's word. God's word has been rendered in human words from the past—assertions and doctrines—so that they function as predictable norms for any future theological articulation.

125. Marshall, *Trinity and Truth*, 124.
126. Ibid., 157: "The unrestricted epistemic primacy of central Christian beliefs thus seems quite compatible with the requirement that a plausible set of epistemic priorities exhibit inclusive power."
127. Ibid., 204, 212.

The *Deus dixit* is framed as doctrine that constitutes a Christian worldview authorizing itself. All the Holy Spirit may now do is convert people to it (or not). Theology as system grounded in God's reality is replaced by Christianity as a worldview, with theology's function restricted to pointing to doctrines in their epistemic function within that worldview.

II. THE END OF DOCTRINE

On what grounds do believers justify their theological system? This for me is the intriguing problem left by the theological trajectory I have traced. Theologians following in Barth's wake insisted on God's word as ground. But for Barth, God is ground as a transcendent reality. Barth has established a dialectical relationship between human words and the transcendent reality of God; within this dialectic, doctrinal theology's task is to explicate the word of God in terms of its content. But theology always stands under the possibility of the divine judgment. Yet by the time we arrive at the epistemic-advantage model, there is no longer interest in content or referent. Rather, theology's status within the church is analytic, with creed as the normative hermeneutic for Scripture. The specific ground of truth is the church-creed analytic. The church's identity is determined by the specific doctrines it uses to read Scripture. The past shapes doctrine, and recollection of the past has a monopoly on the theological task of explicating doctrine in the present. Doctrine's sole task is to identify, articulate, and relate specific articulations from the past and apply them in the present. There appears to be no way beyond assertion construed as normative on the basis of the past, as captured by the church-creed analytic. Because content is not significant in this system, there is no place for novelty in theological development. It is enough to press diverse Christian authors to say the same thing across language and time periods. Church-creed analytic establishes coherence for the Christian worldview, which then is grounded on what is deemed to be the norm in the church.

At this point, doctrine has come to an end. Doctrine without dialectic, theology without discovery, church without history, and language without meaning—this is what is left when doctrine loses its transcendent reality and becomes the norm of its own truth, a self-enclosed system incapable of communicating to others on the outside. This is what the end of doctrine means: the totalizing of Christian discourse in a worldview sealed off from God except in the person of the Holy Spirit relegated only to the task of converting persons. From some points of view, such splendid isolation may appear advantageous, if only for allowing theologians to go about their work without needing to address critical questions from others who are seeking to understand. The disadvantage is that theologians lose the content of the faith; and without content and reality, theology becomes a cabinet of curiosities from the past. When doctrine is fixed as assertions of belief, what reason is there to teach or to learn, to discuss, or even to disagree?

I cannot imagine a sharper contrast between ways of conceptualizing theology: theology as a living practice versus theology as an endeavor of restriction; theology as dialectic and interpretation versus theology as that which is already received; and theology in full and open conversation with men and women living out their times in good faith versus theology limited to those who already share the Christian worldview. On the one hand, theology speaks with other disciplines in the university because, like these other endeavors, theology is a human enterprise. On the other hand, theology is intentionally isolated from other academic disciplines precisely so that it can make its assertions without justification or reasons. But it is the fate of the relationship between the living God and theology that is most vexing in this catalog of contrasts. When God is cut off from doctrine, doctrine loses itself.

The overarching question is whether a theology may make doctrinal claims about God in view of God's reality rather than in view of words fixed in the past. In thinking about this, I am inspired by Barth's clear sense of theology's exigency. Theology is the discipline that erects the emergency signal and witnesses to the divine reality while at the same time looking at self, world, and God through the lens of human language and concepts. Theology so conceived is capable of honest assessment of how language comes to make claims about the reality of God, informed by history and semantics. So it was among theologians at the origins of Christianity. But this requires a recovery of the referent of theological discourse, at the very least for the task of working out how language makes claims about God, whether analogically or by means of the *via negationis* (way of negation), or the *via eminentiae* (way of eminence), or any other way. It also requires a good look at how any theological activity may be open to novel and creative formulations. The intriguing thing about doing theology, as Barth said early in his career, is that theology is a sign that something is not right in the world. Into this work, God's word comes, the word that is not predictable but faithful, open to novelty, and at the same time recognizable.

The truth of God has to do with God's reality, and theology's task has the recovery of divine reality as its subject matter. Humans may speak about God while at the same time referring to God's reality as living word. I am proposing that theology recover a sense of the God who speaks in spite of and sometimes in contradiction to doctrine. In this spirit, we may look to Count Nikolaus von Zinzendorf's (1700–1760) argument that the Holy Spirit is the mother of Christ, or to Schleiermacher's emphasis on the Trinity as the unfinished history of God's relationship with the world. Who is to say that these are not rich and compelling possibilities? Doctrine is formulated in novelty and intersubjectivity. Investigation into what words mean may yield difference, even when the words seem fixed. Although the church may confess words whose meaning has been lost long ago, these words may be filled again with content because their referent continues to live. Doctrine too lives only when it is connected to the living God, whose word invites men and women to express, praise, witness, explain, and narrate in their own words.

4

Language and Reality

*A Theological Epistemology
with Some Help from Schleiermacher*

I. AT THE END, A (TENTATIVE) BEGINNING

Where are we at this juncture? I have examined the historical trajectory of key strands of twentieth-century theology and arrived at the point where doctrine's demise has been twice pronounced. First, the end of doctrine was laid at Schleiermacher's doorstep, as we saw in chapter 1. Experience grounded in a prelinguistic core, rather than the biblical text, was said to be what Schleiermacher understood to be the source of doctrinal normativity, thereby compromising God's truth by an alien anthropological category. The end of doctrine was also pronounced in chapter 3. There doctrine was seen to have merged with an epistemic function as it shaped the Christian worldview. Christian faith was single-mindedly oriented to the linguistically articulated articles of faith. Belief was wholeheartedly discursive and coherent, with an indefinite epistemic extension. But doctrine collapsed into the grammatical structure of a worldview; as I argued, it ended up losing its connection to the transcendent reality whose identity it purported to circumscribe. Normativity of the letter had replaced the spirit of the articles of faith. The language of doctrine had lost its relation to the living God.

With an end comes a beginning. At least it has been my hope that the genealogy described in the first part of this book has surfaced some of the key issues driving the contemporary theological situation. And we have enough information about these issues now that we may begin to transform an end into a beginning. In this chapter I will initiate a "tentative," rather than entirely new, beginning by picking up the problem with Schleiermacher. Schleiermacher has tracked the history of twentieth-century theology by providing a negative foil to key affirmations concerning word and doctrine, as we have seen. Historiographical periodization suggests that the central issue at stake in the problem with Schleiermacher is modernity set in opposition to the "faith world" of the Bible and Protestant Reformers. Yet if Schleiermacher is regarded as the father of modern theology, the challenges he presents concerning modernity will not go away, even if one seeks to overcome them by a nostalgic appropriation of precritical values in a postcritical time.

I.1. Bible and Doctrine

The contrast between two types of biblical interpretation illustrates the way word rests uneasily with modernity. If the Bible is viewed as "the book of books,"[1] then strategies applied to its interpretation must be guided by the principles derived from its internal practices and meanings. The Christian church reads the canon as authoritative when it applies the hermeneutical rule of faith taken from the Bible in the first place. Strategies deployed within Scripture that create theological connections between different parts are privileged by the church when it reads Scripture as a unified text. Doctrines, such as Christology and Trinity, are more than mere historical interpretations of biblical meaning; they also are true representations of the God revealed in Scripture. The contrasting position holds that if the Bible is to be read "like any other book," then hermeneutical strategies—from historical, literary, and grammatical, and onward to psychological, philosophical, and religious—may legitimately be applied to understand this text that human authors composed. The Bible, as a text communicating in human words the complexity of relations between God and world, can be understood by its human readers. Does this second interpretative option necessarily result in the controversial legacy of the European Enlightenment for biblical hermeneutics, converting the Bible's meaning into extrabiblical idioms? This either/or opposition is the hermeneutical dilemma confronting theologians today.[2]

The second contrast between modernity and the precritical era concerns doctrine. With Brunner's criticism of Schleiermacher, we have seen that the concern with truth is exclusively tied to the spiritual valence of God's

---

1. The balance between interpreting the Bible "like any other book" and interpreting a book that has claims to a unique truth, "the mind of Christ and His Apostles," is carefully explained by Benjamin Jowett, "On the Interpretation of Scripture," in *The Interpretation of Scripture and Other Essays* (London: G. Routledge & Sons, 1907), 35, 72; repr. from *Essays and Reviews*, ed. F. Temple et al. (London: Parker, 1860), 330–433.

2. Lindbeck (*Nature of Doctrine*, 118) sums up one side of the either/or: "Intratextual theology redescribes reality within the scriptural framework rather than translating Scripture into extrascriptural categories. It is the text, so to speak, which absorbs the world, rather than the world [absorbing] the text."

word. The association of nature and mysticism in Brunner's terminology led to the conclusion that the word is falsified when it is rendered into human consciousness. This understanding of Schleiermacher's view of interiority remains unchanged at the end of the twentieth century. Although the terminology is slightly different—prelinguistic experience is substituted for nature mysticism—the repercussions for doctrine are the same. Schleiermacher is accused of arguing for an accidental relation between linguistically articulated doctrine and a prelinguistic religious experience. There is no necessary relation between doctrinal signifier and experiential signified; the signifier has no external instance by which its truth can be verified. The norm of human experience judges doctrinal truth, not the other way around. The implication of this critique of Schleiermacher is that the truth of doctrine is not compatible with modernity's values.

I.2. Reception and Production

The relation between word and doctrine—or in other terms, between Scripture and tradition, as I have analyzed it in terms of the binary opposition introduced by Brunner—points to a deeper question that occupies me in this chapter. The issue has been initially circumscribed in terms of language, the linguistically composed biblical text, and the linguistically articulated articles of faith as embedded at the depth dimension of the Christian worldview. But the problem with Schleiermacher has identified another instance of opposition located in the notion of the competition between human nature and the truth of God's word. Human consciousness and experience, or "nature mysticism," as in Brunner, are judged to compete with the linguistically available biblical text and doctrine, setting up an oppositional principle. The issue all along with Schleiermacher has been his understanding of language in relation to a reality that is demarcated by religious consciousness; in the terms of his theology, this reality is the mystical relation of the believer with Christ that is available in the Christian community. Ultimately the question of language and reality comes to the fore.

I propose to open up the language/reality question by introducing yet another binary opposition in order to sharpen the issue at hand. For the purpose of addressing the problem of language and reality, let me take a firmer hold on what is at stake for Schleiermacher as viewed through the lens of the production/reception distinction.

When the problem is identified in terms of reception, Schleiermacher is judged to have failed. Reception privileges the givenness of a religious tradition for subsequent appropriation. A tradition that conveys its truths, beliefs, and rituals to the following generations does so by accepting aspects of the tradition as given and available for communication. In this context Lindbeck refers to the Bible: "How can a religion claim to preserve 'the faith which was once for all delivered to the saints' (Jude 3), as all religions in some sense do, when it takes so many forms in both the past and present?"[3] Posed this way, the question of reception lends itself to describing and analyzing given discursive aspects of a religious tradition, such as word, doctrine, or articles of faith, as well as discursive relations to liturgical and devotional practices, as all these are correlated with a community's identity through time. The question concerning the appropriation of belief focuses its search for an answer in word and doctrine as shaping and informing ongoing practice. To cite Lindbeck again, "To become a Christian involves learning the story of Israel and of Jesus well enough to interpret and experience oneself and one's world in its terms. A religion is above all an external word, a *verbum externum*, that molds and shapes the self and its world, rather than an expression or thematization of a preexisting self or of preconceptual experience."[4] The story must first be told in order that it might be heard and then made one's own. Looking at a religious tradition from the perspective of reception opens up a vocabulary that connotes shaping and informing, a conceptuality that isolates the givenness of particular tradition as significant for what comes later and identifies specific elements of that tradition as significant for the tradition's identity through time.

But there are other questions that might be asked of a religious tradition generally, and specifically of the authoritative texts of the Christian religion. How are the literary artifacts that constitute identity produced in the first place? Rather than focus on the literary givenness of word and doctrine, one can look at their *production* to see why specific words and texts have come to be articulated in the first place and then regarded as significant for a particular group of persons. How did canonical texts arise and under what conditions?

The question of the production of the canon, both scriptural and confessional, is a historical issue. As Brevard Childs has shown, the development of the "final form" of the Christian Bible can be both exegetically and historically tracked. The production of a canonical Scripture has to do with a variety of pressures identifiable by source, form, tradition, and redaction criticism.[5] The production of doctrine is likewise addressed by historical study. In recent years new historiographies have contributed to a deeper understanding of how the doctrine of the Trinity, for example, was being produced in the debates leading up to the Councils of Nicaea (325) and Constantinople

3. Ibid., 78.
4. Ibid., 34.
5. See Brevard S. Childs, *Biblical Theology of the Old and New Testaments: Theological Reflection on the Christian Bible* (Minneapolis: Fortress Press, 1992).

(381).[6] Although it is a truism that in Scripture one cannot find the Trinity as given in its orthodox formulations, its appearance in the fourth century has a strong precedent in early Christianity. Its production may be traced as development from proto-Trinitarian intimations in the Bible, as in the Johannine Farewell Discourses and Pauline epistolary greetings and benedictions, to its explicit confessional and creedal articulation in the fourth century.

But what if we engage the question of the production of canonical texts from another angle, by framing production as an epistemological rather than strictly a historical issue? By epistemological, I intend a generous sense of the term that grasps how a word or words come to be articulated under the pressures of particular reality. Epistemology might be misunderstood in a sense I do not mean here, as grounding theology in human psychology and reason and thereby falsifying the true theology, which has revelation as its source. Rather, I take epistemology as concerning how theological statements, doctrines, and even systems are produced in relation to reality. This perspective on epistemology is decisively theological. When the question is posed concerning the particular way in which theology makes its claims in relation to God's reality, it adds a significant theological dimension to the philosophical analysis of reason and its limits undertaken by Kant.

With the help of Schleiermacher, my aim is to reconstruct a theological epistemology that will show how a distinct understanding of language in relation to reality is at the root of production of the New Testament, as well as a consistent parameter shaping the history of doctrine. Theological epistemology, as I define it for the purpose of this chapter, has a speculative reconstructive dimension. It explains how distinct texts are produced by authors who have experienced something so transformative that they are compelled to talk about it. Original speech lays the foundation for subsequent doctrinal formulation and theological reflection. A theological epistemology may be reconstructed to include a developmental dimension and the possibility for novelty. The development of concepts about God, self, and world is a transhistorical history of the formation of key theological concepts. I will rely on Schleiermacher's account of concept formation to explain how theological concepts remain consistent once they have been established, even while holding open the possibilities for new insights. For Schleiermacher, the Christian religion is a living tradition to the extent that experiences with the Christian reality of God in the world, the *Christus praesens*, are not relinquished to the past, but are possibilities in present and future.

6. See, e.g., a volume introducing new historiographies by contemporary theologians, among them Lewis Ayres and Christopher Beeley, in Sarah Coakley, ed., special edition on "The God of Nicaea: Disputed Questions in Patristic Trinitarianism," *Harvard Theological Review* 100, no. 2 (2007).

There are two parts to the theological epistemology explored in this chapter. The first section has to do with the production of the New Testament. This is Christianity's canonical text, according to Schleiermacher, and the textual basis on which the christological association between Jesus of Nazareth and work of redemption has been established. The second section explores how significant theological concepts are produced in the history of Christianity. In this latter instance my aim is to show how doctrine arises and develops in view of the language-reality relation established on the basis of the New Testament and to account for the possibility of novelty in concept formation. The focus in both parts is the construction of an epistemology that explains how word in Scripture and doctrine is produced. Such an epistemology is theologically necessary in order to show how the specific issue of language and reality in Christianity informs the ongoing theological task. Here are several main questions: How does language change under the new pressure of experience? How are consciousness and intentionality (meaning reference to a reality outside oneself) part and parcel of linguistic framing? And how does theological language refer to Christ's saving deeds? The language-reality relation is construed theologically from the perspective of its subject matter, and from this perspective it explains the liveliness of the Christian religion in relation to its God.

I.3. Qualifying the Help from Schleiermacher

Schleiermacher's theology, although often referred to in exclusive relation to a philosophy of consciousness, also treated the issue of language, not least as the vehicle by which Christ is communicated in the church.[7] He discusses different genres of Christian discourse in an important section in the prolegomena to his work *Christian Faith*, for instance, in which he deals with the relation of the state of Christian self-consciousness to faith statements (*CF* §§15–19). Language also arises as a significant topic in the *Dialectic*, Schleiermacher's philosophical lectures on the production of scientific knowledge. According to Schleiermacher, knowledge is only available to the extent that it is articulated linguistically in communication with others. This explains why he wrote philosophical lectures on hermeneutics alongside and as companion to the *Dialectic*. Since the *Dialectic* considers the production of knowledge through the linguistic articulation of claims and debate about these claims, hermeneutics is required in order for scholars to understand each other's

---

7. *CF* 77 (§15.2): "The whole work of the Redeemer Himself was conditioned by the communicability of His self-consciousness by means of speech, and similarly Christianity has always and everywhere spread itself solely by preaching."

respective knowledge claims. Hermeneutics is, as Schleiermacher defines this discipline that he is credited with founding, the "art of understanding particularly the written discourse of another person correctly."[8] Both dialectics and hermeneutics presuppose an intimate relation between language and reality.

Although the topic of the relation between language and reality in Schleiermacher can be analyzed through a number of different texts, my interest is the way Schleiermacher explicates the relation of language to the experience of Christ that he identified as the foundational layer of the New Testament. This is especially relevant with regard to the problem of Schleiermacher in contemporary theology. Both the problem of biblical interpretation (the translation of biblical truth into culturally relative idioms) and the problem of interiority (experience is prior to and distinct from linguistic expression) may be resolved together by studying how Schleiermacher dealt with the question of how the New Testament arose as a text in the first place. Schleiermacher's account presupposes a soteriological core that both prompts the production of the New Testament and explains the novelty that is required at any stage in the Christian religion for its liveliness.

Schleiermacher's contribution to the study of the New Testament was significant for the field. Indeed, the translation of his lectures on Luke (1817) into English in 1825,[9] before the translation of his *Christian Faith* in 1928, resulted in his reception as a New Testament scholar in the English-speaking world, rather than as a systematic theologian. He was an avid and vital interlocutor in discussions of the Synoptic Problem,[10] and although he erroneously dated John's Gospel as the earliest (rather than the latest) Gospel, he opened the question of exploring the production of the New Testament in view of its proximity to Jesus. His interpretations of 1 Timothy (1807) and Colossians (1832) set parameters for the field, particularly for deuteropauline studies, that remain salient in New Testament studies today.[11] In addition to

8. Friedrich Schleiermacher, *Hermeneutics and Criticism and Other Writings*, trans. Andrew Bowie, Cambridge Texts in the History of Philosophy (Cambridge: Cambridge University Press, 1998), 3. The lectures on *Hermeneutics* were first published in the *Sämmtliche Werke* (*SW*) edition of Schleiermacher's works, yet in the philosophical section rather than the theological section.

9. Friedrich Schleiermacher, *Critical Essay on the Gospel of St. Luke*, trans. and intro. Connop Thirlwall (London: John Taylor, 1825); repr. with further essays, emendations, and other apparatus by Terrence N. Tice, *Schleiermacher: Studies and Translations 13* (Lewiston, NY: Edwin Mellen, 1993).

10. For a discussion of the New Testament scholarship in the nineteenth century, see John S. Kloppenborg, *Excavating Q: The History and Setting of the Sayings Gospel* (Minneapolis: Fortress Press, 2000), 275–328.

11. On Schleiermacher's interpretation of these and other biblical books, see Hermann Patsch and Dirk Schmid, "Einleitung [to Schleiermacher's exegetical writings]," in *KGA* I/8, ed. Hermann Patsch and Dirk Schmid (2001), vii–lvii; my

lecturing on individual books in the New Testament (many of these lectures remain unpublished) at the University of Berlin,[12] Schleiermacher delivered lectures on "Introduction to the New Testament" (published in 1845) and the course in 1831/32 on the "Life of Jesus." Student notes of these lectures were published thirty years after his death in 1864.[13]

Because Schleiermacher did not write a theory on the production of the New Testament, the topic requires reconstructing a number of pertinent texts in systematic relation to each other in order to fill in one perspective's gaps with insights from another. The biblical and theological texts in Schleiermacher's corpus are obvious sources for this study, but dialectics and hermeneutics are also brought into the reconstructive project. With appeals to texts outlining Schleiermacher's methodology for the intersubjective pursuit of knowledge, I fill in the gaps of his New Testament research with (what I take as) the important presuppositions informing the language-reality relation. Schleiermacher's understanding of the way in which the New Testament documents the experience of Jesus of Nazareth presupposes concepts of consciousness, experience, reality, and linguistic context. Hence a close look at the intersection between language and consciousness sheds light on how Schleiermacher conceives the epistemology behind the composition of the New Testament, considering the epistemology in as intimate a proximity to the experience of the historical Jesus as possible.

A treatment of Schleiermacher's understanding of the Christian canon is not without controversy. I am aware that for Schleiermacher, the New Testament rather than the Old Testament is the canonical text for Christian faith

---

"Schleiermacher's Exegetical Theology and the New Testament," in *The Cambridge Companion to Friedrich Schleiermacher*, ed. Jacqueline Mariña, Cambridge Companions to Religion (Cambridge: Cambridge University Press, 2005), 229–48; as well as my "The Consummation of Reality: Soteriological Metaphysics in Schleiermacher's Interpretation of Colossians 1:15–20," in *Biblical Interpretation: History, Context, and Reality*, ed. Christine Helmer, Society of Biblical Literature Symposium Series 26 (Atlanta: Society of Biblical Literature Press, 2005), 113–32.

12. From 1804 to 1834, Schleiermacher regularly lectured on books in the New Testament. For a list of all the New Testament lectures that he delivered, see Andreas Arndt and Wolfgang Virmond, *Schleiermachers Briefwechsel (Verzeichnis) nebst einer Liste seiner Vorlesungen*, Schleiermacher-Archiv 11 (Berlin: de Gruyter, 1992), 300–330.

13. Friedrich Schleiermacher, *Einleitung ins neue Testament*, in *SW* I/8, ed. G. Wolde (1845); idem, *Das Leben Jesu*, *SW* I/6, ed. K. A. Rütenick (1864); ET as *The Life of Jesus*, trans. S. MacLean Gilmour, ed. and intro. Jack C. Verheyden, Lives of Jesus Series (Philadelphia: Augsburg Fortress, 1975; repr., Mifflintown, PA: Sigler Press, 1997); Catherine L. Kelsey, "A Reading of Schleiermacher's *Life of Jesus* Lectures: An Historian at Work," in *Schleiermacher, Romanticism, and the Critical Arts: A Festschrift in Honor of Hermann Patsch*, ed. Hans Dierkes, Terrence N. Tice, and Wolfgang Virmond (Lewiston, NY: Edwin Mellen, 2007), 209–26.

(as stated above).[14] His insistence on this was criticized from the first publication of his claim in the *Brief Outline* in 1811, and it continues to be a serious difficulty for any sympathetic reading of his understanding of the Christian canon.[15] But this understanding of "canon," likewise, requires some qualification. For Schleiermacher, both Old and New Testaments make up the Christian Bible, which he regards as the text that exhibits the unity of the church and that was read as a unity by the church since its earliest traditions. Since its origins, Christianity has continued to rely on both Testaments as liturgically significant.[16] Yet "Bible" is distinguished from "canon," by which Schleiermacher means the specific text that was produced under the pressure of the historical person of Jesus of Nazareth, and that has authority for Christian faith and morals. Since Schleiermacher restricts the Christian experience to the person of Jesus as recounted by eyewitnesses in the New Testament, for making Christian theological claims he excludes any text not directly concerned with the experience of this person. This restriction is tied to Schleiermacher's understanding of the relations between language, Christ, and experience, as I will discuss in more detail below. More critical work needs to be done on the historical restrictions that Schleiermacher places on experience from Christian theological perspective. At this point, however, I am using Schleiermacher in order to excavate the concern with language and reality in the hope that this will pave the way for more critical and constructive engagement with the topic in contemporary theology.

II. LANGUAGE AND REALITY
IN THE NEW TESTAMENT

I begin with Schleiermacher's understanding of the New Testament as literary document fixed solely on Jesus of Nazareth. This gives us a clearer glimpse

---

14. For Schleiermacher, the term "canon" seems to be an idea rather than a concrete list of distinct books. In the first edition of the *Brief Outline* (1811), he uses the term "idea of the canon." See Friedrich Schleiermacher, *Kurze Darstellung des theologischen Studiums zum Behuf einleitender Vorlesungen (1810/30)*, ed. Heinrich Scholz, 3rd ed. (Leipzig: A. Deichert, 1910); repr. in the series Bibliothek klassischer Texte (Darmstadt: Wissenschaftliche Buchgesellschaft, 1993), I, §§1–2 (cited as *KD*). This is the regulative idea in Kant's sense as the object of infinite approximation. Cf. *KD* I, §10. In *KD*, 2nd ed. (1830), Schleiermacher refers to canon as the "collection of those writings which contain the normative presentation of Christianity" (*BO* §104).

15. The first published review of the *Brief Outline* is clear in its rejection of Schleiermacher's view of the Old Testament. See F. H. Chr. Schwarz, "Review of Schleiermacher's *Brief Outline*," *Heidelberger Jahrbücher der Litteratur* 5, no. 33 (1812): 526–27.

16. *BO* §115.

into the issue at hand between language and experience, looking closely at how Jesus' relationships with those in his proximity are significant in the composition of stories told about him in the New Testament. Schleiermacher sees an original relation between the historical Jesus and Christian discourse. I want to show how Schleiermacher understands the specific discourse of Christ and his work to be produced under the impact of personal experience of Jesus. But first I begin with the historical question that prompted Schleiermacher to be preoccupied with this relation.

II.1. Jesus and the New Testament

At the turn of the nineteenth century, the issue occasioning much New Testament scholarship had been articulated by Hermann Samuel Reimarus (1694–1768) half a century before Schleiermacher's time. In 1750, Reimarus, a professor of Oriental languages at Hamburg University, had written a text titled *An Apology for, or, Some Words in Defense of Reasoning Worshipers of God*, calling into question the reliability of the New Testament witnesses to Jesus. According to Reimarus, Jesus' disciples deliberately falsified their master's message and established Christianity on fraudulent foundations. In his view, the task of historical criticism is to get back to the historical Jesus and his authentic message. After Reimarus's death, around 1769/70 his daughter Elise and son Johann Albert Heinrich Reimarus gave a draft copy of the 1750 text to Gottfried Lessing (1729–81), who published excerpts from it between 1774 and 1778 in the journal *Zur Geschichte und Literatur: Aus den Schätzen der Herzoglichen Bibliothek zu Wolfenbüttel*. The duke of Braunschweig had lifted the censorship requirement for Lessing's journal, thereby making a publication of the controversial fragments possible. Lessing veiled the text's author under the title *Fragmente eines Ungenannten* (*Fragments*), claiming that he had discovered the manuscript in the Wolfenbüttel library.[17] The fragment controversy, as it came to be known, swiftly established the key questions for the study of the New Testament Gospels, particularly the sources of the Synoptic Gospels, their mutual dependence, and their relation to the Gospel of John. Schleiermacher was a major voice in this discussion. His contribution consisted of demonstrating that the historical relation between Jesus and the texts composed about his life and word, in effect the New Testament, was unbroken. The gap that Reimarus had driven between Christ and the

---

17. See Ernst-Peter Wieckenberg, *Johan Melchior Goeze*, Hamburger Köpfe (Hamburg: Ellert & Richter Verlag, 2007), 186–90; Volker Leppin, "Fragment-Controversy," *EBR*, vol. 9 (forthcoming). The German title of Reimarus's text is *Apologie oder Schutzschrift für die vernünftigen Verehrer Gottes*. Albert Schweitzer credited Reimarus with the origins of the quest for the historical Jesus.

New Testament would be closed, according to Schleiermacher, by a historical account of the New Testament's production.

In demonstrating the indivisible connection between Jesus and New Testament, Schleiermacher's historical work had another motivation. The issue of redemption was the hinge on which this connection turned. It was the historical Jesus of Nazareth who accomplished redemption.[18] Hence Schleiermacher valued the New Testament's proximity to Jesus in soteriological terms. A successful portrait of Jesus of Nazareth would be more than a historically reliable document. It would convey its subject matter in a way that would establish the origins of a community redeemed by Jesus, and thus would also explain the continued redemptive action of Christ in the Christian community through the ages. Physical proximity to Christ—whether in his antemortem body to his disciples or as the postmortem *Christus praesens* after the resurrection[19]—was the means by which redemption was communicated. If the New Testament was to be regarded as the reliable witness to Christ, it needed to be seen as the original text that communicated efficaciously and continuously the gospel of divine love distributed according to the divine wisdom through Jesus of Nazareth.[20] In Jesus' identity with God's redemptive work, the person of Jesus would continue to be rendered present, and soteriologically communicative, by these texts.

Some of the assumptions informing Schleiermacher's line of questioning are controversial. His definition of redemption restricts the agent to the historical Jesus, excluding all speculation regarding the preexistent Christ from his understanding of Jesus and thereby questioning the normativity of the Athanasian form of the Trinitarian doctrine.[21] His evaluation of the Gospel of John as the most historically proximate to Jesus on the grounds of its literary coherence would be dismissed as early as 1820, when John was deemed

18. Schleiermacher defines the essence of Christianity in the proposition of *CF* 52 (§11): "Christianity is a monotheistic faith; . . . everything in it is related to the redemption accomplished by Jesus of Nazareth."

19. Schleiermacher acknowledges a distinction in the type of presence that Jesus has before and after his resurrection. Yet the difference does not in any way detract from the soteriological efficacy that is intimately connected with Jesus' presence. Redemption is accomplished through Jesus by his presence with his disciples and with following generations of Christians.

20. In *CF* §§170–72, Schleiermacher describes the two mutually connected divine attributes of love and wisdom that are the cause of God's redemptive activity in the world.

21. For an article that astutely situates Schleiermacher's innovations vis-à-vis the Trinitarian doctrine in continuity with the normative tradition of Trinitarian reflection, see Francis Schüssler Fiorenza, "Schleiermacher's understanding of God as Triune," in Mariña, *The Cambridge Companion to Friedrich Schleiermacher*, 171–88.

to be the last Gospel and Mark the first Gospel.[22] These errors eventually led to a dismissal of Schleiermacher's historical claims concerning the New Testament, particularly after David Friedrich Strauss published his scathing attack on Schleiermacher's lectures on the life of Jesus that Strauss had heard him deliver in Berlin during the winter semester of 1831/32. Strauss's 1865 critical review, published just one year after the posthumous publication of Schleiermacher's own "Life of Jesus" lectures, is a significant marker in the negative reception history of Schleiermacher's scholarship on the New Testament Gospels.[23]

Although much could be said to address the controversial positions that Schleiermacher took on Jesus and the Trinity, the question guiding my study is Schleiermacher's concern with the language-reality relation as he seeks to dismiss Reimarus's rumors of a hoax. Schleiermacher's interest is infused with a theological concern: the text-reality relation must be able to explain the unique contribution that Christianity makes in history, which is its soteriologically significant relation to Christ. The New Testament is not merely an eyewitness account of a man who lived in first-century Galilee. It is a portrait of a person who dramatically transformed people who encountered him so that their documented memories continued to serve as media by which his personal presence was rendered in following generations. Jesus' transformative work was not restricted to early Christianity but would be the same source enlivening the entire history of Christianity. Soteriology, not history, is the theologically significant factor in Schleiermacher's account of the production of the New Testament.

II.2. Mysticism Again

At this point I reach back to chapter 2 and briefly pick up the discussion of mysticism that provoked Brunner's ire with Schleiermacher.[24] Although Brunner's critique makes it seem that the term "mysticism" is pervasive in Schleiermacher's vocabulary, the opposite is actually the case, particularly if one considers the later Schleiermacher of the *Christian Faith*. There the term "mystical" shows up in one particular paragraph (*CF* §100), where Schleiermacher is discussing the theological difficulty of distinguishing between Christ and the community that evokes his presence by proclamation and the

22. In 1820, Karl Bretschneider published *Probabilia*, which assigned a late date to John. See Verheyden, "Introduction" to Schleiermacher, *Life of Jesus*, xxxi.

23. David Friedrich Strauss, *The Christ of Faith and the Jesus of History: A Critique of Schleiermacher's "The Life of Jesus"* (1865), trans., ed., and intro. Leander E. Keck, Lives of Jesus Series (Philadelphia: Fortress Press, 1977).

24. See section IV.2. in chap. 2 above.

difficulty of relating Christ to that community. Only reluctantly does Schleiermacher appeal to the term "mystical" as he alludes to the controversies swirling around the term in his own day.[25] The use of the term to discuss the Christ-community relation is particularly significant in Schleiermacher's case because it points to the specific experience of Christ that characterizes the soteriological focal point of Christianity from its origins to the present day.

Schleiermacher's understanding of a mystical relation with Christ takes seriously the ecclesial context in which this experience takes place. The theological issue at stake is precisely Schleiermacher's insistence that *the church* is the communal context in which the believer can come into the presence of Christ. Soteriology requires a community that "circulates" Christ. In Schleiermacher's understanding, Christ's redemptive influence is coterminous with the creation of the church. The theological difficulty that emerges from this coterminous relation between Christ and church is precisely the conceptualization of how Christ can be present to the community without becoming identical with it. At stake, in other words, is the agency of redemption. If Christianity is a religion that refers unambiguously to Jesus of Nazareth as the person who has accomplished redemption (as Schleiermacher claims in *CF* §11),[26] it cannot confuse Christ with the church.

Schleiermacher's solution is to insert the term "mystical" in order to distinguish the specific relation between Christ and individual believer from the community's circulation of Christ in its ritual and proclamation. The "mystical element," meaning the individual's relation to Christ, is distinguished from the "churchly element," the corporate life of believers.[27] But both elements must be held together because Christ cannot be separated from the community that he creates and continues to enliven with his Spirit. Schleiermacher thus holds the term "mystical" as a middle path between two other positions that theoretically emphasize one of the constants in the Christ-church relation to the detriment of the other: (1) A "magical" view holds Christ's relation to the believer as independent from the community. (2) An "empirical" view collapses Christ's influence into the moral perfection stipulated by the community. "Mystical" thus denotes a precise christological term that distinguishes, but does not isolate, Christ's redemptive agency from church proclamation.

With this definition of "mysticism," Schleiermacher is simultaneously holding on to two important points about the Christ-believer relation. The

25. The term, Schleiermacher writes, is "so extremely vague that it seems better to avoid it" (*CF* 429 [§100.3]). Discussants in this controversy include Schelling Fichte, and Jacobi.

26. *CF* 52 (§11, proposition): "Everything in it [Christianity] is related to the redemption accomplished by Jesus of Nazareth."

27. *CF* 428–31 (§100.3).

first point is that experience transcends language. A mystical encounter with Christ cannot be captured in the third-person objective discourse of theology. Rather, it is "mystical" in the sense that a specific relation with Christ is decisively unique and transcends linguistic determination. The second point is that Schleiermacher gives "mystical" a christological precision. It does not refer to a generic religious experience that can be described apart from Christian discourse. Schleiermacher's description of the mystical element in his theology of redemption focuses on the Christ-believer relation that itself cannot be considered independently from the Christian community in which Christ is proclaimed in the first place. When Christ is preached in the community, this proclamation provides the occasion for a personal encounter with Christ. Even if it is ultimately the experience with Christ that is constitutive of the believer's redemption, the community's ritual and proclamation precede this experience.

II.3. Total Impression

The term mystical must also be clarified vis-à-vis another issue. Brunner, as we have seen in chapter 2, had castigated Schleiermacher's mysticism as a confusion between nature and sprit. Mysticism marks the slippery experiential slope to confusing God with human consciousness.

Schleiermacher cannot be correctly interpreted on the matter of experience, however, without considering his relation to the Kantian inheritance. For both Kant and Schleiermacher, experience of the external world is available through sense perception. For Schleiermacher, sensible self-consciousness (or temporal self-consciousness) is the aspect of human consciousness that makes sense of external objects perceived through the senses. Objects in space and time are perceived and then schematized according to distinct categories so that the understanding may more easily handle concepts that refer to these objects. It is significant for his theory of consciousness that Schleiermacher takes over Kant's causal reference theory. Concepts rendered by the understanding refer to external objects that have originally been passively sensed by perception before they are actively categorized in concepts. The process of thinking that occurs in sensible self-consciousness refers immediately to external objects as its cause.

Religion, like sense perception, is experienced as an encounter with an external element. Yet there is a crucial difference between the character of religious experience and the kind of consciousness that apprehends it. Although sense perception plays a role in all experience, it is overcome when an external object is perceived in its totality rather than as a function of its parts. This perception of a totality requires the availability of sensible consciousness that perceives and conceptualizes the distinct object as the sum of its parts. In order for the object to be perceived as a totality that is more than the sum of its parts, the unifying participation of immediate self-consciousness in the experience is required. Immediate self-consciousness, according to Schleiermacher, is the psychological condition that unifies distinct moments of sensible self-consciousness in a feeling that the self in a unity with the world is absolutely dependent on a Whence. This is the particular "province" for religion as outlined in the famous section 4 of *Christian Faith*: the unique capacity that humans have for religion requires a perception of a distinct object as its condition, and then, with the unifying capacity of immediate self-consciousness, the person approaches that object in the totality of the self-world relation. For Schleiermacher, temporal and immediate self-consciousness are the two inseparable parts of one consciousness. They cannot be separated from each other in order to yield two distinct objects of perception. Rather, sense perception delivers to consciousness an object that is then experienced as a "total impression" under the condition of immediate self-consciousness. Schleiermacher uses the term "total impression"[28] to denote the experience of Jesus' personal presence. Jesus is the cause of a particular perception that is apprehended in its totality by immediate self-consciousness.

How does the total impression relate to the feeling of absolute dependence? In light of the above, I will briefly answer this crucial question. The feeling of absolute dependence is, as the abstraction of immediate self-consciousness from sensible consciousness (an abstraction that is never an actuality), the feeling that self and world as a totality are absolutely dependent on a Whence. When Schleiermacher explicates the meaning of this feeling in the famous §4 of *CF*, he intends merely to give the barest determination of this feeling in abstraction from the content of positive religion. Given his understanding that human consciousness is a unity between temporal and immediate self-consciousness, it is not correct to say that the feeling of absolute dependence offers a determination of God independently of the content of positive religion. Rather, in Schleiermacher's conceptuality, the feeling of absolute dependence is a sense of a lack of a ground for the self, which by an immediate reflex in self-consciousness assigns the cause of this lack of a ground to an external cause outside of the self-world totality. When this feeling of absolute dependence is construed according to the positivity of Christianity, as it inevitably is for Schleiermacher, it is a feeling that the redemption of the self-world totality as mediated through the historical person of Jesus has its cause in the Christian God. There is no feeling of religion in the generic

28. *CF* 72 (§14, postscript).

sense. Rather, religious feelings are always united with the content given to experience through positive religion.

Yet the mere impression of a totality caused by an encounter with an external Other is not sufficient to account for the soteriological generosity that is attributed to Jesus by the Christian religion. At this point Schleiermacher adds to his account the soteriological essence required by a Christology that has informed the course of Christianity's history. The total impression perceived through the unity of temporal and immediate self-consciousness is identical with an effect that cannot be attributed to a cause immanent in self-consciousness. Schleiermacher insists that the effect of Jesus' total impression is so transformative as to elicit in the perceiving subject the attribution of causality to Jesus himself. The presence of Jesus transforms the person who encounters the reality of his person. The transformation is, as Schleiermacher alludes to the language of his Protestant orthodox predecessors, person-forming. The total impression of Jesus has a transforming effect at the core of individual personhood. Immediate self-consciousness, the psychological site at which the self is aware of her own lack of a ground to the self, receives the person-forming influence of Jesus' presence in the sense that Christ grounds personal existence. "So if anyone is in Christ," Schleiermacher can agree with the apostle Paul's original words, "there is a new creation" (2 Cor. 5:17a). Christ's presence effects a transformation of the soul by grounding it in his personal presence. Nothing less is at stake in Schleiermacher's account of Christ's transformative presence than the externality of Jesus as cause for the redemption of the world.

II.4. Acclamation

The question of language is addressed at precisely this point in Schleiermacher's account of the earliest encounters with Jesus of Nazareth. Schleiermacher's concern is to access the most original historical layer of the New Testament and thereby show that the connection between experience and language precludes the possibility of interruption and distortion. To meet Reimarus's challenge that the disciple's linguistic articulations about their master are deliberate falsifications of Jesus' person, teaching, and actions, language cannot be a secondary layer added onto experience. Schleiermacher's response is keenly committed to showing that although language can never be identical with the experience, it may be so proximate to the original experience of Jesus that it is inseparable from it.

There is a further theological reason why Schleiermacher insists on the proximity of language to experience at these earliest layers of the New Testament. When a person encounters Christ and perceives him in a total impression, the impression that emanates from Christ's person transforms consciousness in a specific way. A new and unprecedented state of consciousness is initiated by Christ. This state of consciousness is felt as unprecedented because it registers a transformation for the good that has not been achieved in that person's consciousness until that point in her existence. Schleiermacher adds an additional ingredient to this account of the transformation experienced as a result of encountering Christ. The cause of transformation is not attributed to self but is referred immediately and inevitably to an external subject, to Jesus of Nazareth. The unambiguous referral to an external cause is an original reflex in the soul that perceives a transformation in relation to an encounter with Jesus of Nazareth. This reflex is linguistically articulated. It identifies Christ as subject of transformation in speech from a first person to a second person. Hence at the earliest level of the New Testament is the genre of acclamation: "[I say that] you are the Messiah [Christ], the Son of the living God" (Matt. 16:15–16).

At the origins of Christianity is a personal encounter, recorded in the first-to-second-person exchange of question and answer. Whether the answer is articulated as a claim of identification or as a claim of sight,[29] an experiential encounter with Christ elicits a unique exclamation concerning Christ. Furthermore, the expression is registered in terms of Christ as source of an unprecedented and often unnerving work. A relationship with Christ is one in which Christ does something so dramatic and transformative that only Christ can be identified as its source. Saul's conversion on the road to Damascus (Acts 9:3–8) is the paradigmatic case among transformative experiences. The encounter is so dramatic that a conversion of personal identity is attributed to Christ alone.[30]

The grammatical structure of the acclamation exhibits the reality. The mechanism of consciousness attributes its transformation to an external cause. It is at this point that language arises. The first-to-second-person direct speech emerges spontaneously, provoked by the total impression of Christ's person: "You are the Christ, the Son of the living God," lauds Peter in response to Jesus' question to his disciples at Caesarea Philippi, "But who do you say that I am?" (Matt. 16:15). The genre of Peter's answer is an acclamation in direct speech: "You are . . ." Jesus' dead body on the cross elicits a similar reaction. "Truly this man was God's Son!" exclaims the Roman centurion who

---

29. The Easter story in Luke 24:13–35 tells of two disciples who were accompanied by the unrecognized Jesus on the road to Emmaus. It was only after they had invited him to dinner, and after Jesus had blessed and broken the bread, that "their eyes were opened, and they recognized him" (Luke 24:31).

30. In Acts 9:5, it is Saul who asks, "Who are you, Lord?" The reply comes, "I am Jesus, whom you are persecuting."

faces Christ as he dies (Mark 15:39). The acclamation is so closely intertwined with the recipient's experience of Jesus that it arises as a spontaneous claim of identity. The cause of transformation, the person of Jesus, elicits a particular linguistic formulation that discloses the nature of the experience. Acclamation attributes causality of the experience to Jesus and does this in a way that makes a claim about Jesus' identity. The particular kind of transformative experience communicated by Christ's person through the total impression of him cannot be distinguished from the linguistic acclamation that reveals the external cause in a statement about identity. Jesus is no ordinary human being. He is Redeemer of the world. Experience and language are one. Both are intentional, referring to an external cause, and both have a subjective dimension, in consciousness that is transformed and in language that documents this transformation; thus the intentionality of the reflex in language is an attribution of identity as causing the transformation in the first place.

The specific grammatical structure of the acclamation is predication. "You are" points to the subject, Jesus; the predicate, which signifies the transformative experience as it is provoked by the external subject, completes the sentence. A theological epistemology can be developed from the philosophical discussion that explains how predication of an individual takes place. The case of the individual, Christ, determines the specific rationale for a predication structure that allows for an increase in knowledge to take place in view of the individual subject. When Christ questions his disciples at Caesarea Philippi, "Who do you say that I am?" Christ asks for a judgment that predicates a specific term of his person, whether it is prophet, Messiah, or Son of the living God. The predicate is evoked in relationship with Jesus. Each act of judgment refers a predicate to this specific Christ with whom the person is in relationship. The exclaimed predication as answer to Christ's question is the linguistic articulation of who Jesus is for the individual who has already formed a judgment about Jesus—by virtue of predicates gleaned from personal experience, friends, and context.

II.4.1. Predication and Intensional Logic

The particular logic of predication that characterizes Schleiermacher's thoughts on this topic is noteworthy. Although he does not explain the mechanism of predication in his theological writing, Schleiermacher works through the logic in his *Dialektik*, where he discusses the process of concept formation as the intellectual work of predicating terms of a subject. A concept refers to a subject, which is characterized by distinct predicates, so that concepts can be identified by and distinguished from other concepts by virtue of the distinct predicates that characterize them. The particular logical relation of predicate to subject term is called intensional logic, a commitment that Schleiermacher shares with the eighteenth-century philosopher Gottfried Wilhelm Freiherr von Leibniz (1646–1716).[31]

The philosophical question addressed by intensional logic is the epistemological problem concerning knowledge of an individual.[32] The question of clear and distinct knowledge of an individual, as Leibniz posed it, had to do with being able to distinguish one monad (or individual substance) from another. Each monad must have more than one predicate in order for it to be distinguished from another. Yet predicates are related to the subject term by a logic of containment. A predicate is contained in the subject term when the subject term can be identified by its having that particular predicate.[33] For Schleiermacher, the way in which knowledge of a subject proceeds is when new predicates are added to the subject term. These predicates are grasped when one has an experience of the subject. In an act of judgment, the predicate that is gleaned from experience is predicated of the subject term. When the subject has acquired a new predicate, so to speak, the subject term includes the new predicate by virtue of containment. Later, when someone else experiences the subject, that person will experience the predicates already included in the subject term as well as another and new predicate. This new predicate can then be added to the subject term. As long as the subject exists, new experiences of the subject are possible, and new predicates can be applied to the subject term through acts of judgment. Thus a subject term exhibits a history of predicates that have been attributed to it.

When we apply Schleiermacher's understanding of predication to the New Testament acclamations of the type "Jesus is the Christ," we see that this logic of containment picks out the individual, Jesus, by virtue of at least one predicate, for example, the Christ. The predicate is attributed to the subject term in a judgment that identifies the individual by virtue of the containment of predicate in the subject term. There is only one individual: this one is Jesus the Christ.

---

31. The complex relationship of Schleiermacher's dependence on Kant and Leibniz as well as the productive reception of their thought in the post-Kantian context is wonderfully sketched out by Jacqueline Mariña, "Schleiermacher between Kant and Leibniz: Predication and Ontology," in *Schleiermacher and Whitehead: Open Systems in Dialogue*, ed. Christine Helmer with Marjorie Suchocki, John Quiring, and Katie Goetz, 73–92, Theologische Bibliothek Töpelmann 125 (Berlin: de Gruyter, 2004); as well as by Manfred Frank's contribution in the same volume, "Metaphysical Foundations," 15–34.

32. For a detailed discussion of the problem of predication from philosophical perspective, see Donald Davidson, *Truth and Predication* (Cambridge, MA: Belknap Press of Harvard University Press, 2005), esp. 120–63 (chaps. 6–7).

33. I am grateful to Professor Jacqueline Mariña for clarifying the difference between Leibniz and Kant on the topic of predication.

The specific genre of acclamation as predication according to the intensional logic applied by Schleiermacher is precisely the theological speech-act at the center of Christianity. The reality of Jesus' person and work are acclaimed in acts of predication that articulate an identity for Christ as the one who accomplishes both personal and corporate redemption. When these speech-acts are collected in stories and texts, they are translated from their original first-to-second-person acclamation ("You are the Christ, the Son of the living God") to third-person statements (person x reported, "Jesus is the one who healed me"). Various titles, metaphors, predications of action, in short, various descriptions of Jesus in their experienced variety are knitted into the chain of concept formation by predication. Christological titles emerge from this variety, formulations identifying the subject term, Jesus, by claims about his person and work. The seeds of these linguistic predications are reaped as doctrine, as we shall see.

II.4.2. Predication in a Linguistic Milieu

The final question concerning predication has to do with the origin of the predicates. If predicates are taken as referring to the reality of experiencing Jesus, then they must come from the linguistic milieu in which that reality is experienced. For Schleiermacher, predicates for making claims about Jesus' identity are taken from the already-existing possibilities of linguistic terms and expressions. The particular New Testament authors are Greek speakers who reflect elements of Hebrew in their Greek composition. Their particular bilingualism must be taken into account when interpreting the grammar of the Koine Greek.[34] Although this assumption reflects contemporary consensus in New Testament scholarship, which sees New Testament authors as native Greek speakers in the Greco-Hellenistic context of the first century CE, it shows Schleiermacher's sensitivity to the particularities of the linguistic milieu of authors he studies.

The status of the predicates' relation to a subject term is a question that also has relevance in contemporary theological discussions. The issue turns on whether the predicates used to characterize a subject term in effect translate the subject term into the cultural idiom in which the predicate circulates or whether a judgment of this sort exhibits the acquisition of new knowledge about the subject term. The task of biblical interpretation likewise turns on this question. When the Bible is interpreted in a postbiblical context, is hermeneutical knowledge acquired by translating the biblical concept into the cultural idiom *imposed on it* by the interpreter or by exhibiting a predicate

---

34. Schleiermacher, *Hermeneutics*, 42: "To understand N.T. language one must consider the issue of bilingualism."

term *already contained* in the range of possible meanings of the biblical passage? The question has to do, in short, with the "new language" of Christian discourse.

According to Schleiermacher, via the particular predicates attributed to Jesus, the historically original layer of predication in the New Testament succeeds in exhibiting the novelty of the person of Jesus. Predicates—such as Christ, prophet, and living water—are all available to the cultural-linguistic milieu of first-century Palestine. Yet when attributed to Jesus, they express a judgment that exhibits the novelty of Jesus' distinctive person. Through the structure of intensional logic, an act of predication renders a claim about Jesus that expresses the novelty of who he is. Let me illustrate Schleiermacher's point with an example. When John reports that Jesus says, "I am the true vine" (John 15:1), the evangelist claims that the predicate renders the subject term, Jesus, according to a judgment in which "vine" articulates an actuality contained in the subject term. Since the predicate is taken from the agricultural context of Jesus' background, it comes to have a new meaning when identified with the subject term. When Jesus claims that he is a vine, he is no ordinary branch on which grapes grow. He is the source of abundant life for all. There is no issue of translating the distinctiveness of the subject term into a cultural predicate in the judgment "Jesus is the vine." Rather, the judgment articulates a distinctive aspect of Jesus' person, in this case the life-giving force of his personal presence.

The choice of which predicate to take from the cultural-linguistic milieu rests with the individual uttering the acclamation. Jesus' personal presence is experienced in a distinctive way by the individual encountering him. The transformation that Jesus causes in the person's existence is so dramatic that it elicits an acclamation identifying the change from personal perspective. The Samaritan woman at the well is struck by Jesus' knowledge of her private life and tells him, "Sir, I see that you are a prophet" (John 4:19). In the village of Nain, the crowd that witnesses Jesus' raising the widow's son from the dead exclaims in the third person, "A great prophet has risen among us!" and "God has looked favorably on his people!" (Luke 7:16). Although Jesus is sometimes portrayed as making predications about himself, the dominant motif in the New Testament Gospels reports expressions of individuals who acclaim Jesus as cause of a particular life-transforming effect. Jesus' presence elicits the acclamations. Their specificity has to do with the individual's distinct experience of Jesus and her capacity to choose one predicate from her personal linguistic repertoire.

A distinctive theological epistemology underlies the composition of the New Testament. This epistemology can be reconstructed by identifying the particular logic that is presupposed by the structure of predication while its theological distinctiveness is fitted to the particular subject term—the impact of Jesus' person on individuals making the locution. It is Christ himself who elicits the locution. Language comes to refer to a new reality by virtue of Christ, who makes all things new.

II.5. Consciousness, Language, and Doctrine

Reimarus's charge concerning the falsification of Jesus' message by his disciples challenged New Testament scholars to develop constructive arguments concerning the genesis of the New Testament at its earliest layers. Schleiermacher's response can be understood to have two aspects. The second, the theological epistemology I have reconstructed from texts in Schleiermacher's philosophical and theological corpus, offers an explanation for how language can be related to experience at an immediate point of contact. With this I have attempted to provide a model that addresses Reimarus's charge. This concern has extended into contemporary theology with a suspicion about distance between experience and language and with Schleiermacher as protagonist of this problem. But a more accurate interpretation of Schleiermacher on this issue arrives at the opposite conclusion: the earliest layer of linguistic articulations attributing causality to Christ predicate novel titles for this unique person. Jesus is, for these early believers, the Christ, a faith statement at the origins of Christology.

My primary concern in going through the steps of reconstructing a theological epistemology is to show that we can learn from Schleiermacher if we carefully interpret him on the specific issue of experience in relation to language. For Schleiermacher, the issue is not an either/or, but a relation that involves a complicated combination of psychological, causal-referential, religious, and linguistic elements. As a living religious tradition, Christianity holds open the possibility for persons in any generation to experience Jesus' personal presence. Christian witness is necessarily related to experience. Both elements together—experience and witness—are understood as a distinct theological account of transformation, its attribution to an external agent, and the linguistic acclamation of this attribution to Jesus. Novelty of experience and word is the catalyst of a living Christianity, while the continuity of this mechanism is referred to "Jesus Christ," who "is the same yesterday and today and forever" (cf. Heb. 13:8). Acclamations in the New Testament, in Easter liturgies, in pentecostal praise—all participate in and contribute to the lively Christian praise of God in Christ.

Thus experience-language relation is contextualized in intersubjective reality, whether in a specific community or in the transhistorical flow of Christian traditions. The givenness of Christian discourse for both intragenerational and transhistorical intersubjectivity is, as Schleiermacher saw it, available in the circulation of ideas, liturgies, and practices. Human consciousness is formed, informed, and re-formed by religious ideas and practices. Human consciousness is also sometimes affected in mystical ways when words and gestures convey the personal presence of Christ in a particularly dramatic way. Experiences that refer through words to their subject matter and words that open possibilities for experience—both are the given ingredients of religious life. The experience of Jesus Christ is the origin of doctrine.

III. THEOLOGICAL EPISTEMOLOGY AND DOCTRINE

The theological epistemology I have developed here explains how discourse is first produced in such a way that doctrine may then serve as the linguistic repertoire of subsequent proclamation and theology. Once produced, discourse is available for reception; then reception is an open invitation for experience and the articulation of its novelty. The discussion has focused on Schleiermacher's proposal because his systematic thinking offers the dialectical, hermeneutical, religious, and theological tools for a theological epistemology that can explain how word is related to consciousness and reality. There may be other ways to construct an explanatory mechanism for connecting discourse to reality, such as an emerging discussion in religious studies concerning the recovery of the real in religion.[35] My purpose is not a recovery tout court of Schleiermacher, but the beginning of a discussion in theology concerning the resources for recognizing and explaining how reality can be related to doctrine, which is both produced and received. The question concerns how doctrine refers to its subject matter while accounting for its articulation in an intersubjective milieu that has taken "lived religion" to heart. Epistemology is integrally related to content.

Now I turn to the question of how a theological epistemology might explain the production of doctrine, assuming its ongoing reception, as catalyst

---

35. See Robert A. Orsi, "The Problem of the Holy," in *The Cambridge Companion to Religious Studies*, ed. Robert A. Orsi, Cambridge Companions to Religion (New York: Cambridge University Press, 2012), 84–105; Christine Helmer, "Recovering the Real in the New Testament: A Case Study of Schleiermacher's Theology," in *The Multivalence of Biblical Texts and Theological Meanings*, ed. Christine Helmer with Charlene T. Higbe, Symposium Series 37 (Atlanta: Society of Biblical Literature, 2006), 161–76. See also the website of a workshop held in March 2013 at the Helsinki Collegium for Advanced Studies, "Beyond Deconstruction: New Engagements in Religious Studies," http://www.helsinki.fi/collegium/events/beyond-deconstruction.html.

for the living tradition of Christianity. I continue to explore Schleiermacher's model—acknowledging that there might be others—by pressing the question of how doctrine continues to be a significant intellectual practice in the church's history. The discussion focuses on the theological epistemological aspect of doctrinal development, particularly as it emerges from the Bible with distinct fixed parameters while also being open to novelty. The central question is how doctrinal production retains an original connection, as documented in the Bible, between word and reality at later historical points in articulation. This issue is of central import to the liveliness of Christianity. If doctrinal faithfulness can be established in terms of the word's connection to reality, rather than by word alone not connected to reality, then its transhistorical continuity can be open to the novelty that characterizes Christianity as a living religion. Significantly in our contemporary global context, Christian doctrine might look differently than what has been conveyed since the earliest centuries of the Common Era. The theological epistemology that follows is intended to help explain how faithfulness and novelty can be joined without fear. The argument is that this connection must refer to the reality of Christian experience.

III.1. The Origins of Doctrine

Jesus' personal presence is an effective presence. It accomplishes a work so dramatic that spontaneous eruptions of speech attribute work to agent. This relation between work and person that is embedded in the original acclamations will have normative force for subsequent doctrinal development concerning descriptions of Jesus' uniqueness. The uniqueness of his person is reciprocally related to work while dramatic work is attributed to his agency alone. Schleiermacher identifies the act of judgment concerning the reciprocity between person and work to be at the center of Christianity. The novelty of this religion rests on the christological claim that redemption is fully accomplished by the Redeemer (*CF* §11, proposition), while subsequent doctrinal formulations are regulated by the christological rule established at the earliest layers of the New Testament. The person of Jesus is identified with the transformation that he effects in people's lives, and his person-forming influence is attributed to his person. In the case of Jesus, person implies work and work refers immediately to person.

The origin of Christology is in fixing the subject term, Jesus, by the original predicate: Christ, vine, or any other attribute for Jesus found in the Bible. Some might disagree that "bread of life" (cf. John 6:35) is a fitting predicate for Jesus; others might think that the vine metaphor is more apt (cf. John 15:1). Yet agreement and disagreement are made possible only on the basis of an original consensus concerning the significance of Jesus' person in terms of his work. Original acclamations expressing acts of judgment shape the fundamental christological rule that connects person to work. Christ is the "bread of life" and "true wine" because his person effects works of a life-giving quality. The fundamental grammar of predication funds the person-work reciprocity that is rendered as axiomatic in Christology. Once established, the doctrinal grammar is opened to a history of predication. Individuals experience Jesus' presence in different ways, contextualized in different linguistic milieus, cultures, and intersubjective groupings. Yet these different ways are all related to each other in an agreement concerning the original doctrinal grammar. Different predications arise once the fundamental act of judgment concerning Jesus' unique personhood has already been established.

The foundational structure of predication identifies the origins of Christology together with an ecclesial element. For Schleiermacher, acclamations concerning Christ are linguistically expressed. Language is the intersubjective medium by which acts of judgment are rendered real for others. As an original aspect of its articulation, the linguistically communicated acclamation creates intersubjectivity. When Peter proclaims, "You are the Messiah, the Son of the living God" (Matt. 16:16), his acclamation refers particular predicates to Jesus in the context of the original disciples. In this intersubjective situation, the disciples are brought into the dynamic of relating to Peter's "confession of faith." Peter's act of judgment is coterminous with the intersubjective relating to Christ; in other words, doctrine is related to church. In his systematic theology, Schleiermacher structures Christology in intimate relation to ecclesiology. Christ and his work are together and necessarily oriented to the creation of an intersubjective community whose mission is to communicate Christ by acclamation in worship, by rendering his real presence via word and material reality, and by participating in the working out of new predications in the production of doctrine.

Yet in the process of communication, either intersubjectively or transhistorically, an essential element cannot be lost, namely, Christianity's living essence, core, or center. As a living religious reality, Christian experience cannot be captured but can be conveyed, and as such, it must constantly infuse the living stream with fresh water. The theological epistemology outlined here has taken this essence into account by the word-reality relation that lies behind the linguistic acclamations, the third-person faith statements about Christ, or the sophisticated distinctions in doctrinal formulation. When acclamations are conveyed in other literary genres, whether as first-person worship and narrative or third-person theology, these discursive acts are fueled by a connection, whether proximate or remote, to an impression of a totality that may have been experienced as a glimpse or fragment, a promise of new life. The communication of Christian discourse continues to convey its religious center in ways that might be audacious, as in the explicit preaching of the good news, or theologically dangerous, as in challenging assumed habits of doctrinal thinking. The former boldly creates opportunities for becoming immediate to Christ's presence; the second is dangerous for its introduction of individuality into the consensus. Whether primary or secondary, Christian discourse is ultimately soteriological at its core. Even when immediate forms of discourse become objects for intellectual reflection and thereby enter into the concept formation that is the production of theology, Christian discourse gestures toward, and sometimes even explicitly refers to, the reality of God in Christ in the world. Christianity is a positive religion, in Schleiermacher's terms, where positivity is created by the development of Christian discourse that both depends on original parameters set in Scripture and creates possibilities for novelty, which in turn precipitates new acclamations.

The biblical witnesses are directly related to doctrine. Schleiermacher's theological epistemology addresses the question concerning the historical discrepancy between Bible and doctrine by orienting the solution to a conceptual relation between earliest literary discourse, the acclamation, and the structure of predication undergirding this acclamation. The reciprocal relation between Jesus' person and work thus grounds both biblical discourse and doctrine. Schleiermacher's explanation likewise preserves the necessary ingredient for characterizing Christianity as a religion with the possibility for new life. The reality of Jesus is consistently connected to discourse evoked by his presence. As such, the discourse conveys the "inner essence" of the doctrine concerning his person and work. The soteriological dimension of Christian discourse is reproduced in, although not produced by, doctrine because doctrine is grounded conceptually in the language-reality encounter between believer (or acclaimer) and Christ. The production of doctrine is the theme of the next sections. How is doctrine open to novel predications in light of new encounters with the *Christus praesens* while continuing to be oriented by the parameters of original predication? This concerns doctrine's development as necessary to the liveliness of the Christian tradition and is relevant to current theological concerns with doctrine in a global context.

III.2. The Development of Doctrine in Intersubjective Milieu

The filling-in of the foundational christological proposition introduces elements of novelty and continuity. Any nontrivial discussion proceeds in the wonderful and relatively unique identifier of the human species—language—which is simultaneously Babel and Pentecost, community ruin and community building. Yet language is grammatically constructed by concepts and by verbs or logical connectors joining concepts in distinct configurations. Given language's grammatical structure, the question becomes how to organize grammatical elements in such a way as to work out linguistic arrangements as these arrangements refer to reality. Each time an exclamation is made about Christ's impact in one's life, or each time a claim is made attributing a predicate to the subject "Christ," terms are added to the determination of the subject. Multiple determinations add to knowledge about who Christ is and what he does. As such, they communicate something of significance to others.

Communication proceeds on the assumption that significant determination can be effectively communicated. The recipient is able to understand the communicated content by virtue of an underlying agreement that linguistic arrangement of grammatical elements results in an increase in the determination of the subject term by a predicate term. "You are the Messiah" predicates a term of the subject, Christ, and its communication increases our knowledge of who Christ is. It may not be the case that every determination is effectively communicated or fully understood. It may even be recognized that human communication and understanding proceed in fragments and glimpses. Yet the intersubjective commitment to language's grammatical arrangement is the reason for discussion in the first place. Commitment to language reveals commitment to the intersubjective milieu as the only context in which meaningful content can be communicated about a subject.

Predication is a process that occurs when experience is instantiated in language. Experience assumes that language has already circumscribed an area that permits an experience of a distinct sort to be available, and so experience is exclaimed, described, interpreted, and narrated in language. The relation between experience and language is more intimate than a standard one-directionality of language that expresses a prior experience or an experience that is thoroughly structured by language so as not to admit novelty. Experience, if it is interpreted at all, is "more than" its interpretation. Language is asymptotic in its attempt to capture experience. This is demonstrated by subsequent efforts to describe, interpret, and narrate an original experience. Language also establishes the contours of experience. Experience is always culturally located so that the language of exclamation, description, interpretation, and narrative inevitably takes up cultural nuances of the day.

The question of predication is crucial to demonstrating this claim because ongoing predication occurs in the present tense, which is the tense of living reality. Christianity's vital sign is the ongoing instantiation of Christ's unique work in human hearts. Even if predication refers to a new experience entirely in terms of language that has already been used in every respect to characterize past experiences, the mere fact of its repetition in the present tense indicates the present reality of a living tradition. The particular challenge for

Christian theology today consists precisely in admitting plural predications into the tradition's present reality on a global scale, which is as yet without precedent in Christian intellectual history. *Discovering a theological way for plural predication to occur in the context of a global Christianity has the opportunity to transcend, in an exciting way, predications that have to a large extent been determined contingently (although not accidentally) in the history of Western Christianity.* The question of plural predications asks how new predications can be related to prior predications (and their categorizations into doctrines and theological concepts). In the following, I present some reflections on the issues at stake in challenging theology toward plural predication and its initial categorization.

III.3. Doctrine in a Global Context

Today's global Christianity is an invitation to an unprecedented plurality of predication. It is a contemporary consensus in both West and non-West that Christian theology today requires taking the global scope of Christianity into account. Vítor Westhelle, a Brazilian theologian based in Chicago, makes this case in a recent essay in specific view of a Protestant denomination that has, since the sixteenth century, been associated with primarily German and Nordic countries and their immigrants. Lutheranism is rapidly spreading to all parts of the world so that in ten years' time more Lutherans will be living in the global south than the global north.[36] Other theologians from around the world could be mentioned that state this same case, although I cite here the example of Lutheranism as paradigmatic for the predication challenge because of German Protestantism's extensive and powerful history of determining Western theological predication. Martin Luther, Friedrich Schleiermacher, Karl Barth, and Karl Rahner have established the foundational parameters for theological predication in the modern West; many other biblical scholars, church historians, and systematic theologians have both set the conceptual contours of major theological concepts and infused them with content. The challenge of predication presented to theology today is to acknowledge and appreciate that until this point the history of predication has been dominated by a German intellectual elite, and then—without denying this experientially, conceptually, and linguistically structuring history—to invite plural predications as they accurately open up the scope of Christian experience today.

Initial difficulty arises in promoting plural predication of a global scope. Where can we begin? The matter of a starting point turns on an

---

36. Vítor Westhelle, "Incursions in Luther's Theology," in *The Global Luther: A Theologian for Modern Times*, ed. Christine Helmer, chap. 17 (Minneapolis: Fortress Press, 2009).

epistemological issue that also has to do with a historical contingency. When new languages instantiating new experiences are summoned, the process can only begin relative to what has gone on before. In epistemological terms, there can be no absolutely original starting point once the process of predicating is under way. Predication of the concept of Christ occurs in an epistemological sense "in the middle" because the concept of Christ available to predication already constitutes the Christian tradition and has already been given to it.

The epistemological process is closely related to a historical issue. The West's alliance with Christianity (and here we are speaking primarily of Western Christianity and its missions to non-Western parts of the globe) is a recognized historical contingency. And if historicity is metaphysically constitutive of human existence, as I believe it is, then inevitable historical contingency will mark all features of temporal change and development. Concepts of Christianity that have arisen as the result of predications in the West have taken on distinct linguistic and conceptual shaping in Greek and Latin, eventually in German, and currently in English. The concepts, made available in "new tongues" as the good news is "proclaimed" to "the whole creation" (Mark 16:15–17), were further taken up by developments in Western philosophy, culture, and actions. The controversy regarding a Western imposition onto global predication cannot be solved by the prescription that non-Western predication must reject its Western givenness.[37] Rather, the controversy could be met with creative proposals that allow for mutual interaction between many predicative traditions. Global predication should be free to critically engage with and build on its contingent epistemological and historical Western shape, while Western predication should not confuse contingency with superiority. Nevertheless, the controversy of current global predication requires that necessary questions concerning the truth of specific predications be raised. The process of working out the truth of Christianity must be aimed at promoting a Christianity that is adequate to its claims of justification and justice.

An epistemic orientation that is attuned to the predication of novel experiences of Christ dovetails with characteristics constituting the particular theological perspective from which predication should be framed in the first place. Theological assumptions for an adequate epistemic orientation are derived from the central Christian confession concerning Christ's unequivocally unique work of salvation that emanates from Christ's unequivocally unique person. Theology's attunement to individual novelty is constituted by the

37. English, e.g., has emerged as the lingua franca of international biblical scholarship.

unique Christian confession. Its fundamental capaciousness to plural predication must also be constituted on the same ground.

Yet theological attunement to plural predications of unique experiences of Christ is a cultivated habit, a disposition that is a learned art of listening at different levels of "hearing." True attentive listening requires the maturity to listen for spiritual resonances accompanying explicit linguistic articulation. Listening with ears open to another's account requires a seasoned personality, particularly in unblocking one's own prejudices, which prevent true hearing of what the other person has to say. Listening also requires the cultivation of intellectual resources in order to hear cultural, historical, political, and social notes that harmonize with the attribution of a redemptive experience to Christ. Contemporary theology ought to be open to ethnography as a method and to theories exploring hybrid identities, colonial legacies, and polyvalent accounts of sexuality and gender. By borrowing from diverse sources to listen attentively to factors in religious experience that have not been considered in the past, theology would develop its intellectual resources to refine the conceptual apparatus by which it hears and appreciates novel experiences. The cultivation of theology's capaciousness would then serve to embody the central Christian claim that every experience of Christ dignifies each human person as loved by God eternally.

Predication, as constituted by historicity and as taking place in relation to theological work, is fraught with challenges. Theology is a practice that, like other areas of study, disciplines its adherents to conform to standards of normativity. Authority is invoked in order to request conformity, or in dramatic cases to enforce conformity. The spirit of small-mindedness is theology's destructive nemesis, particularly when authority is invoked precisely in order to enforce normativity without permitting questioning of either authority or normativity. Sometimes even the invocation of the discipline of theology itself—both its circumference and its content—is enough to block predications without conversation or even a hearing. Absolutes cover up for theologians' insecurities concerning threats to prestige and power. Dogmatic appeal to predications in the name of their unique otherness—without acknowledging the common history shaping, even to a limited degree, any novel experience of Christ—poses one kind of challenge. The rush to identify unique areas of experience in antithesis to traditions long associated with Christianity, whether "Western" or "male," also exposes implicit dogmatic appeals to authority and normativity. Theology's disciplining of its boundaries, content, and methods is a frightening obstacle to its own existence as a living tradition of reflection in the many and various ways in which God is manifest among God's people (cf. Heb 1:1). If it were not for the reformers, the mystics, and the prophets, many of whom have been persecuted in the name of a normative theology, theology would be condemned to reciting empty formulas and meaningless propositions.

Yet the Holy Spirit continues to transcend structures of ecclesial and academic disciplining, as the Spirit has done throughout Christian history, in order to enliven Christianity as a living tradition. If left up to humans, theological predication would be the death sentence of Christianity. But as God is still God of Christianity, God can transcend human small-mindedness and self-satisfied arrogance and invite persons to open up to experiences of the Spirit's joyful novelty. Entry into divine transcendence requires the sacrifice of one's own dogmatism. By dying to self, as the mystics loved to impress upon Christian spirituality, a healthier, more God-focused epistemic attention is cultivated. The cultivation of theological habits that better discern the Spirit's working is participation in God's work to transcend human theological disciplining. The Spirit, moving in mysterious ways, has the mind of Christ, so that the very appreciation of novelty in Christ's creation of new experiences is part and parcel of the Spirit's work. If transcendence is a mark of Christianity, if the Christian religion is engaged in the task of promoting new possibilities for "abundant living," then transcendence also has a part in the art and task of theological predication. Plural predications, embraced by careful epistemic attention, expand traditional conceptual boundaries, break down walls that would deny the right to speak of Christ's work in particular lives and particular persons, and rejoice that Christ's gospel of newness is experienced all over the world.

III.3.1. Categorization

Plural predication goes hand in hand with the process of mapping predicates onto a conceptual grid. Predications, even if they are repetitions, generate larger conceptual areas that sustain the memory of prior predications and serve as the reservoir for future possible predications. When new predications take place, they are fitted to these conceptual areas, while at the same time the new predications critically expand or destabilize these concepts. The full history of Christianity bears witness to multiple predications that are generated and then mapped onto conceptual areas by a theological process of categorization. Theological categorization makes sense of predications, whether old or new, by showing relations among predications and by questioning existing relations. The querying of predication's meaning and explanation tends to categorization so that conceptual areas function in explaining what is meant and why.

The epistemological perspective for categorization has to do with slotting predicates into fuller determinations of subject terms. Judgments of the sort "s is p" make a claim concerning an individual predicate that adds to the determination of the subject term. Subsequent judgments add claims concerning an array of predicates about the specific subject term. The predicates can either instantiate new experiences of the subject or are contained in the subject term as possibilities for future instantiation. As plural predicates are added to the subject term, new questions arise. Hence the categorization of plural predicates into a subject term invites exploration as to the relation between predicates—whether actual or possible—and the subject term, and further, exploration as to how the subject is related to other subjects. New determinations pose questions of an already-categorized subject that, in turn, compel explorations of relationships into other domains. A simple predication of hair color to a person, for example, opens up questions concerning genetic determination—the specific person's relationship to parents and relatives, individual behavior in effecting the specific hair color (such as diet or hair dye), environmental factors (such as a chlorine pool), or dictates of role models—that map judgments onto the larger world.

As predicates are mapped onto a conceptual grid, they may destabilize concepts or they may secure them. Certain predicates are elevated into key determinations of concepts while others are taken to be less central. The grid is "in process," a living process of fitting predicates to concepts as those concepts are determined in relation to each other. The categorization process is both critical and constructive. Sometimes the process elicits fear, particularly when destabilization threatens the perceived continuity of specific concepts. Feminist theology, for example, was perceived in the 1980s to threaten the traditional naming of the triune God according to terms that conjured up male persons: Father and Son. Yet feminist theology opened up new areas of investigation into the experience of God from women's perspectives that resulted in richer determinations of God's maternal character. In the context of global predications, the challenge remains for primarily Western theologians to replace fear with a curiosity concerning the Spirit's work in the world and to question retrenchment into familiar patterns of categorization. This challenge, however, should not come at the expense of critical curiosity. Destabilization and new ways of mapping can also obscure key determinations of the gospel. The prosperity gospel in the contemporary United States, for example, maps Christ onto a late capitalist and neoliberal grid as framed by the Calvinist theological tradition. The stabilization of Western patterns of heteronormativity, to use another example, with accompanying limitations of women's personhood and roles, should be critically called into question on the grounds of new predications from both women's experiences and from theological reflections on the divine will that truly desires women's freedom.

As categorization further succeeds in mapping predicates onto a conceptual grid, it becomes the explanation for why predicates are related to each other and to particular concepts in particular ways. In this way categorization dovetails with theology's tendency toward "systematization." The development of system requires categorization together with a degree of self-consciousness concerning the reasons why relations between predicates and concepts are mapped in particular ways. The process of categorization must concur with a process of testing how it is occurring. Categorization cannot be a predictable slotting of pegs into the pigeonholes of systematic theology, but an invitation to test explanations for familiar ways of conceptualizing reality and to open up new ways to understand the categorization perceptions. The questioning of early Christian and traditional theological categorizations may result in retrieving pertinent relations or disclosing new ways in which predicates are related to the subject. A living system is precisely one that is characterized by transcendence.

III.3.2. Construction

Theology, particularly its systematic form, is a constructive process. Construction opens up new possibilities for orienting system to central ideas and querying the explanations for this mapping. In the process of assigning predicates in specific relations to each other and to subject terms, construction takes a systematic shape. I look at construction in this subsection and show how it requires a speculative dimension. A theological epistemology has a speculative outlook that characterizes the transcendence of a living system.

In the history of Christianity, system developed as a dominant form of categorizing predication. The first four centuries of Christianity were crucial in setting the systematic parameters as questions were asked concerning Jesus and his relation to God, whom he called on as "Father." A number of narratives reconstruct this development of the church's two dogmas: Trinity and Christology. Schleiermacher proposed an alternative narrative to what he called the dominant "Athanasian" narrative and showed how a refocusing of parameters concerning history and eternity resulted in a "Sabellian" construal of the historical sources.[38] Lewis Ayres undertakes a rewriting of the doctrinal conflicts in the early church and proposes another path to understanding

---

38. Schleiermacher's position is a significant modification of the "Sabellian" position of early Christianity. The divine modes coexist after their dispensation so that the distinctions between "persons" is maintained rather than one mode dissolving into a subsequent mode, thereby erasing distinctions between them. See Friedrich Schleiermacher, "Über den Gegensatz zwischen der Sabellianischen und der Athanasianischen Vorstellung von der Trinität," in Kritische Gesamtausgabe, ed. Hans-Friedrich Traulsen, vol. I/10 (Berlin: de Gruyter, 1990); ET, "On the Discrepancy between the Sabellian and Athanasian Method of Representing the Doctrine of the Trinity (1822)," trans. Moses Stuart, Biblical Repository and Quarterly Observer 5 (April 1835): 31–33; 6 (July 1835): 1–116.

the development of the "pro-Nicene" position on the Trinity.[39] Whatever
content results from a narrative rehearsal of dogma's development, the epistemological point is the same. The categorization of plural predicates of
Christ, whether "Son of God" or "son of David" (cf. Rom 1:3–4), gives rise
to questions that ultimately become questions of Trinity and Christology.
The early Christians struggled to best articulate a Trinitarian doctrine that
would account for Christ's relation to the eternal Father and also Christ's
temporal sojourn on earth. The parameters of the system of Christian theology were established as philosophical questions were addressed concerning
time and eternity, substance and accidents, persons and works. These speculative aspects were the structural building blocks of Christianity's system. From
Arius to Hegel, the speculative dimension designated theology's central question of relating time to eternity. From questions concerning Christ's metaphysical status to speculations concerning world history in relation to the
Absolute, the system's development is precipitated by speculative parameters
arising during the process of categorization.

The current malaise in systematic theology actually discloses the questioning of both the validity of system itself and, along with it, the speculative
restructural shaping of system. Regional theologies—theologies articulated
from the perspective of particular regions of experience—question system's
claim to comprehensiveness. How can plural predications be subsumed under
one categorization that speaks for all? The criticism has primarily in mind the
Western system as articulated by (German) male intellectual elites intend-
ing to speak universally. Yet another aspect to this questioning concerns the
authority of a universal metaphysic that is allegedly necessary for the construction of system. Is it true that only one type of metaphysic can establish
the parameters required for a true exposition of doctrine? Even the legitimation of an axiomatic starting point through the process of construction
is disclosed to be a problem in construction. If a specific Christian form of a
doctrine is assumed to be axiomatically true, then what method of discovery
might facilitate the construction of system? Challenges such as these necessarily expose pretensions to authority and dominance. They are met with
more modest theological proposals. The ambition to systematic construction
is rejected, countered by the categorization of distinct doctrines according to
regional parameters. Constructive theology is currently critical and regional.

The current state of theology, however, does not necessarily entail the
demise of system. On the basis of the theological epistemology outlined
here, system is an inevitable epistemological feature of categorizing plural

---

39. Lewis Ayres, *Nicaea and Its Legacy: An Approach to Fourth-Century Trinitarian
Theology* (Oxford: Oxford University Press, 2006).

predications. The challenge for imagining future systems rests precisely on the courage to speculate. The current and ongoing radical influx of plural predicates and their multiple epistemological mappings show that there is not just one speculative solution to the metaphysical questions of systematic structuring. Rather, new metaphysical possibilities need to be articulated in order to categorize predications that may not be in line with the established system. The inclusion of the relational category in *A Native American Theology* points to a novel metaphysic, required by the regional predications, yet one that opens up avenues for comparing with and questioning other systems.[40] Construction requires speculation in order to transcend established categorizations—and thus be able to see new experiences of God in Christ.

Plural predication can assist speculation by pointing to new possibilities to be contained in the subject term. Plural predications arise from experience, yet the categorization of predication cannot be limited to experience. If the conceptual determination of the subject term is restricted to experience, then the resulting subject term would be limited. Reality is always bigger—and in the case of Christ, more beautiful—than can be accounted for by predication. The speculative dimension comes in to assist predication by widening it to imagine possible experiences, not just actual experiences. By imagining new predicates, the predication process will stretch the borders of subject terms and rearrange relations among predicates in relation to each other and to the subject term. Such daring would extend the range of possible predicates so as to attune categorization to the possibility of new mappings. The possibility for seeing new things is, to a certain extent, preset by speculation.

The example of Luther's radical insight into the distinction between law and gospel is a case in point. The categories he applied to understand certainty in the moment of absolution ended up terrifying his conscience. When he discovered joyful solace in the certainty of Christ's work of forgiveness, without human contribution, he found a new conceptual tool to categorize his experiences of terror and demonic assault.[41] The central distinction between law and gospel as two functions of divine agency facilitated his idea of justification as entirely attributed to divine agency, even while sin was maximally uncovered by the divine function of law. The speculative development in Luther's theology—fueled by experience, but then worked out through

40. See Clara Sue Kidwell, Homer Noley, and George E. "Tink" Tinker, *A Native American Theology* (Maryknoll, NY: Orbis Books, 2001), and my review of this book in *Pro Ecclesia* 12, no. 2 (Spring 2003): 240–42.

41. There are a few accounts of Luther's "conversion" as urban legend. See Risto Saarinen's essay, "Luther the Urban Legend," in *The Global Luther: A Theologian for Modern Times*, ed. Christine Helmer, 13–31 (chap. 1) (Minneapolis: Fortress Press, 2009).

intellectual engagement with Bible, philosophy, and theology—yielded new possibilities for understanding Christ's work of salvation without presupposition of human agency or the subsequent imposition of a new law.

What is needed for theology's construction is a concept of speculative "anchoring" or "benchmarking." These terms connote the psychological and rational aspects of framing data. Data is framed differently depending on which choices are made for structuring it. In theology, the comfort zone in structuring spiritual realities is established by spiritual and theological benchmarks, what is commonly accepted as "normative." One of theology's great contributions to the history of ideas is its insistence on benchmarking human experiences of God according to divine agency and radical transformation. Theologians insist on Christ's givenness, which cannot be controlled by human agency or contained in a human concept. The accompanying commitment to terms such as "alien," "*verbum externum*," and "externality" stretches vocabulary by insisting on divine agency in radical disjunction to human agency. Although these terms occur within the repertoire of human language, they point to a reality that is different from human existence while changing it in deep and often hidden ways. Theology's benchmarking consists of keeping a speculative dimension of reality open to Christ's uniqueness. Theological truth, then, requires speculative skill to benchmark uniqueness adequately. Theology must secure God's work that is distant from common experiences of a world in which humans make or break themselves in a battle of winners and losers. God, as distant from the world of the *homo faber* (man the worker), is also radically proximate to this world. God is seen as giver of all good things and our defender from all evil, as Luther interprets the first article of the Apostles' Creed in the confession of faith.[42]

Speculative benchmarking is a characteristic of theological construction that aims to represent divine agency as other to human reality, yet it is at the same time transformative of human reality. Its epistemological legitimation rests with the process of plural predication and categorization. Predications occur by assuming the axiom of Christ's uniqueness while speculative anchoring categorizes predicates explicitly in view of Christ's uniqueness. The question of predication and construction does not inevitably entail a choice for either privileging Christ or culture in the directionality of predication or in the mapping of predicates onto a conceptual grid. Rather, a theological epistemology is useful in demonstrating the inevitability of predication in a cultural milieu that consistently keeps the predication open by epistemological glimpses of transcendence. Whether predication or construction, both

---

42. Martin Luther, "Explanation to the First Article of the Creed," in the "Large Catechism (1529)," *BC* 432–33.

epistemological procedures can be understood from theological perspective to establish and preserve the anchoring of reality in the reality of a God who continuously transcends the present with new possibilities for doctrine.

IV. FROM EPISTEMOLOGY TO CONTENT

It was Barth who taught us that reality is significant, that theology has a special calling to witness to the transcendent reality of God, and that the truth of theology depends on its capacity to remain open to divine truth when God speaks the living word today. Yet early twentieth-century theology, which acquired its distinctive tonality in relation to a particular social, political, and intellectual environment, may not be useful as a model for theology today. Especially problematic, given the place of the idea of social construction in contemporary theology, is the earlier era's rejection of what it saw as Schleiermacher's foundationalist theology of experience. My response to this reading of Schleiermacher was to show how reality figured in a complex mechanism in his thought. My goal was to rehabilitate Schleiermacher's understanding of the New Testament as social construction by putting his work in close relationship to Reimarus's question, which may be taken as analogous to the gap between experience and expression that so haunts Schleiermacher and so haunts theology today.

My aim here and especially in the next chapter is to find a path from epistemology to content. A first step on this path is a theory that explains the relationship between experience and reality, between words and experience, and between the individual and the intersubjective. I have taken this step here by taking apart one account of how the New Testament was *produced*, rather than approaching it as a canonical text that is *received*. It then became possible to appreciate the text's social constructedness in particular and varied historical contexts. Schleiermacher did not posit a dichotomy of *either* production *or* reception; he created a conceptual tool that was able to explain both the New Testament and its doctrinal parameters from the perspective of encounters with Christ. The Christian community encountered the *Christus praesens*, Schleiermacher argued, in continuous experience.

In this chapter I have considered the development of doctrine from Scripture by using the perspective of a theological epistemology rather than the perspective of history. An historical treatment would illuminate how scriptural themes and concepts led to the urgent questions addressed by theologians in the first centuries of the early church. A theological epistemology, on the other hand, offers an analytical angle to pinpoint a distinct way of explaining how language arose in intimate proximity to the experience of Christ. The aim is to produce a conceptualization that is able to explain how Scripture and doctrine have the same epistemological structure in their generation, from the earliest layers of the New Testament to contemporary global Christianity.

Approaching the topic from this angle has made three things possible: (1) We were able to take into consideration relations between language and consciousness, reality and acclamation, self and Christ, within a social-linguistic milieu. With a little help from Schleiermacher, we could see how a specific experience of Christ might lead to particular verbal expressions having specific structures of predication, which then served as ground for the doctrine attributing the work of redemption to the Redeemer. (2) We saw how Schleiermacher worked out a particular theological epistemology, with Christ as Redeemer in constant focus. In this way a central core was developed to account for Christianity as a living tradition through time, which is the specific understanding of Jesus the Christ accessible in different times and places, from the earliest appearances of Jesus of Nazareth in Galilee to encounters with Christ across the planet today. (3) Finally, the method was open to applying psychological, linguistic-historical, metaphysical, and religious resources in its explanation.

Hence theological epistemology is theological because it contributes to the production of the doctrine of Christ, and it is an epistemology because of its central claim that humans are the ones doing the theological work of speaking of God.

In sum, I use the reconstruction of a theological epistemology to demonstrate how the doctrine of the person and work of Christ emerged at early layers of the New Testament and how the same mechanism may explain the constant throughout the history of Christianity. This constant is the articulation of claims of predication when encountering Jesus, claims that then inform the history of how the concept of Jesus Christ as cause of redemption was formed. On the basis of this look at the empirical-historical experience of the encounter with Jesus Christ, it was possible to document the way language bore the imprint of the experience and created the possibility for producing knowledge. Different groups at different times speak about their encounter with Christ in different ways. The interactions among specific elements—including consciousness, word and work, social experience, and mysticism—come together in particular historical and cultural contexts to produce doctrine. Doctrine requires philosophical and academic resources in order to make its claims to knowledge. It also requires an ongoing experience of Christ, which injects the personal, perhaps even the mystical, into tradition and into the experiential in relation to the community. In this way the production of doctrine emerges from within the living Christian tradition. It is not merely the hermeneutical review of the origins of Christianity nor a *regula fidei* that normatively constructs the origins but a living reality open to new ways of predicating the experience of Jesus Christ in contemporary global Christianity.

Developing a way forward does not end by putting Schleiermacher in conversation with Barth. It requires pushing on to contemporary efforts to recover reality generally, religious reality in particular, in its intellectual, bodily, intersubjective, and experiential dimensions. This is the move from epistemology to content. Making this step will take us more deeply into the production of doctrine as it is approached in between theology and religious studies. How may the conversation with religious studies aid in orienting the production of doctrine concerning the way God is experienced?

5

Acknowledging Social Construction and Moving beyond Deconstruction

Doctrine for Theology and Religious Studies

I. DOCTRINE AS INEVITABLE SOCIAL CONSTRUCTION

The previous chapters traced the history of doctrine to its end, as I diagnosed it, through the lens of developments in early twentieth-century theology, specifically German theologians' appropriation of certain cultural and philosophical elements, principally neo-Kantian categories, for their theological work. The aim was to show that doctrine is a human social construction that takes into its compass particular views of reality, both divine and human. Barth emerged as the protagonist of this thesis. Throughout his life Barth maintained the conviction that theology is a human enterprise that stands as much under God's judgment as any other human activity. Theology does not have a privileged place, either among the human sciences or in culture and society. Even its distinctive responsibility to witness to its subject matter, which is the transcendent reality of God, does not grant theology special access to divine truth. What is distinctive about theology, rather, is its task to witness to God in language and categories that nevertheless and inevitably are social constructions. This dimension of Barth's thought was at the forefront of my historical examination of twentieth-century German theology.

By the turn of the twenty-first century, Barth's theological interest in preserving the difference between divine and human reality for doctrine had disappeared from theological analysis. Theology took a new and dogmatic direction. The unlikely switching point in this transition was George Lindbeck's accepting anthropologist Clifford Geertz's account of culture and religion and applying it to theology. In making this move, Lindbeck's intention was to find a way of overcoming the impasse in ecumenical conversation between Lutherans and Roman Catholics. He wanted to clarify the nature of doctrine for the specific purpose of discussing the doctrinal differences precipitated by Luther's Reformation theology of justification. But as it happened, the anthropological idea that Lindbeck borrowed became transposed into a dogmatic register. Social constructivism and the notion of culture as meaning-making were used to frame a *theological* account of religion and as a way of talking about doctrine's constitutive role as "grammar" in a religious worldview. The social-scientific meanings and implications of the concept of social construction were eclipsed by the discourse of a biblical worldview taken as the matrix for viewing an entire world.

The irony, in short, is that Lindbeck's irenic effort to clarify the social and cultural meanings of doctrine led to the decoupling of doctrine from its role as witness to a transcendent reality. This is precisely what I mean by *the end of doctrine*. Doctrine reaches its terminus when its own status as social construction is no longer acknowledged and when it takes the place of the transcendent reality to which it is meant to refer. I illustrated this development with a discussion of the epistemic-advantage model of doctrine, which, as I argued, ended up losing not only the reference to God but also to the reality of historical difference. The irony of Marshall's position is that by insisting on the immanence of linguistically articulated doctrines, he turns them into the social constructions that he wants to excise from theology. The further irony of this story, then, is that at the end of doctrine there is no ecumenical conversation. There may be no conversation at all. The model originally proposed to overcome impasses in ecumenical discussion ends up in solitary dogmatic silence.

To summarize up to this point: When social construction is not acknowledged for what it is, namely, social construction—when this is forgotten or denied—it becomes a chamber without light or air. The constructions of one particular world at one time are mistaken for the truth of the world itself for all time. Transcendent reality as the font of ontological diversity is eclipsed as the social construction that constitutes one's own perspective is elevated to the position of normativity. Thus doctrine's coherence becomes its own normative "truth."

In the volume of essays that so influenced Lindbeck, Geertz tells a story about an Englishman who hears that people in India—Geertz says he heard this as an "Indian story"—believe the world rests upon a platform that sits atop an elephant that stands upon a turtle.[1] "What does the turtle stand on?" the Englishman asks a South Asian interlocutor. "Another turtle," he is told. "What about *that* turtle?" "Well," comes the response, "after that it is turtles all the way down." One hears this phrase often in academic discourse, "all the

---

1. Clifford Geertz, "Thick Description: Towards an Interpretive Theory of Culture," in *The Interpretation of Cultures: Selected Essays* (New York: Basic Books, 1973), 29.

way down," and I am about to use it here. The theological task of articulating doctrine is the practice of social construction all the way down. As an intellectual enterprise, as the work of theologians, the discipline of theology is bound up fully with all other aspects of human life, with human actions and human thoughts. Theology is a cultural production that conveys the social, political, historical, and religious origins, involvements, and values of its own production. It is not exempt from the social construction all-the-way-down model of human culture, even if—or perhaps especially when—theology purports to hold a distinctive place and responsibility among other academic pursuits in its mission of studying God in relation to the world. As theologians create doctrines by way of connecting the Christian past and its lived present, these doctrines are inevitably cast within cultural references.

So the question becomes: What is at stake in denying this? The failure to acknowledge that theology is a social construction may be the result of a desire to inoculate theology against relativism, secularism, and liberalism—three ideologies that allegedly compromise the truth of which theology is asserted to be sole proprietor. Or perhaps it is that the commitment of a particular theology to the truth of "the one holy apostolic church" requires the erasure of historical difference, even as this difference manifests itself in biblical and creedal attempts to formulate the doctrine of God. Maybe the rhetoric of "translation into a cultural idiom" keeps certain theologians from openly acknowledging the historical realities that inform any theological practice. Or perhaps the referent of doctrinal claims, which is the transcendent reality of God, calls every theological formulation into question. So what is at stake?

Whatever its reason(s)—and I lean with Barth toward the last one given—the consequence of the failure to acknowledge that theology is a social construction all the way down is a view of theology as normative all the way down. In other words, while many theologians today would agree that theology is a social construction, there is disagreement about what it means to say this. For example, it may mean (1) history and culture all the way down, as Geertz intended. Or it may mean (2) normativity all the way down, as in the epistemic-advantage model of doctrine. Recognizing such fundamental differences among theologians, all using the language of social construction, is a necessary precondition for further conversation.

At issue here is the nature of doctrine itself, along with the prospects for a theology that generates doctrines ultimately concerned with the triune God and with this God's "passion for material creation."[2] Doctrine comes

---

2. The phrase is from Marilyn McCord Adams, *Christ and Horrors: The Coherence of Christology*, Current Issues in Theology (Cambridge: Cambridge University Press, 2006), 39.

alive when it arises out of an intellectual tradition dedicated to the task of reflecting on the lived experience of men and women. Such a theology will produce ideas faithful to religious life in the past while being open to the novelty that comes in the experience of a God whose mercies are "new every morning" (Lam. 3:23). Doctrine is formulated in conversation among theologians and other Christians talking in earnest with each other about the God with whom they are in relationship, about the glimpses they have in their lives of the inbreaking of redemptive reality, as they struggle to articulate what they know and what they have experienced of the truth that sets them free (cf. John 8:32).

The beginning of doctrine is thus the admission that it is "turtles all the way down." I use the phrase here not as a metaphor for a relentless hunger for explanation that scratches toward a first cause but in recognition that all linguistic constructions are just that: cultural productions. But here is a twist, and I began to work it out in my choice of unlikely conversation partners, Barth and Schleiermacher: theology's social constructedness all the way down is specifically theological because it has to do with a distinct reality that has its being and existence outside social construction. Outside, to use the inevitable but unsatisfactory spatial language, but also involved in the lives of individuals and communities who undertake the necessary theological task of constructing doctrine to represent as best they can the truth of God as they know it. Barth maintained the externality of God's reality while arguing that Scripture, doctrine, and proclamation are the human words that accomplish what he saw as the theological imperative of his times. Likewise, Schleiermacher was interested in how human language may make claims about divine reality. Language has to do with the real.

The necessary questions then become about how human words may be analyzed in close relation to particular religious experiences and how language gives a place to the externality of the linguistic referent. The special responsibility of theological language is to be the sign that keeps social constructedness open to a reality beyond it. Beyond it, but always with this proviso: that God's encounters with and engagements in material creation are inevitably historical. Hence all efforts to bring these encounters and engagements to linguistic expression are governed by the particularities of historical location. The point is that to keep from being an insulated set of doctrinal formulas, one needs to have an account of language that makes it answerable to and engaged with the transcendent reality of God, on the one hand, and the historical and cultural reality of lived religion, on the other hand.

Before going on to develop my idea of doctrinal production from a theological perspective, I need briefly to allude to a conversation parallel to the one I have been tracing in theology. Theologians were among the founders of the academic study of religion at the turn of the twentieth century, in Germany and the United States in particular, and the two intellectual enterprises have long been entwined with each other. Although today theology and religion have a divided or even mutually hostile existence in the academy, the study of religion in recent years has taken a direction analogous to modern theology's track, which has brought it to an analogous impasse. It will be useful to compare their trajectories with particular emphasis on how the idea of social construction plays out its role. To recover the reality of religion for theology, it is necessary to be concerned with the fate of "religion" in modern understanding. One place this fate is played out is in religious studies.

II. BEYOND DECONSTRUCTION

Braided as the histories of theology and religion are, the two academic disciplines (with all their internal variations) have different vocabularies and have taken different, if parallel, directions in the modern academy in relation to the humanities and social sciences. Going forward, theology and religious studies may find it constructive to pay attention to the respective steps each is taking in their different spheres toward recovering their subject matter.

The study of religion has its origins in the same period that was so important, as we have seen, for the history of the idea of doctrine. As was the case with theology, the categories of neo-Kantianism were crucial to the formation of the *Religionsgeschichtliche Schule*. The philosopher Jakob Friedrich Fries (1773–1843) was a key figure in the transmission of Kantian terminology into the new study of religion. At the same time, Luther scholars, in particular those working in Berlin, turned to historical methods to chart the "Reformation breakthrough" in Luther's religious and intellectual biography. Karl Holl (1866–1926), for example, the historian and theologian credited with initiating the new interest in the historical Luther, the *Lutherrenaissance*, used historical, experiential, and religious categories to understand Luther's discovery of God.[3] Among the important figures in the Lutherrenaissance were Rudolf Otto (1869–1937) and Ernst Troeltsch (1865–1923), whose early careers included a debate with each other over the question of how to divide Christian history into epochs, specifically, where to locate the break between the medieval and the modern in Western history. Both made significant contributions to the study of the historical, cultural, and sociological aspects of religion.

3. Karl Holl, *What Did Luther Understand by Religion?*, ed. James Luther Adams and Walter F. Bense, trans. Fred W. Meuser and Walter R. Wietzke (Philadelphia: Fortress Press, 1977).

Otto is important to the story I want to tell about the braided histories of theology and religious studies in modern scholarship. There is a recent resurgence of interest in Otto in religious studies, where he has long been relegated to a marginal position.[4] Otto is a connecting link between the theological past of religious studies, its emergence as a discipline in its own right, and one scenario for its future direction. He is an avatar of a more generative interconnection between theology and the study of religion than has been offered in some time.

Otto was trained as a Lutheran theologian. He wrote his doctoral dissertation on Luther's pneumatology, which was the inspiration for Otto's own concept of the *mysterium tremendum et fascinans*. Otto acknowledges this explicitly in his famous 1917 work, *Das Heilige*, where he dedicates one full chapter to "the numinous in Luther." As Otto writes, "The reason I introduced these terms above ["absolute numen," *maiestas, tremendum*] was in fact just because I recalled Luther's own expressions, and borrowed them from his *divina maiestas* and *metuenda voluntas*, which have rung in my ears from the time of my earliest study of Luther."[5] Otto's search for a concept of God that exceeds the rational and political domestication of Luther's God in the Lutheranism of his times brought him back to Luther's concept of God in *The Bondage of the Will*, which Luther wrote against Erasmus in 1525. In this work Otto found an account of God that destabilized his own rationalist formation in the early twentieth-century Ritschlian school.

Otto found additional inspiration for the concept of God he was seeking in Schleiermacher. "Schleiermacher was the first to attempt to overcome this rationalism," Otto writes in *Das Heilige*, "most boldly and uncompromisingly in the rhapsody of his *Discourses*, with less heat and more subdued tone in his *Glaubenslehre* and his theory of the 'feeling of absolute dependence,' which in point of fact give a representation . . . of the first stirring of the feeling of the numinous."[6] Otto republished the first edition of the *Speeches* in a special centenary edition in 1899, with a new introduction, and then again in 1906.[7]

---

4. See the volume on *Rudolf Otto: Theologie, Religionsphilosophie, Religionsgeschichte*, ed. Jörg Lauster, Peter Schüz, Roderich Barth, and Christian Danz (Berlin: de Gruyter, 2013).

5. Rudolf Otto, "The Numinous in Luther," in *The Idea of the Holy: An Inquiry into the Non-Rational Factor in the Idea of the Divine and Its Relation to the Rational*, trans. John W. Harvey, 2nd ed. (Oxford: Oxford University Press, 1950), 94–108, here 99.

6. Ibid., 108.

7. Friedrich Schleiermacher, *On Religion: Speeches to Its Cultured Despisers*, intro. Rudolf Otto, trans. John Oman (New York: Harper Torchbooks, 1965). The 1906 reprint included an expanded introduction and commentary, reprinted again in 1913 and 1914. See Todd A. Gooch, *The Numinous and Modernity: An Interpretation of Rudolf Otto's Philosophy of Religion*, Beihefte zur Zeitschrift für die alttestamentliche Wissenschaft 293 (Berlin: de Gruyter, 2000), 7.

The familiarity and engagement of the author of *Das Heilige* with Schleiermacher, specifically with the Schleiermacher of the *Speeches on Religion*, was deep.

Otto's project in *Das Heilige*, to discover a way of conceptualizing religious experience beyond the most narrowly construed limits of reason, was clearly grounded in and inspired by his reading of Luther and Schleiermacher. For a methodology that related experience and feeling to objective reality, Otto turned as well to the then-current discussion of Kant, in particular to Fries's theory of schematization. Although the relationship between God and the religious subject eluded rational classification and thereby rational analysis, the feeling typology that Otto developed demonstrated the possibility of studying religion by means of the distinct *instrumentarium* of religious experience. Religion, Otto concluded, is ultimately not about reason or the logical life of the mind. It is the experience of a transcendent reality that inspires distinctive feelings in the religious subject.

As a theologian whose interest in religion in human experience led him to the development of a distinctive category for its analysis, Otto is representative of a generative period in the history of the academic study of religion. Theologians understood the study of the history of religions and of comparative religion—of religious experience, narrative, and ritual—as integral to their work as theologians. Along with Otto, other examples of this outlook are Cornelius Petrus Tiele, who lived a little before Otto, and W. Brede Kristensen, who came a little afterward. Both were Lutheran churchmen and theologians, and both were contributors to the early study of comparative religion. Given this background, it is not surprising that until very recently a theological education was considered to be a prerequisite for an academic career in religious studies and theological ideas served as a seedbed of critical religious theories.

This is not the case any longer (although, as we will see, such matters are constantly shifting, constantly being rethought and rearranged). For the past several decades the division between the two areas of inquiry has steadily and seemingly inexorably widened. Figures from both parties have contributed to this parting of the ways. For their part, theologians have expressed hostility to approaches to Scripture and tradition that would translate them into alien categories, meaning into the categories of contemporary critical analysis used in religious studies. Meanwhile a number of scholars of religion have seen fit to caricature theology in such a way that the discipline's dogmatic interests are represented as confessional and catechetical, impervious to critical methodologies. Theologians are said to import and impose faith categories onto the study of religion's more rigorous objective, nonnormative, and historicist methods. This dismissal of theology comes with a concomitant determination either to quarantine religious studies from theological contamination or else to so thoroughly identify religious studies with various caricatures of theology as to render departments of religious studies alien to the secular academy—as prelude to their closing. Either way, theology is an infection. This is evident even from the most passing glance at works written by religious studies scholars.[8]

In the past one reason why some scholars of religion were hostile to theology had to do with anxiety over admission to and status within the secular academy. To be taken seriously as a legitimate academic discipline, religious studies apparently needed to clearly have nothing to do with the study of belief or its inculcation, especially nothing to do with personal religious commitments and affiliations, and above all nothing to do with theology—in that order. To claim a place in the secular academy, religious studies banished theology's distinctive terminology, such as transcendence, the holy, spirit, soul, and divinity. But one consequence of the gradual dislocation of the two fields from each other—as theology took a turn to the word of God dogmatically construed while religious studies anxiously went about divesting itself of its theological inheritance—was the dismantling of the specifically religious dimension of religion in academic inquiry. The focus not only shifted away from belief and toward social institutions and practices; the practices themselves were also stripped of their religious quality. Devotional practice, religious experience, religious identity, and identity formation—these and other aspects of religion have all been thoroughly deconstructed, reframed as purely and sufficiently social phenomena. This was the vaccine offered against the contagion of theology, deployed to inoculate academic work (and perhaps also academic life and academics) against religion's perceived (and real) excesses, its destabilizing powers, and its capacity to trouble critical certainties by bringing into the conversation a concern for what lies beyond human control and conceptualization.

A number of arguments were offered for the imperative of such deconstructive work. (1) Religion is a historical and cultural phenomenon and therefore is to be analyzed specifically within the limits of modern historiography and cultural studies. (2) Politics and power explain religion while the human sensorium registers the political processes that create it.[9] (3) Religion as a discrete phenomenon is a concept introduced by Western (meaning German) theologians, who have so tainted the study of religion with theology that it ought to be abandoned entirely as a discrete academic field. This third argument

---

8. I discuss this at greater length in "Theology and the Study of Religion: A Relationship," in Orsi, *The Cambridge Companion to Religious Studies*, 230–31.

9. For an example of this view, see Talal Asad, "Thinking about Religion, Belief, and Politics," in Orsi, *The Cambridge Companion to Religious Studies*, 36–57.

for the abandonment of "religion" as a category of analysis is usually made in terms of discourse analysis since it proposes that the discourse of religion rather than its subject matter be the object of inquiry.[10] (4) Religion must be tamed in order to render it compatible with modernity's secular values and imperatives. Contemporary versions of this taming are haunted by specters of the nineteenth-century masters of suspicion, who understood religion as psychiatric deviation, an aberration of human nature, or a political distraction and emollient. Yet like their nineteenth-century counterparts, contemporary demolishers of "religion" subsume the various aspects of religion under one deconstructive enterprise: a distinct genre of religious naturalism in which religion can be explained with reference to a single primary explanandum,[11] whether psychological, social, political, or economic. (5) They turn to bodily practice and technology at the expense of the ideas of religion, in order to exorcise the ghosts of Protestant belief and faith.

After two decades into this effort, however, the field of religious studies is beginning to recognize the intellectual consequences of such internecine strife as well as its theological anxiety. At the end of deconstruction, what is left of the subject matter of religion? What is left even of religion as the subject of an academic discipline? The reality of religion has been subsumed within the category of social construction, into political processes and historical analysis, with the result that the area for what can be claimed specifically as religious experience—even within the limits of politics, society, and history—has shrunk to nearly nothing. While theorists of a new materialism outside both religious studies and theology have sought to broaden the discussion of matter beyond the confines of the positivism of nineteenth- and early twentieth-century natural and social sciences, the old materialism was alive and well in religious studies.

So a change seems to be coming, of which the resurgent interest in Rudolf Otto is an harbinger. There is talk of a "more," in William James's word, to religion as a human phenomenon and as the object of study, a deepening

10. For an example of this view, see Masuzawa, *The Invention of World Religions.*

11. Andrew C. Dole constructs a helpful typology of religious naturalism showing that just one kind of naturalism is prone to the deconstructive enterprise. See his "Introduction" in *Schleiermacher on Religion and the Natural Order,* AAR Religion, Culture, and History Series (New York: Oxford University Press, 2010), 3–34. The Deweyan type of religious naturalism, as espoused by the philosopher of religion Sami Pihlström, e.g., admits religious sentiments and an openness to mystical experience that would not be tolerated by the strict causation naturalists. See his "Deweyan Pragmatic Religious Naturalism," in *Pragmatic Pluralism and the Problem of God* (New York: Fordham University Press, 2013): 47–72. On the "compulsion of explanation," see Ludwig Wittgenstein, *Remarks on Frazer's "Golden Bough,"* trans. A. C. Miles, rev. Rush Rhees (Gringley-on-the-Hill, UK: Brynmill, 1979), 2e.

apprehension that the reigning sociocultural and sociohistorical tools are not completely adequate to refer to the excess a religious event holds. To speak in a Schleiermacherian vein here: the encounters with Jesus of Nazareth narrated in Christian Scripture have such an excess that preachers for two millennia have explored the Gospel texts in their sermons and still not exhausted them. These preachers hope that their communications and interpretations of the texts may evoke some of the excess in such a way that their hearers may experience at least intimations of it in their own lives. This is a different relationship between present and past, text and reader, speaker and hearer, the one and the many—different from the relationships conceived by modern critical inquiry. There are hints of this now in contemporary texts in religious studies, which are both concerned with the really real of religion and with evoking it in such a way that readers and hearers may catch a glimpse of a reality that so gripped a particular community at a particular time and place and that so gripped the scholar of religion.[12]

The search for a language that might serve this purpose has curiously brought scholars of religion back toward the theological. In a recent essay, anthropologist of Christianity Joel Robbins, for example, appeals to the term "transcendence" as a conceptual device to mark the conceptual distinction between Protestants and Catholics.[13] Transcendence, according to Robbins, characterizes a Protestant and in particular a Pentecostal understanding of the relationship between the believer and her God, while immanence is characteristic of the sacramental ethos of Catholic Christianity. Another anthropologist, Matthew Engelke, deploys the term "real presence" effectively as an analytic in studying a contemporary Christian movement in Zimbabwe.[14] Yet another anthropologist, Tanya Luhrmann, in a much-celebrated and widely noted book, examined the reality of occasions when "God talks back" to contemporary American evangelical Protestants.[15] It is striking that so much of this turn to the "more" in contemporary scholarship on religion, and more broadly on the human imagination, appears outside the boundaries of religious studies, as if the recent preoccupation with shedding theology's influence has left behind an intellectual timidity. At least on this score, anthropologists may be bolder.

12. See the discussion of the distinctive poetics of religious studies in Daniel Gold, *Aesthetic and Analysis in Writing on Religion: Modern Fascinations* (Chicago: University of Chicago Press, 2003).

13. Joel Robbins, "Transcendence and the Anthropology of Christianity: Language, Change and Individualism (Edward Westermarck Memorial Lecture)," *Journal of the Finnish Anthropological Society* 3, no. 2 (2012): 14.

14. Matthew Engelke, *A Problem of Presence: Beyond Scripture in an African Church* (Berkeley: University of California Press, 2007).

15. Tanya M. Luhrmann, *When God Talks Back: Understanding the American Evangelical Relationship with God* (New York: Vintage Books, 2012).

This search for a vocabulary of religious experience, reality, imagination, agency, and transcendence is an open invitation to theology to rejoin the religious studies conversation. Theology, after all, has for long been interested in the relations between the historical and the conceptual, between experiential and discursive, as my allusion to Schleiermacher above was meant to suggest, and it has developed a toolbox of categories to discover a metaphysics that can account for a transcendent dimension of human experience while also being attentive to the local and particular. Thus we find medieval theologians concerned with the relation between the universal and the particular, early modern theologians interested in experience and text, and later modern historicist theology, as exemplified by Troeltsch and Ritschl, seeing human agency in close relationship to historical and social development while retaining a concept of the individual; all of these explorations belong to the shared history of religious studies and theology. This is so not only because of the fact of common origins but also in terms of shared concepts, theoretical terms, and problematics.[16]

But can theology be a resource for scholars of religion, in religious studies and more broadly in the humanities and social sciences? With doctrine at the end I have described, is theology capable of addressing questions of cultural production again? Or is theology now so completely positioned as enterprise for the churches, so thoroughly imagined as the negation of culture, that its wider academic relevance is lost? In the past, theologians stretched the intellectual, rational, methodological, and analytical resources of academic thought, and this legacy stands as a challenge to contemporary theologians. It would be tragic today if, just when theology has the most to contribute to the humanities and social sciences, it has the least to say to them. It would likewise be tragic if, just when theology has the most to learn from other disciplines and from being in conversation with other fields, it lacks the language to engage them.

III. GETTING CLEAR ON THE SOCIAL CONSTRUCTION OF REALITY

Social construction becomes a problem only when it masquerades as the real, either for theologians or for scholars of religion. The way out, therefore, is to hold together two ideas: (1) social construction is just that, and (2) there is

16. Jörg Dierken, "Transcendental Theories of Religion: Then and Now," in *Schleiermacher, the Study of Religion, and the Future of Theology*, ed. Brent W. Sockness and Wilhelm Gräb, Theologische Bibliothek Töpelmann 148 (Berlin: de Gruyter, 2010), 151–64.

a reality beyond itself that social constructions attempt to convey. Holding these seemingly disparate notions in productive tension allows for the articulation of difference and the beginning of conversation between theology and religious studies. Recovering the subject of religion, which is also the subject matter of theology albeit in another perspective, has been the subtext of this book all along. This was the point of my historical effort to recover both the categories and the depth of theological categorization when theologians were actually concerned with reality, as Barth was, and when theologians explored the complicated mechanisms by which reality was construed and articulated in religious contexts and language, as Schleiermacher did. This is the question I come to now. In our present circumstances, and with the aid of Schleiermacher and Barth, how may we think through the dimensions of reality that theology is responsible for recovering, selecting, and organizing as it produces doctrine for another generation of Christians excited about the living God?

I want to consider different perspectives on how theology may do this. All is premised on the assumption that doctrine's content has to do with divine and human reality, with human historical context and human witness, and with a living language as the medium of witness that changes as we talk about the God who both transcends time and engages deeply in history and with human lives in the world.

III.1. Conversation with Religious Studies

One area in which theology has recently taken an empirical interest in religious experience is the ethnography of religion. This is a novel development for the field of theology, which has usually restricted itself to the conceptual and abstract and to doctrinally prescriptive analysis. One impetus for this turn to the empirical in the recent past is liberation theology, with its emphasis on praxis. Liberation theologians ask how Christians in their respective political contexts articulate and enact their faith in order to change their lives and societies.

While its origins are in Latin American political exigencies, liberation theology has by now had a broad impact. Finnish theologian Elina Vuola[17] and American theologian Mary Fulkerson[18]—who work at the intersections of the study of religion, theology, and anthropology—have appropriated ethnographic methods in order to study the making of theology "on the ground" in

17. Elina Vuola, "Patriarchal Ecumenism, Feminism, and Women's Experience in Costa Rica," in *Gendering Religion and Politics: Untangling Modernities,* ed. Hanna Herzog and Ann Braude (New York: Palgrave Macmillan, 2009), 217–38.

18. Mary McClintock Fulkerson, *Places of Redemption: Theology for a Worldly Church* (New York: Oxford University Press, 2010).

their respective contexts. Their research has led them to the conclusion that the development of theological categories and concepts by religious practitioners is a necessary corrective to reigning theological abstractions and to the draw that such abstractions have in theology. Ethnographic research also challenges theological assumptions regarding the impact of official church teaching on ordinary practitioners; it does so by calling attention to the plurality of ways these Christians have reflected on the theological categories of sin, grace, divinity, and human nature. The academic theologian has a limited textual repertoire from the history of the tradition that she uses to articulate theological claims. Ethnography, in all religious contexts, extends the horizon of theological discourse by widening the range of sources for religious reflection and by expanding the range of interlocutors. Geertz said that anthropologists provided "another country heard from" by means of their fieldwork, another perspective from which to reflect on human experience. In this spirit it might be said that the turn to ethnography offers theologians other minds to hear from, other embodied lives to learn from.

Also contributing to the new turn to the ethnographic and to lived experience in theology are practical theologians. While systematic theology ordinarily concerns itself with doctrine, practical theology is allocated the task of engaging the content of Christian life as it is expressed and lived by ordinary religious practitioners rather than by a religious elite. But what happens when systematic theology actually takes an interest in lived religion, in the life of embodied ideas that inform the reality with which doctrine is concerned? Tanya Luhrmann is not a theologian, but theologians can surely learn from her. Theologians might use the self-reflective methods of conversation, observation, and participation to explore the ways Christian ideas and practices are formed by human experience of the reality of God, by the seeming absence of God when presence is most sought, by long-term relationships with God and others, and by miraculous interruptions. Such experiences do not in and of themselves ground normative discourse, although they may influence it. We know from history that pivotal experiences, encounters, and events have urged doctrine on to deeper truths, from Mary Magdalene's experience of Jesus to Mechthild von Magdeburg's and Adrienne von Speyr's visions of the Trinity to contemporary mystics. Systematic theologians, responsible for the formation of theological theory, will want to stay open in these spaces of experience, taking care to see and hear, so that lived experience may eventually make its way into doctrinal formulation. In other words, lived experience is not a source alien to theological reflection; that it may be thought so is an emergency sign for theology. Rather, lived experience is integral to theological formation and to the production of doctrine, imbuing it with the experiences and understandings of Christians in relation to each other, in a shared conversation about religious ideas and practices. Without the road to Damascus, there would be no Pauline Epistles.

III.2. The Return to History

While there is consensus on historical scholarship being a major contributor to modern knowledge, there is considerable variation among the historiographies proposed to approach human life in time. In chapter 3 we saw how the epistemic-advantage approach to doctrine collapsed or ignored historical difference between Luther and Thomas Aquinas in the instance cited. Because the historical-critical method admittedly does not have a monopoly either for reading the Bible or for examining religious history, it does not follow that it may be abandoned altogether. The return to history is a recovery of the reality in which humans exist and which they help to change as agents of history. When history is recovered as significant for understanding the reality that shapes the production of doctrine, from initial acclamations to doctrinal statements, from religious experience to their narration in texts that inspire future generations, then its study is imperative for understanding the way doctrines are produced and interpreted.

A new beginning to doctrinal work requires a historical methodology that is capable of describing and analyzing historical differences among varied social constructions of doctrine. History is the discipline that best gets at the reality that human beings are both (acting) subject of and (receiving) subject to their specific life circumstances. Historical claims do not require positivistic reduction. Rather, historians may open up their historiographical horizons to bring into view aspects of history that are approachable by historical method and yet exceed a narrow empirical grasp. Theology may contribute to historical study by encouraging historians to pay attention to a wider range of phenomena, including those that push against the limitations of modern historiography.

A number of scholars in religious studies as well as in history are currently challenging the consensus on what counts as historical knowledge and what is admissible as a historical topic. Theology may stand in productive solidarity with these colleagues as they go about the work of imagining more expansive theories of history that appreciate the religious dimension of human reality.[19] Likewise, religious studies scholars may learn from theologians that the

19. Lewis Ayres, "Into the Cloud of Witnesses: Catholic Trinitarian Theology Beyond and Before Its Modern Revivals," in *Rethinking Trinitarian Theology: Disputed Questions and Contemporary Issues in Trinitarian Theology*, ed. Giulio Maspero and Robert J. Woźniak (London: T&T Clark, 2013), 16: "This focus on the distinctive qualities of texts and people that were once easily placed within a unitary narrative certainly disrupts some ways of relating to figures."

history of Christian thought bears witness to a great diversity in religious experiences of the divine-human encounter that press toward distinctive predicates for the meaning of inherited doctrinal formulations. In other words here is a language forged and reforged over and over in different times and places for conceptualizing the various aspects of divine-human interaction. The history of theology could make both theology and religious studies aware of the varieties of religious experience and formulations across the ages.

We have seen how Ritschl, for example, engaged the doctrine of justification in the philosophical terminology and political realities of his time, while Barth in his context a few years later insisted on divine reality as transcendent. Schleiermacher retained the mystical designation as a descriptive term for Christ's transformative effect on religious consciousness. Two centuries forward, other theologians would frame doctrine in linguistically constituted terms as a function of religious worldviews. So an unapologetic and bold return to historical analysis would be an exercise in discovering the differences over time in the meanings of key doctrinal terms, in understanding the kinds of reality that are presumed by the concept of "doctrine" itself, and in analyzing the complexity of relations among thought and language, experience and reality, continuity and novelty that constitute doctrine's meanings.

In this regard an intriguing case study is the history of the doctrine of the Trinity. Recent theologians have concentrated on the development of Trinitarian doctrine in the early centuries of the new Christian religion.[20] The Trinity was also the subject of lively debate, bitter contestation, and creative innovation in Reformation theology as well; and then during the Enlightenment, the Trinity was again the subject of intense study, as contemporary historian of Christianity Paul C. H. Lim has shown.[21] The Protestant concept of *sola scriptura* lent an urgency to these debates. Because the Trinity as a spelled-out doctrine is not found in Scripture, Protestant theologians and laity defended or denounced the doctrine in vigorous debates that raged from pubs to classrooms, farmhouses to the British Parliament. The result was a range of theologies reflective of diverse Catholic and Protestant sensibilities and understandings. In that period, the contemporaneous rise of historical criticism and empirical historiography added to the intense preoccupation with the truth of the Trinity. Historians and theologians contributed their

---

20. See, e.g., the essays in part 1 ("The Trinity in Scripture") and part 2 ("Patristic Witnesses to the Trinitarian Faith") in *The Oxford Handbook of the Trinity*, ed. Gilles Emery, OP, and Matthew Levering, Oxford Handbooks in Religion and Theology (Oxford: Oxford University Press, 2013).

21. Paul C. H. Lim, *Mystery Unveiled: The Crisis of the Trinity in Early Modern England* (New York: Oxford University Press, 2012).

methodological tools to make sense of the relation of the Christian God encountered in the Bible to the doctrine of the Trinity articulated in history.

Such debates attest to the challenge and vigor of the doctrine. They do not settle the question of its truth. After that time, in the modern period, the history of the doctrine of the Trinity saw the increasing deployment of speculative *and* historical tools in its development. While the early church developed the concept of the Trinity as a way of answering questions about Christ's divinity, modern debates approached the Trinity in the gap between the Bible and the early church. Precisely as the result of their efforts to think through the Trinity in its interstitial position between being and history, Schleiermacher and Hegel expanded the possibilities of Western historiography, using both historical and speculative tools to conceptualize the Trinity in terms of a metaphysics of becoming.[22] By the time of Barth's prolegomena to his *Church Dogmatics*, the Trinity had been firmly anchored in the history of modern theology as the motivation and inspiration for developing systems that integrated the historical and the speculative.

Doctrines are produced over time as social constructions in the terms available in any historical and cultural context and also as a catalyst to social construction. Doctrine is always both the product and the producer of social construction, the shaper and the shaped. There is always this both/and historical dialectic to doctrine. The pressures of modern historicism set the agenda for considering the Trinitarian doctrine in terms of historical development, to refer to Schleiermacher's example, but this understanding of doctrine in turn troubled other foundational dichotomies in modern thought, provoking new ideas about the systematic theological significance of the Trinitarian doctrine, as is the case with Barth. On the one hand, modern historiography directs our attention to the inheritances that have shaped Trinitarian doctrine; on the other hand, Trinitarian doctrine—with its particular metaphysical and ontological questions, its concerns for the relationship between communities and ideas—opens new conceptual possibilities for thinking about some of the major questions of modern critical thought. Far from immunizing itself against culture, theological study, in its productive engagement with the Trinity, actually expanded rational and imaginative possibilities. Doctrinal work led to an opening out, not to a closing in.

To return to the relation between doctrine and reality, history is an invitation to see that doctrine has to do with the living reality of God as God

---

22. For more on this subject, see my essay "Between History and Speculation: Christian Trinitarian Thinking after the Reformation," in *The Cambridge Companion to the Trinity*, ed. Peter C. Phan, Cambridge Companions to Religion (Cambridge: Cambridge University Press, 2011), 149–69.

encounters humans in time. Doctrine comprises claims to truth made about the living God. It is the work of human hands. And the work of doctrine includes the perennial recognition that God may decide to surprise humans with the unexpected and unforeseen, which will require them to correct their doctrinal formulations again and again.

IV. LANGUAGE, DOCTRINE, REALITY

The claim that doctrine is the reception of normative formulations was not Barth's position, nor Schleiermacher's, nor Luther's, as I have argued.[23] Doctrine is about divinity and its manifold relations to the created world. It has to do with the living reality of God. Doctrine presses toward knowledge and truth while at the same time remaining cognizant of its human origins and historical particularity. Spiritual discernment is required to see and to understand the relations that God creates and transforms in different yet often hidden ways. God cannot be domesticated by doctrine, even when doctrine insists on divine faithfulness to specific ways of relating to the world and on specific forms of divine being, as in the doctrines of the Trinity and of Christ. Doctrine can only present its content according to the spiritual and intellectual capacities of human theologians operating under the cultural conditions of their intersubjectivities. The deepest ground of doctrine's epistemic humility is the recognition that the theologian stands before a divine reality that is capable of rejecting human efforts and of shattering human expectations with novelty.

As contemporary theologian Francesca Aran Murphy argues in *God Is Not a Story*, theology must look beyond its tradition of bracketing reality by means of narrative models in order to promote a sustained interest in content that includes metaphysics.[24] To make Murphy's suggestion into a proposition: if theology is about the realities of personhood, of God, and of intersubjectivity, as she and I both think it is, then its mandate is to be concerned above all with historical and religious content rather than being preoccupied by questions of method.

---

23. For Luther's position on doctrine as gift from God, see Risto Saarinen, "Luther und humanistische Philosophie," in *Lutherjahrbuch 80: Jahrgang 2013*, Organ der Internationalen Lutherforschung (Göttingen: Vandenhoeck & Ruprecht, 2013), 91–99.

24. Francesca Aran Murphy, *God Is Not a Story: Realism Revisited* (New York: Oxford University Press, 2007), 112: "Storied rationality doesn't go anywhere or do anything, and doesn't permit the existence of anything outside itself." Also: "For narrative theology, Scripture is, not a picture, but a picturing, the rule-governed process by which reality is construed" (3).

With a renewed and constructive interest in doctrine, language, and content from historical and global perspectives, theology invites scholars of religion to pursue the study of religion qua religion. This is especially so if theologians accept the academic responsibility of finding ways to communicate with scholars of religion, to share theology's distinct ways of exploring the relation of language to religious reality and the description of religious experience.[25] On these matters theologians and scholars of religion can partners in the work of recovering the study of religion's subject matter, its particular take on reality as religious reality, with theology offering conceptual terms, possibilities for analysis, and historical perspective for understanding present-day usage and constructive application. In such matters theology has more freedom to draw on conceptual and even speculative resources than is permitted to its more empirically oriented colleagues. Theologians can make this invitation attractive by sharing the distinctive ways theology has discovered of using language to describe religious realities.

The reality of God is discussed, debated, communicated, and contested in history, and in the process the limits of history as a venue for discussing, contesting, and communicating reality are tested. The Trinity, which the Russian Orthodox theologian Pavel Florensky famously posited as the dead end of rationality,[26] has made and continues to make a crucial contribution to the distinctive dynamics of Western thought by challenging philosophers to expand their repertoire in thinking through reason's logics and semantics. The Trinity has also inspired what might be called a mysticism of history by introducing into historiography a glimpse into mysteries of eternity, or at least a peek into the possibility of such mysteries. Time and what happens in time look different from this perspective than they do when the horizon is closed. The development of doctrine expands inherited conceptions of reason and experience; as doctrine pays attention to God's movements in history, it opens new ways of looking at reality, at the reality of God first of all, but then also at what counts as rational consensus.

---

25. In a recent article Jörg Lauster has proposed that more historical and constructive theological work should be done on the concept of religious experience, a term that in English elides at least three German terms, *Erfahrung*, *Erlebnis* (which has the character of an event), and *Widerfahrnis* (which emphasizes the passive dimension of experiencing an object or reality outside the self). The term *Erlebnis* originated in a neo-Kantian context of early twentieth-century Germany, specifically Marburg. See Jörg Lauster, "Liberale Theologie: Eine Ermunterung," *Neue Zeitschrift für systematische Theologie und Religionsphilosophie* 49, no. 3 (2007): 291–307.

26. Pavel Florensky, *The Pillar and Ground of the Truth: An Essay in Orthodox Theodicy in Twelve Letters*, trans. Boris Jakim (Princeton: Princeton University Press, 1997), 41: "The single word *homoousios* expressed not only a Christological dogma but also a spiritual evaluation of the rational laws of thought. Here rationality was given a death blow."

Language and reality are conjugated in different ways in different conditions. Theologians in various and particular times and places may speak the same words but mean different things by them (cf. Matt 24:5), or they may say seemingly quite different things but mean something similar by them.[27] All doctrinal investigation requires analysis and comparison by means of concepts that may unite and distinguish, analyzing content in distinction from form even while form is indispensable.

Theological practice also has a communal dimension. It is here that the difference between ways of studying religion generally, and in particular the relationship between the individual and the community, becomes especially dichotomous. Theology is said to focus on the community's normative doctrines that have binding force on the individual, whereas empirical studies on the ground can reveal a plethora of beliefs, interpretations, and practices that can be seen to deviate from theological norms or offer innovations. From the point of view that doctrine equals authority, there is little reason to study religious experience as it is lived other than to correct it when it strays from received doctrinal norms. Among some contemporary theologians, moreover, resistance to the idea of individual religious experience constituting an alternative authority to word, text, and tradition has a political edge. Giving priority in this way to individual experience seems to be a restatement of neo-liberal values in theological and philosophical language, if not actual capitulation to the contemporary order of being.

I take the first point about the disconnection between normative inheritances and lived polyvalence as a conceptual challenge (as Schleiermacher did too), and I take the second point about the problem of emphasizing the individual as a welcome ethical and political caution. But truth is not diminished when it is understood as historical interpretation(s). Rather, being attuned to the historical brings truth into the medium of human intersubjectivity, where disagreement and explication, competing perspectives and various proposals—all are part of the process of its formulation. Theology is always intersubjective and social. Historical and social embeddedness are constitutive of theology. Likewise doctrine exists—has always existed—in production, negotiated in discussion and debate. It requires evidence, and it benefits from comparative perspectives. If this sounds too benign, let me add that the realities of power and enforcement are also implicated in the history and making of doctrine and must be acknowledged and studied. Doctrine is open to

---

27. For ecumenical theology, Theodor Dieter proposes a process of negotiating between language, meaning, and reality; see his "Ein Blick zurück und ein Blick nach vorn: Vortrag beim 45. Internationalen Sommerseminar in Strasbourg am 1. Juli 2011," http://www.ecumenical-institute.org/wp-content/uploads/2012/10/Seminar-2011-Dieter.pdf.

the reality of the incarnation, the reality of God become human; doctrine is shaped by the formation of concepts; and doctrine is always at risk of error, including or especially the error of mistaking power for truth.

A theology that is attuned to the realities of God, personhood, and inter-subjectivity will also necessarily address the question of language as the indispensable tool for communicating the knowledge and experience of these realities. As we have repeatedly seen in the preceding chapters, the question of language invites inquiry into the relation of reality to discourse. In relation to doctrine, the question of language requires that we ask how discursive formations convey knowledge and truth between persons, across linguistic barriers, and transhistorically. How is the truth of the Trinity apprehended and lived within particular local congregations, for example? How have African and Asian Christians apprehended and lived the reality of the Trinity? And how has the Trinity been known in the fourth century and in the twenty-first century? Moving ahead with these questions, we might take theologian and philosopher Risto Saarinen's lead in considering how the relationship between language and particular doctrinal exigencies may be studied. Saarinen calls on theologians to acquaint themselves with recent work in semantics and cognitive theory in order to open up doctrine to a new study of its referent.[28] So too the present book has proposed that a renewed interest in doctrine means once again taking up the issue of the relationship of language and reality in order to better understand the mechanisms by which doctrine has been (and is) produced in Christianity, and to better appreciate the ways in which linguistically articulated doctrines are related to—and may be judged by—the divine reality with which they ultimately have to do.

At the very least, what is needed is greater critical transparency in the rhetoric concerning the relation between doctrine and church and fuller attentiveness to the historical and cultural specificity of linguistic formulations. Better still, there needs to be more investigation into the role of normative statements in communal contexts, specifically assessing the relative obligations of doctrine on individuals and also exploring openness to the reality of God and the reality of human experience. To call for faithfulness to the story in the biblical text does not by its very proclamation guarantee that its

---

28. Risto Saarinen seeks to move beyond the "traditionalist" readings of doctrine by "postliberal theologians" and articulates his aim: "The present paper will show how linguistic utterances in themselves incorporate the resources to speak about the mysteries of faith. They may do so even better than in postliberal theories, since many postliberals locate the mystery to the social and cultural context of the church rather than to the text as a linguistic entity." See his "Reclaiming the Sentences: A Linguistic Loci Approach to Doctrine," *Neue Zeitschrift für systematische Theologie und Religionsphilosophie* 54, no. 1 (2012): 1–2.

referent is the living God; novel formulations cultivated by a soul at prayer might have deeper insight into knowledge and love of God.

My introduction of the example of Trinitarian doctrine in post-Reformation theology was meant to underscore again the necessary interplay of theology and modern thought. In its relationship to historical, cultural, and philosophical developments, doctrine is opened to new ways of thinking in such a way that doctrine then may make positive and generative contributions to thought in turn. Here I think of the model of the helix, with doctrine, historical contingency, human experience, and philosophy twining around each other, reaching toward the reality of the living God. As doctrine makes claims about God in relation to human reality, it contributes distinct content to theology's quest for knowledge; at the same time, theology may refine rationality's methodologies in productive ways. Thus doctrines may subtly alter the cultural idioms in which they are produced in such a way that there will be room to develop new possibilities for addressing the big questions about God, reality, truth, and world, and thus stir up new prospects for recovering the subject matter of religious studies and theology.

Theologians are not museum docents. Their—our—role is not to point out doctrinal artifacts from lost civilizations. Rather, it is to show how God still has to do with humanity. The transhistorical dimension of theological work takes cognizance of the longevity of theological ideas, which is much greater than the lifespan of any individual theologian, and of the inherited bonds that transcend the lived affiliations of any contemporary congregation or church. God will relate to human beings in their communities in unexpected ways, because God is God; yet at the same time God's engagements with humans will be recognizable because God has an ongoing relationship with humanity. Theology as the study of doctrine must accept the challenges posed by these two present realities: discernment and remembering.

Ultimately theological concern with doctrine is about God's reality, approached through the study of human reality to discern the divine presence that transcends and indwells it. Out of these multiple and entwined relationships—God's relationship with human beings and communities, the theologian's relationship with religious experience—new stories come. The horizon of an unexpected future appears. Doctrine, then, is a preparation for recognizing this reality when it touches us, and God's new reality is the beginning of doctrine.

Bibliography

Abraham, William J. "Systematic Theology as Analytic Theology." In *Analytic Theology: New Essays in the Philosophy of Theology*, edited by Oliver D. Crisp and Michael C. Rae, 54–69. New York: Oxford University Press, 2009.

Adams, Marilyn McCord. *Christ and Horrors: The Coherence of Christology*. Current Issues in Theology. Cambridge: Cambridge University Press, 2006.

Arndt, Andreas, and Wolfgang Virmond. *Schleiermachers Briefwechsel (Verzeichnis) nebst einer Liste seiner Vorlesungen*. Schleiermacher-Archiv 11. Berlin: de Gruyter, 1992.

Asad, Talal. "Thinking about Religion, Belief, and Politics." In *The Cambridge Companion to Religious Studies*, edited by Robert A. Orsi, 36–57. Cambridge Companions to Religion. New York: Cambridge University Press, 2012.

Assel, Heinrich. *Der andere Aufbruch: Die Lutherrenaissance—Ursprünge, Aporien und Wege: Karl Holl, Emanuel Hirsch, Rudolf Hermann (1910–1935)*. Forschungen zur systematischen und ökumenischen Theologie 72. Göttingen: Vandenhoeck & Ruprecht, 1994.

Ayres, Lewis. "Into the Cloud of Witnesses: Catholic Trinitarian Theology beyond and before Its Modern Revivals." In *Rethinking Trinitarian Theology: Disputed Questions and Contemporary Issues in Trinitarian Theology*, edited by Giulio Maspero and Robert J. Woźniak, 3–25. London: T&T Clark, 2013.

———. *Nicaea and Its Legacy: An Approach to Fourth-Century Trinitarian Theology*. Oxford: Oxford University Press, 2006.

Barth, Karl. "Brunners Schleiermacherbuch." *Zwischen den Zeiten* 8 (1924): 49–64.

———. "Concluding Unscientific Postscript on Schleiermacher." In *The Theology of Schleiermacher: Lectures at Göttingen, Winter Semester of 1923/24*, edited by Dietrich Ritschl and translated by Geoffrey W. Bromiley, 261–79. Grand Rapids: Eerdmans, 1982.

———. *The Epistle to the Romans*. ET of the 6th German ed. (1933). Translated by Edwyn C. Hoskyns. London: Oxford University Press, 1968.

———. *The Göttingen Dogmatics (1924–25): Instruction in the Christian Religion*. Edited by Hannelore Reiffer. Translated by Geoffrey W. Bromiley. Vol. 1. Grand Rapids: Eerdmans, 1991.

————. "The New Word in the Bible (1917)." In *The Word of God and Theology*, translated by Amy Marga, 15–30. London: T&T Clark, 2011.

————. "The Righteousness of God (Lecture in the City Church of Aarau, January 1916)." In *The Word of God and Theology*, translated by Amy Marga, 1–14. London: T&T Clark, 2011. ET of "Die Gerechtigkeit Gottes." In *Das Wort Gottes und die Theologie: Gesammelte Vorträge*, 5–17. Munich: Chr. Kaiser, 1925.

————. "The Word of God as the Task of Theology (1922)." In *The Word of God and Theology*, translated by Amy Marga, 171–98. London: T&T Clark, 2011. ET of "Das Wort Gottes als Aufgabe der Theologie (Elgersburg, October 1922)." In *Das Wort Gottes und die Theologie: Gesammelte Vorträge*, 156–78. Munich: Chr. Kaiser, 1925.

Bayer, Oswald. *Martin Luther's Theology: A Contemporary Interpretation*. Translated by Thomas H. Trapp. Grand Rapids: Eerdmans, 2008.

————. *Theologie*. Handbuch systematischer Theologie 1. Gütersloh: Gütersloher Verlagshaus, 1994.

Beiser, Frederick C. *The German Historicist Tradition*. New York: Oxford University Press, 2011.

Birkner, Hans-Joachim. *Schleiermachers christliche Sittenlehre: Im Zusammenhang seines philosophisch-theologischen Systems*. Theologische Bibliothek Töpelmann 8. 1964. Repr., Berlin: Alfred Töpelmann, 2012.

Brunner, Emil. *Erlebnis, Erkenntnis und Glaube*. 4th and 5th eds. Zurich: Zwingli-Verlag, 1923.

————. *Die Mystik und das Wort: Der Gegensatz zwischen moderner Religionsauffassung und christlichem Glauben dargestellt an der Theologie Schleiermachers*. 1924. 2nd ed., Tübingen: J. C. B. Mohr (Paul Siebeck), 1928.

————. *Religionsphilosophie evangelischer Theologie*. Munich: R. Oldenbourg, 1928. Repr., Munich: Leibniz, 1948.

Büchsel, Friedrich. "*Krisis.*" *TDNT* 3 (1965): 941–42.

Büttgen, Philippe, Ruedi Imbach, Ulrich Johannes Schneider, and Herman J. Selderhuis, eds. *Vera Doctrina: Zur Begriffsgeschichte der Lehre von Augustinus bis Descartes / L'idée de doctrine d'Augustin à Descartes*. Wolfenbütteler Forschungen 123. Wiesbaden: Harrassowitz Verlag, 2009.

Chalamet, Christophe. *Dialectical Theologians: Wilhelm Herrmann, Karl Barth and Rudolf Bultmann*. Zurich: Theologischer Verlag Zurich (TVZ), 2005.

————. "Reassessing Albrecht Ritschl's Theology: A Survey of Recent Literature." *Religion Compass* 2, no. 4 (2008): 620–41.

Chignell, Andrew, Terence Irwin, and Thomas Teufel, eds. Special edition on Neo-Kantianism. *Philosophical Forum* 39, no. 2 (June 2008).

Childs, Brevard S. *Biblical Theology of the Old and New Testaments: Theological Reflection on the Christian Bible*. Minneapolis: Fortress Press, 1992.

Christian, William A., Sr. *Doctrines of Religious Communities: A Philosophical Study*. New Haven: Yale University Press, 1987.

Coakley, Sarah, ed. Special edition on "The God of Nicaea: Disputed Questions in Patristic Trinitarianism." *Harvard Theological Review* 100, no. 2 (2007).

Davaney, Sheila Greeve. *Historicism: The Once and Future Challenge for Theology*. Guides to Theological Inquiry. Minneapolis: Fortress Press, 2006.

Davidson, Donald. *Truth and Predication*. Cambridge, MA: Belknap Press of Harvard University Press, 2005.

Dierken, Jörg. "Transcendental Theories of Religion: Then and Now." In *Schleiermacher, the Study of Religion, and the Future of Theology*, edited by Brent W. Sockness and Wilhelm Gräb, 151–64. Theologische Bibliothek Töpelmann 148. Berlin: de Gruyter, 2010.

Dieter, Theodor. "Ein Blick zurück und ein Blick nach vorn: Vortrag beim 45. Internationalen Sommerseminar in Strasbourg am 1. Juli 2011." http://www .ecumenical-institute.org/wp-content/uploads/2012/10/Seminar-2011-Dieter .pdf.

————. "Why Does Luther's Doctrine of Justification Matter Today?" In *The Global Luther: A Theologian for Modern Times*, edited by Christine Helmer, 189–209. Minneapolis: Fortress Press, 2009.

Dole, Andrew C. *Schleiermacher on Religion and the Natural Order.* AAR Religion, Culture, and History Series. New York: Oxford University Press, 2010.

Emery, Gilles, OP, and Matthew Levering, eds. *The Oxford Handbook of the Trinity.* Oxford Handbooks in Religion and Theology. Oxford: Oxford University Press, 2011.

Engelke, Matthew. *A Problem of Presence: Beyond Scripture in an African Church.* Berkeley: University of California Press, 2007.

Fabricius, D. Cajus. "Albrecht Ritschl und die Theologie der Zukunft." *Preußische Jahrbücher* 140 (1910): 16–31.

————. *Positives Christentum im neuen Staat.* Dresden: Hermann Püschel, 1935. ET, *Positive Christianity in the Third Reich.* Dresden: Hermann Püschel, 1935.

Fiorenza, Francis Schüssler. "Schleiermacher's Understanding of God as Triune." In *The Cambridge Companion to Schleiermacher*, edited by Jacqueline Mariña, 171–88. Cambridge Companions to Religion. Cambridge: Cambridge University Press, 2005.

Florensky, Pavel. *The Pillar and Ground of the Truth: An Essay in Orthodox Theodicy in Twelve Letters.* Translated by Boris Jakim. Princeton: Princeton University Press, 1997.

Ford, David F. *Shaping Theology: Engagements in a Religious and Secular World.* Malden, MA: Blackwell, 2007.

Frank, Manfred. "Metaphysical Foundations: A Look at Schleiermacher's *Dialektik.*" Translated by Jacqueline Mariña and Christine Helmer. In *The Cambridge Companion to Schleiermacher*, edited by Jacqueline Mariña, 15–34. Cambridge Companions to Religion. Cambridge: Cambridge University Press, 2005.

Frei, Hans W. *The Eclipse of Biblical Narrative: A Study in Eighteenth and Nineteenth Century Hermeneutics.* New Haven: Yale University Press, 1974.

————. *Types of Theology.* Edited by George Hunsinger and William C. Placher. New Haven: Yale University Press, 1992.

Fulkerson, Mary McClintock. *Places of Redemption: Theology for a Worldly Church.* New York: Oxford University Press, 2010.

Geertz, Clifford. *The Interpretation of Cultures: Selected Essays.* New York: Basic Books, 1973.

Geisler, Ralf. *Kants moralischer Gottesbeweis im protestantischen Positivismus.* Göttinger theologische Arbeiten 51. Göttingen: Vandenhoeck & Ruprecht, 1992.

Gilland, David Andrew, trans. and ed. *Karl Barth–Emil Brunner Correspondence.* Edinburgh: T&T Clark, 2013.

Gold, Daniel. *Aesthetic and Analysis in Writing on Religion: Modern Fascinations.* Chicago: University of Chicago Press, 2003.

Gooch, Todd A. *The Numinous and Modernity: An Interpretation of Rudolf Otto's Philosophy of Religion.* Beihefte zur Zeitschrift für die alttestamentliche Wissenschaft 293. Berlin: de Gruyter, 2000.

Hart, John W. *Karl Barth vs. Emil Brunner: The Formation and Dissolution of a Theological Alliance, 1916–1936.* Issues in Systematic Theology 6. New York: Peter Lang, 2001.

Heimburger, Martin, ed. *Begründete Freiheit: Die Aktualität der Barmer Theologischen Erklärung; Vortragsreihe zum 75. Jahrestag im Berliner Dom.* Neukirchen/Vlyun: Neukirchener Verlag, 2009.

Heit, Alexander. *Versöhnte Vernunft: Eine Studie zur systematischen Bedeutung des Rechtfertigungsgedankens für Kants Religionsphilosophie.* Forschungen zur systematischen und ökumenischen Theologie 115. Göttingen: Vandenhoeck & Ruprecht, 2006.

Helmer, Christine. "Albrecht Benjamin Ritschl" In *Metzler Lexikon christlicher Denker,* edited by Markus Vinzent, 586–87. Stuttgart: J. B. Metzler, 2000.

———. "Between History and Speculation: Christian Trinitarian Thinking after the Reformation" In *The Cambridge Companion to the Trinity,* edited by Peter C. Phan, 149–69. Cambridge Companions to Religion. Cambridge: Cambridge University Press, 2011.

———. "The Consummation of Reality: Soteriological Metaphysics in Schleiermacher's Interpretation of Colossians 1:15–20," 113–32. In *Biblical Interpretation: History, Context, and Reality.* Edited by Christine Helmer. Society of Biblical Literature Symposium Series 26. Atlanta: Society of Biblical Literature Press, 2005.

———. "Luther, Religious Studies, and the University." In *Lutherrenaissance: Past and Present.* Edited by Christine Helmer and Bo Kristian Holm. Forschungen zur Kirchen- und Dogmengeschichte. Göttingen: Vandenhoeck & Ruprecht, forthcoming.

———. "Recovering the Real in the New Testament: A Case Study of Schleiermacher's Theology." In *The Multivalence of Biblical Texts and Theological Meanings,* edited by Christine Helmer with Charlene T. Higbe, 161–76. Symposium Series 37. Atlanta: Society of Biblical Literature, 2006.

———. Review of *A Native American Theology,* by Clara Sue Kidwell, Homer Noley, and George E. "Tink" Tinker. *Pro Ecclesia* 12, no. 2 (Spring 2003): 240–42.

———. "Schleiermacher." In *The Blackwell Companion to Nineteenth-Century Theology,* edited by David Fergusson, 31–57. Malden, MA: Wiley-Blackwell, 2010.

———. "Schleiermacher's Exegetical Theology and the New Testament." In *The Cambridge Companion to Friedrich Schleiermacher,* edited by Jacqueline Mariña, 229–48. Cambridge Companions to Religion. Cambridge: Cambridge University Press, 2005.

———. "The Subject of Theology in the Thought of Oswald Bayer." *Lutheran Quarterly* 14, no. 1 (Spring 2000): 21–52.

———. "A Systematic Theological Theory of Truth in Kathryn Tanner's *Jesus, Humanity and the Trinity: A Brief Systematic Theology.*" *Scottish Journal of Systematic Theology* 57, no. 2 (May 2004): 203–20.

———. "Theology and the Study of Religion: A Relationship." In *The Cambridge Companion to Religious Studies,* edited by Robert A. Orsi, 230–56. Cambridge Companions to Religion. New York: Cambridge University Press, 2012.

———. "United and Divided: Luther and Calvin in Modern Protestant Theology." In *Calvin and Luther: The Unfinished Conversation,* edited by R. Ward Holder, 195–211. Refo500 Academic Studies 12. Göttingen: Vandenhoeck & Ruprecht, 2013.

Helmer, Christine, Christiane Kranich, and Birgit Rehme-Iffert, eds. *Schleiermachers Dialektik: Die Liebe zum Wissen in Philosophie und Theologie*. Religion in Philosophy and Theology 6. Tübingen: Mohr Siebeck, 2003.

Herms, Eilert. "Schleiermacher's *Christian Ethics*." Translated by Jacqueline Mariña and Christine Helmer. In *The Cambridge Companion to Schleiermacher*, edited by Jacqueline Mariña, 209–28. Cambridge Companions to Religion. Cambridge: Cambridge University Press, 2005.

———. "'Weltanschauung' bei Friedrich Schleiermacher und Albrecht Ritschl." In *Theorie für die Praxis—Beiträge zur Theologie*, 121–43. Munich: Chr. Kaiser, 1982.

Hockenos, Matthew D. *A Church Divided: German Protestants Confront the Nazi Past*. Bloomington: Indiana University Press, 2004.

Holl, Karl. "Die Rechtfertigungslehre in Luthers Vorlesung über den Römerbrief mit besonderer Rücksicht auf die Frage der Heilsgewißheit." *Zeitschrift für Theologie und Kirche* 20 (1910): 245–91.

———. *What Did Luther Understand by Religion?* Edited by James Luther Adams and Walter F. Bense. Translated by Fred W. Meuser and Walter R. Wietzke. Philadelphia: Fortress Press, 1977.

Holm, Bo Kristian. "Der Trost kommt vom Sehen—zu Katechismussystematik und Lehrbergiff." In *Denkraum Katechismus: Festgabe für Oswald Bayer zum 70. Geburtstag*, edited by Johannes von Lüpke and Edgar Thaidigsmann, 109–24. Tübingen: Mohr Siebeck, 2009.

———. "Zur Funktion der Lehre bei Luther: Die Lehre als rettendes Gedankenbild gegen Sünde, Tod und Teufel." *Kerygma und Dogma* 51, no. 1 (2005): 17–32.

Howard, Thomas Albert. *Protestant Theology and the Making of the Modern German University*. Oxford: Oxford University Press, 2006.

Hunsinger, George. *How to Read Karl Barth: The Shape of His Theology*. New York: Oxford University Press, 1991.

Hütter, Reinhard. *Suffering Divine Things: Theology as Church Practice*. Grand Rapids: Eerdmans, 2000.

Jenson, Robert W. *Canon and Creed*. Interpretation: Resources for the Use of Scripture in the Church. Louisville, KY: Westminster John Knox Press, 2010.

———. *Systematic Theology*. Vol. 1, *The Triune God*. New York: Oxford University Press, 1997.

Jones, Paul Dafydd. "The Rhetoric of War in Karl Barth's *Epistle to the Romans*: A Theological Analysis." *Journal for the History of Modern Theology / Zeitschrift für neuere Theologiegeschichte* 17 (2010): 90–111.

Jowett, Benjamin. "On the Interpretation of Scripture." In *The Interpretation of Scripture and Other Essays*, 1–76 (chap. 1). London: G. Routledge & Sons, 1907. Repr. from *Essays and Reviews*, edited by F. Temple et al., 330–433. London: Parker & Son, 1860.

Jüngel, Eberhard. *God's Being Is in Becoming: The Trinitarian Being of God in the Theology of Karl Barth*. Translated and introduced by John Webster. Edinburgh: T&T Clark, 2001.

Kelsey, Catherine L. "A Reading of Schleiermacher's *Life of Jesus* Lectures: An Historian at Work." In *Schleiermacher, Romanticism, and the Critical Arts: A Festschrift in Honor of Hermann Patsch*, edited by Hans Dierkes, Terrence N. Tice, and Wolfgang Virmond, 209–26. Lewiston, NY: Edwin Mellen, 2007.

Kidwell, Clara Sue, Homer Noley, and George E. "Tink" Tinker. *A Native American Theology*. Maryknoll, NY: Orbis Books, 2001.

Kirjavainen, Heikki. "Die Spezifizierung der Glaubensgegenstände bei Luther im Licht der Spätmittelalterlichen Semantik." In *Thesaurus Lutheri: Auf der Suche nach neuen Paradigmen der Luther-Forschung*, edited by Tuomo Mannermaa, Anja Ghiselli, and Simo Peura, 237–57. Veröffentlichungen der Finnischen Theologischen Literaturgesellschaft 153, in Zusammenarbeit mit der Luther-Agricola-Gesellschaft A24. Helsinki: Finnische Theologische Literaturgesellschaft, 1987.

Kloppenborg, John S. *Excavating Q: The History and Setting of the Sayings Gospel*. Minneapolis: Fortress Press, 2000.

Knuuttila, Simo. "Luther's View of Logic and Revelation." *Medioevo: Rivista di storia della filosofia medievale* 24 (1998): 219–34.

Lauster, Jörg. "Liberale Theologie: Eine Ermunterung." *Neue Zeitschrift für systematische Theologie und Religionsphilosophie* 49, no. 3 (2007): 291–307.

Lauster, Jörg, Peter Schüz, Roderich Barth, and Christian Danz, eds. *Rudolf Otto: Theologie, Religionsphilosophie, Religionsgeschichte*. Berlin: de Gruyter 2013.

Leppin, Volker. "Fragment-Controversy." In *EBR*, vol. 9 (forthcoming).

Lim, Paul C. H. *Mystery Unveiled: The Crisis of the Trinity in Early Modern England*. New York: Oxford University Press, 2012.

Lindbeck, George A. *The Church in a Postliberal Age*. Edited by James J. Buckley. Radical Traditions Series. Grand Rapids: Eerdmans, 2002.

———. *The Nature of Doctrine: Religion and Theology in a Postliberal Age*. 1984. 25th Anniversary ed., Louisville, KY: Westminster John Knox Press, 2009. ET, *Christliche Lehre als Grammatik des Glaubens: Religion und Theologie im postliberalen Zeitalter*. Translated by Markus Müller and introduced by Hans G. Ulrich and Reinhard Hütter. Theologische Bücherei 90. Gütersloh: Gütersloher Verlagshaus, 1994.

Luhrmann, Tanya M. *When God Talks Back: Understanding the American Evangelical Relationship with God*. New York: Vintage Books, 2012.

Mahlmann, Theodor. "Articulus stantis et (vel) cadentis ecclesiae." In *RGG* 1:799–800.

———. "*Doctrina* im Verständnis nachreformatorischer lutherischer Theologen." In *Vera Doctrina: Zur Begriffsgeschichte der Lehre von Augustinus bis Descartes / L'idée de doctrine d'Augustin à Descartes*, edited by Philippe Büttgen et al., 199–264. Wolfenbütteler Forschungen 123. Wiesbaden: Harrassowitz Verlag, 2009.

Makkreel, Rudolf A., and Sebastian Luft, eds. *Neo-Kantianism in Contemporary Philosophy*. Studies in Continental Thought. Bloomington: Indiana University Press, 2009.

Mariña, Jacqueline. "Schleiermacher between Kant and Leibniz: Predication and Ontology." In *Schleiermacher and Whitehead: Open Systems in Dialogue*, edited by Christine Helmer with Marjorie Suchocki, John Quiring, and Katie Goetz, 73–92. Theologische Bibliothek Töpelmann 125. Berlin: de Gruyter, 2004.

Marshall, Bruce D. "Faith and Reason Reconsidered: Aquinas and Luther on Deciding What Is True." *The Thomist* 63, no. 1 (1999): 1–48.

———. *Trinity and Truth*. Cambridge Studies in Christian Doctrine. Cambridge: Cambridge University Press, 2000.

Martikainen, Eeva. "Der Doctrina-Begriff in Luthers Theologie." In *Thesaurus Lutheri: Auf der Suche nach neuen Paradigmen der Luther-Forschung*, edited by Tuomo Mannermaa, Anja Ghiselli, and Simo Peura, 205–19. Veröffentlichungen der Finnischen Theologischen Literaturgesellschaft 153, in Zusammenarbeit mit der Luther-Agricola-Gesellschaft A24. Helsinki: Finnische Theologische Literaturgesellschaft, 1987.

Masuzawa, Tomoko. *The Invention of World Religions: Or, How European Universalism Was Preserved in the Language of Pluralism.* Chicago: University of Chicago Press, 2005.

McCormack, Bruce L. *Karl Barth's Critically Realistic Dialectical Theology: Its Genesis and Development, 1909–1936.* New York: Clarendon Press, 1995.

McCutcheon, Russell T. "The Study of Religion as an Anthropology of Credibility." In *Religious Studies, Theology, and the University: Conflicting Maps, Changing Terrain,* edited by Linell E. Cady and Delwin Brown, 13–30. Albany: State University of New York Press, 2002.

McDowell, John C. "Karl Barth, Emil Brunner and the Subjectivity of the Object of Christian Hope." *International Journal of Systematic Theology* 8, no. 1 (January 2006): 25–41.

McGrath, Alister. *Emil Brunner: A Reappraisal.* West Sussex, UK: Wiley-Blackwell, 2014.

Meier, Kurt. *Die theologischen Fakultäten im Dritten Reich.* De Gruyter Studienbuch. Berlin: de Gruyter, 1996.

Murphy, Francesca Aran. *God Is Not a Story: Realism Revisited.* New York: Oxford University Press, 2007.

Newman, John Henry, Cardinal. *An Essay on the Development of Christian Doctrine.* 1878. Repr., Westminster, MD: Christian Classics, 1968.

Orsi, Robert A. "Introduction." In *The Cambridge Companion to Religious Studies,* edited by Robert A. Orsi, 1–13. Cambridge Companions to Religion. New York: Cambridge University Press, 2012.

———. "The Problem of the Holy." In *The Cambridge Companion to Religious Studies,* edited by Robert A. Orsi, 84–105. Cambridge Companions to Religion. New York: Cambridge University Press, 2012.

Osthövener, Claus-Dieter. "Schleiermachers kritisches Verhältnis zur theologischen Aufklärung." In *Die Aufgeklärte Religion und ihre Probleme,* edited by Wilhelm Gräb, 511–39. Berlin: de Gruyter, 2013.

Otto, Rudolf. *The Idea of the Holy: An Inquiry into the Non-Rational Factor in the Idea of the Divine and Its Relation to the Rational.* Translated by John W. Harvey. 2nd ed. Oxford: Oxford University Press, 1950.

Patsch, Hermann, and Dirk Schmid. "Einleitung [to Schleiermacher's exegetical writings]." In *KGA* I/8, edited by Hermann Patsch and Dirk Schmid, vii–lvii. Berlin: de Gruyter, 2001.

Pedersen, Else Marie Wiberg. "Mysticism in the *Lutherrenaissance.*" In *Lutherrenaissance: Past and Present,* edited by Christine Helmer and Bo Kristian Holm, forthcoming. Forschungen zur Kirchen- und Dogmengeschichte. Göttingen: Vandenhoeck & Ruprecht, forthcoming.

Pihlström, Sami. *Pragmatic Pluralism and the Problem of God.* New York: Fordham University Press, 2013.

Ratschow, Carl Heinz. *Lutherische Dogmatik zwischen Reformation und Aufklärung.* 2 vols. Gütersloh: Gütersloher Verlagshaus Gerd Mohn, 1964–66.

Reischle, Max. *Ein Wort zur Controverse über die Mystik in der Theologie.* Freiburg im Breisgau: J. C. B. Mohr (Paul Siebeck), 1886.

Ritschl, Albrecht. *The Christian Doctrine of Justification and Reconciliation: The Positive Development of the Doctrine.* ET of vol. 3 of *Die christliche Lehre von der Rechtfertigung und Versöhnung.* Translated by H. R. Mackintosh and A. B. Macaulay. Edinburgh: T&T Clark, 1900.

———. *Die christliche Lehre von der Rechtfertigung und Versöhnung.* 3 vols. 1870–74. 3rd ed., Bonn: Adolph Marcus, 1889.

————. *Die christliche Vollkommenheit: Ein Vortrag; Unterricht in der christlichen Religion.* Edited by Cajus Fabricius. Leipzig: J. C. Hinrichs'sche Buchhandlung, 1924. Repr., *Unterricht in der christlichen Religion.* Edited and introduced by Christine Axt-Piscalar. Study edition of the original (1875) along with changes of the 2nd and 3rd editions. Tübingen: Mohr Siebeck, 2002.

————. *A Critical History of the Christian Doctrine of Justification and Reconciliation.* ET of vol. 1 of *Die christliche Lehre von der Rechtfertigung und Versöhnung.* Translated by J. S. Black. Edinburgh: Edmonston & Douglas, 1872.

————. "Festrede am vierten Seculartage der Geburt Martin Luthers." In *Kleine Schriften*, edited by Frank Hofmann, 148–74. Theologische Studien-Texte 4. Waltrop: Hartmut Spenner, 1999.

————. *Theologie und Metaphysik: Zur Verständigung und Abwehr.* 2nd ed. Bonn: Adolph Marcus, 1887. Repr., *Kleine Schriften*, edited by Frank Hofmann, 68–142. Theologische Studien-Texte 4. Waltrop: Hartmut Spenner, 1999. ET, *Theology and Metaphysics.* In *Three Essays*, translated and introduced by Philip Hefner, 149–217. Philadelphia: Fortress Press, 1972.

Robbins, Joel. "Transcendence and the Anthropology of Christianity: Language, Change and Individualism (Edward Westermarck Memorial Lecture)." *Journal of the Finnish Anthropological Society* 3, no. 2 (2012): 5–23.

Saarinen, Risto. "Luther the Urban Legend." In *The Global Luther: A Theologian for Modern Times*, edited by Christine Helmer, 13–31. Minneapolis: Fortress Press, 2009.

————. "Luther und Humanistische Philosophie." In *Lutherjahrbuch 80: Jahrgang 2013.* Organ der Internationalen Lutherforschung. Göttingen: Vandenhoeck & Ruprecht, 2013:77–109.

————. "Reclaiming the Sentences: A Linguistic Loci Approach to Doctrine." *Neue Zeitschrift für systematische Theologie und Religionsphilosophie* 54, no. 1 (2012): 1–22.

Schleiermacher, Friedrich. *Critical Essay on the Gospel of St. Luke.* Translated and introduced by Connop Thirlwall. London: John Taylor, 1825. Repr. with further essays, emendations, and other apparatus by Terrence N. Tice. Schleiermacher: Studies and Translations 13. Lewiston, NY: Edwin Mellen, 1993.

————. *Dialektik.* In *Sämmtliche Werke*, edited by Ludwig Jonas, vol. III/4.2. Berlin: G. Reimer, 1839.

————. *Dialektik.* Edited by Rudolf Odebrecht. Leipzig: Prussian Academy of Sciences, 1942. Repr., Darmstadt: Wissenschaftliche Buchgesellschaft, 1976.

————. *Hermeneutics and Criticism and Other Writings.* Translated by Andrew Bowie. Cambridge Texts in the History of Philosophy. Cambridge: Cambridge University Press, 1998.

————. *Kurze Darstellung des theologischen Studiums zum Behuf einleitender Vorlesungen (1810/30).* Edited by Heinrich Scholz. 3rd ed. Leipzig: A. Deichert, 1910. Repr. in the series Bibliothek klassischer Texte. Darmstadt: Wissenschaftliche Buchgesellschaft, 1993. ET of the 1810 and 1830 editions as *Brief Outline of Theology as a Field of Study*, with essays and notes by Terrence N. Tice. Schleiermacher Studies and Translations. vol. 1. Lewiston, NY: Edwin Mellen Press, 1990.

————. *The Life of Jesus.* Translated by S. MacLean Gilmour. Edited and introduced by Jack C. Verheyden. Lives of Jesus Series. Philadelphia: Augsburg Fortress, 1975. Repr., Mifflintown, PA: Sigler Press, 1997.

————. *The Life of Schleiermacher as Unfolded in His Autobiography and Letters.* Translated by Frederica Rowan. Vol. 1. London: Smith, Elder & Co., 1860.

————. *On Colossians 1:15–20.* Translated by Esther D. Reed and Alan Braley. In *New Athenaeum / Neues Athenaeum* 5 (1998): 48–80.

————. *On Religion: Speeches to Its Cultural Despisers.* Edited and translated by Richard Crouter, 2nd ed. Cambridge: Cambridge University Press, 1996.

————. *On Religion: Speeches to Its Cultured Despisers.* Introduced by Rudolf Otto. Translated by John Oman. New York: Harper Torchbooks, 1965.

————. "Über den Gegensatz zwischen der Sabellianischen und der Athanasianischen Vorstellung von der Trinität [1822]." In *KGA* I/10, edited by Hans-Friedrich Taulsen with the assistance of Martin Ohst, 223–306. Berlin: de Gruyter, 1990. Translated by Moses Stuart as "On the Discrepancy between the Sabellian and Athanasian Method of Representing the Doctrine of the Trinity (1822)." *Biblical Repository and Quarterly Observer* 5–6 (April 1835): 31–33; (July 1835): 1–116.

————. *Vorlesungen über die Dialektik.* In *KGA* II/10, edited by Andreas Arndt, parts 1 and 21–2. Berlin: de Gruyter, 2002.

Schmid, Heinrich, ed. *The Doctrinal Theology of the Evangelical Lutheran Church.* 3rd ed. Translated by Charles A. Hay and Henry E. Jacobs. Minneapolis: Augsburg, 1961.

Schwarz, F. H. Chr. "Review of Schleiermacher's *Brief Outline.*" *Heidelberger Jahrbücher der Litteratur* 5, no. 33 (1812): 526–27.

Slenczka, Notger. *Der Glaube und sein Grund: F. H. R. von Frank, seine Auseinandersetzung mit A. Ritschl und die Fortführung seines Programms durch L. Ihmels; Studien zur Erlanger Theologie I.* Forschungen zur systematischen und ökumenischen Theologie 85. Göttingen: Vandenhoeck & Ruprecht, 1998.

Soulen, R. Kendall. *The Divine Name(s) and the Holy Trinity.* Vol. 1, *Distinguishing the Voices.* Louisville, KY: Westminster John Knox Press, 2011.

Steinberg, Jonathan. *Bismarck: A Life.* New York: Oxford University Press, 2011.

Strauss, David Friedrich. *The Christ of Faith and the Jesus of History: A Critique of Schleiermacher's "The Life of Jesus" (1865).* Translated, edited, and introduced by Leander E. Keck. Lives of Jesus Series. Philadelphia: Fortress, 1977.

Tanner, Kathryn. *Jesus, Humanity and the Trinity: A Brief Systematic Theology.* Minneapolis: Fortress Press, 2001.

Thiel, John E. "The Development of Doctrine." In *The Blackwell Companion to Catholicism,* edited by James J. Buckley, Frederick Christian Bauerschmidt, and Trent Pomplun, 251–67. Malden, MA: Blackwell, 2007.

Vainio, Olli-Pekka. *Beyond Fideism: Negotiable Religious Identities.* Transcending Boundaries in Philosophy and Theology Series. Surrey, UK: Ashgate, 2010.

Vanhoozer, Kevin J. *The Drama of Doctrine: A Canonical-Linguistic Approach to Christian Theology.* Louisville, KY: Westminster John Knox Press, 2005.

Vuola, Elina. "Patriarchal Ecumenism, Feminism, and Women's Experience in Costa Rica." In *Gendering Religion and Politics: Untangling Modernities,* edited by Hanna Herzog and Ann Braude, 217–38. New York: Palgrave Macmillan, 2009.

Welker, Michael. "Rethinking Christocentric Theology." In *Transformations in Luther's Theology: Historical and Contemporary Reflections,* edited by Christine Helmer and Bo Kristian Holm, 179–92. Arbeiten zur Kirchen- und Theologiegeschichte 32. Leipzig: EVA-Verlag, 2011.

Westhelle, Vítor. "Incursions in Luther's Theology." In *The Global Luther: A Theologian for Modern Times,* edited by Christine Helmer, chap. 17. Minneapolis: Fortress Press, 2009.

Widmann, Peter. "Die Lutherdeutung Albrecht Ritschls in ihrer Frontstellung gegen die liberale Theologie und des Neuluthertum." In *Lutherrenaissance: Past and*

Present, edited by Christine Helmer and Bo Kristian Holm, forthcoming. For-schungen zur Kirchen- und Dogmengeschichte . Göttingen: Vandenhoeck & Ruprecht, forthcoming.

Wieckenberg, Ernst-Peter. *Johan Melchior Goeze*. Hamburger Köpfe. Hamburg: Ellert & Richter Verlag, 2007.

Wiles, Maurice. *The Making of Christian Doctrine: A Study in the Principles of Early Doctrinal Development*. Cambridge: Cambridge University Press, 1967.

Wittgenstein, Ludwig. *Remarks on Frazer's "Golden Bough."* Translated by A. C. Miles. Revised by Rush Rhees. Gringley-on-the-Hill, UK: Brynmill, 1979.

Zachhuber, Johannes. "Friedrich Schleiermacher und Albrecht Ritschl: Kontinuitä-ten und Diskontinuitäten in der Theologie des 19. Jahrhunderts." *Zeitschrift für neuere Theologiegeschichte / Journal for the History of Modern Theology* 12, no. 1 (2005): 16–46.

Index of Ancient Sources

OLD TESTAMENT

Exodus
13:21 — 60

Psalms
23:3 — 20

Lamentations
3:23 — 152

NEW TESTAMENT

Matthew
16:1b — 64n4
16:3b — 64n4
16:15 — 125
16:15–16 — 125
16:16 — 133
24:5 — 167

Mark
15:39 — 126
16:15–17 — 137

Luke
7:16 — 129
24:13–35 — 125n29
24:31 — 125n29

John
1:14 — 99
1:14a — 11
4:19 — 129
6:35 — 132
8:32 — 54, 152
14:23 — 31
15:1 — 129, 132
16–18 — 113

Acts
9:3–8 — 125
9:5 — 125n30

Romans
1–3 — 66
1:3–4 — 142
1:4 — 68n24
1:17 — 9, 29, 70n31
1:18 — 65, 66
2:14–15 — 66
2:15–16 — 68n22
3:1–4 — 66
3:5–6 — 67–18
3:21, — 67, 68nn21–23
3:21–22a — 67
3:24 — 69n26
4:5 — 30

1 Corinthians
6:15, 17 — 31
15 — 93

2 Corinthians
4:14 — 91
5:17a — 124
10:5 — 20
14:4 — 92

Galatians
2:19, 20 — 31
3:27 — 31

Ephesians
5:30 — 31

Colossians
1:17b — 101

1 Timothy — 115

Hebrews
1:1 — 138
13:8 — 130

2 Peter
1:4 — 31

Jude
3 — 14, 112

Revelation
21 — 67

Index of Names

Adams, Marilyn McCord, 151n2
Ailly, Pierre d', 9
Anselm of Canterbury, 86
Aquinas, Thomas. See Thomas Aquinas
Arius, 142
Arnold, Gottfried, 34
Asad, Talal, 156n9
Assel, Heinrich, 66n4
Austin, J. L., 15
Ayres, Lewis, 141–42, 162n19

Barth, Karl, 2, 11, 20, 26–27, 45, 47–48,
        60–90, 103, 105–6, 136, 145, 147,
        149, 151–52, 160, 163–65
Bayer, Oswald, 14–15, 30, 74
Bernard of Clairvaux, 43
Birkner, Hans-Joachim, 52–53
Bismarck, Otto von, 28
Bretschneider, Karl, 120n22
Brunner, Emil, 14, 20, 27, 40–41, 44, 47–57,
        59, 62, 74, 83, 110–11, 120, 122

Chalamet, Christophe, 28n11, 64n5
Chignell, Andrew, 33n27, 35n34, 36n39
Childs, Brevard S., 112

Davaney, Sheila G., 12n10
Davidson, Donald, 127n32
Dierken, Jörg, 159n16

Dieter, Theodor, 8n4, 30, 167n27
Dole, Andrew C., 157n11

Edwards, Jonathan, 3
Elert, Werner, 74
Engelke, Matthew, 158

Fabricius, Cajus, 27, 40–41, 40–47
Fichte, Johann Gottlieb, 121n25
Fiorenza, Francis Schüssler, 119n21
Florensky, Pavel, 166
Frank, Manfred, 50n78
Frei, Hans W., 12n12
Fries, Jakob Friedrich, 153, 155
Fulkerson, Mary McClintock, 160

Geertz, Clifford, 15–16, 25, 102n24, 149–50
Gold, Daniel, 158n12
Gooch, Todd A., 154n7

Hamann, Johann Georg, 51
Hefner, Philip, 28n11
Hegel, Georg Wilhelm Friedrich, 35–36,
        142, 164
Heit, Alexander, 33
Helmer, Christine, 49n72, 74n40, 92n98,
        115n11, 131n35, 156n8, 164n22
Hermann, Wilhelm, 64
Herms, Eilert, 50n78

Holl, Karl, 66, 153
Holm, Bo Kristian, 13n13
Howard, Thomas Albert, 12n12
Hunsinger, George, 63n2
Humboldt, Wilhelm von, 49
Hütter, Reinhard, 14n17, 15n18, 15nn20–21, 16

Irenaeus of Lyons, 95

Jacobi, Friedrich Heinrich, 121n25
James, William, 157
Jenson, Robert W., 17n27, 91–92, 94
Jodock, Darrell, 28n11
Jones, Paul Dafydd, 64n3
Jowett, Benjamin, 110n1
Jüngel, Eberhard, 63n2

Kant, Immanuel, 9, 28, 32–35, 50, 89, 113,
    117, 122, 127n31, 155
Kelsey, Catherine L., 116n13
Kidwell, Clara Sue, 143n40
Kirjavainen, Heikki, 90n92
Kloppenborg, John S., 115n10
Knuuttila, Simo, 100
Kranich, Christiane, 49n72
Kristensen, W. Brede, 155
Kuhlmann, Helga, 28n11

Lauster, Jörg, 166n25
Leibniz, Gottfried Wilhelm Freiherr von, 127
Leppin, Volker, 118n17
Lessing, Gotthold Ephraim, 118
Lim, Paul C. H., 163
Lindbeck, George A., 14–16, 18, 25, 92,
    102n124, 110n2, 112, 149–50
Luhrmann, Tanya, 158
Luther, Martin, 2, 7–10, 12, 14, 16–18, 31,
    42, 54, 60, 63, 66, 90–93, 99–102,
    136, 143–44, 150, 153–55, 162,
    165

Magdeburg, Mechthild von, 161
Mahlmann, Theodor, 23n1, 24, 25
Marga, Amy, 64n6
Mariña, Jacqueline, 127nn31–33
Marshall, Bruce D., 25n8, 26, 60–61, 89,
    91–104, 150
Mary Magdalene, 161

Mary (Virgin), 11, 99
Masuzawa, Tomoko, 4, 157n10
McCormack, Bruce L., 63n2
McCutcheon, Russell T., 4n3
McDowell, John, 48n69
Melanchthon, Philipp, 30
Murphy, Francesca Aran, 165

Newman, John Henry (Cardinal), 19n31
Noley, Homer, 143n40

Orsi, Robert A., 131n35
Otto, Rudolf, 153–55, 157

Patsch, Hermann, 115n11
Paul (apostle), 65, 69–70, 124–25
    See also Saul
Pedersen, Else Marie Wiberg, 42
Peter (apostle), 125, 133
Philström, Sami, 157n11
Plato, 9
Pontius Pilate, 11

Rahner, Karl, 136
Ratschow, Carl Heinz, 32n24
Rehme-Iffert, Birgit, 49n72
Reimarus, Elise, 118
Reimarus, Hermann Samuel, 118, 120, 124,
    130, 145
Reimarus, Johann Albrecht Heinrich, 118
Reimer, Georg, 56
Reischle, Max, 27, 40–44, 47
Ritschl, Albrecht, 27–30, 32–47, 51, 55, 64,
    67, 92n98, 159, 163
Robbins, Joel, 158

Saarinen, Risto, 143n41
Saul, 125. *See also* Paul
Schelling, Friedrich Wilhelm Joseph von,
    121n25
Schleiermacher, Friedrich Daniel Ernst, 2, 7,
    9, 12–14, 17–18, 20–21, 26–27, 40,
    47–59, 63, 76, 83, 87, 106, 109–11,
    113–34, 136, 141, 145–47, 152,
    154–55, 158–60, 163–65
Schmid, Dirk, 115n11
Schmid, Heinrich, 31–32
Schweitzer, Albert, 118n17

Speyr, Adrienne von, 161
Strauss, David Friedrich, 120

Tanner, Kathryn, 89n89
Thomas Aquinas, 9, 92–94, 97–98, 102, 162
Tiele, Cornelius Petrus, 155
Tinker, George E., 143n40
Treu, Martin, 8n5
Troeltsch, Ernst, 153, 159

Vainio, Olli-Pekka, 17n28
Vanhoozer, Kevin J., 17n12

Vuola, Elina, 160

Welker, Michael, 73n38
Westhelle, Vítor, 136n36
Wieckenberg, Ernst-Peter, 118n17
Wiles, Maurice, 19n31
Wilhelm I (King of Prussia), 28
William of Ockham, 9
Wittgenstein, Ludwig, 14, 157n11

Zinzendorf, Nikolaus L. von, 106

Index of Subjects

absolute dependence, 123, 154
absolutes, 138
academy, 6
acclamation, 125–30, 133
actuality, 88
alien categories, 155
alien righteousness, 30
"anchoring," 144
Anfechtungen (spiritual terror), 9
Apostles' Creed, 10, 94, 95, 96, 141
assertion, 60–61, 82, 83, 90–93, 97, 102, 106
Athanasianism, 119, 141
attributes, divine, 36
authority, 138

Barmen Declaration, 72–74, 81, 86
beliefs
    coherence of, 97, 98, 99, 100
    doctrine as grammar of, 15–16
    inculcation of, 156
    package of, 97, 99
    See also faith
"benchmarking," 144
Bible
    and Christian proclamation, 79–80
    communal reading of, 95, 96
    and creed, 96
    final form of, 112
    interpretation of, 110, 115, 128–29

status of, 73
    as tool for theology's task, 65, 70
    See also Scripture
biblical studies, 3, 12
bilingualism, 128n34
body and spirit, 46
Bondage of the Will, The (Luther), 154
Brief Outline (Schleiermacher), 117

Calvinism, 140
canon, 17, 111, 112, 114, 116–17
catechism, 10, 24
categories, alien, 155
categorization, 139–42, 144, 155
Catholicism. *See* Roman Catholicism
causality, 51, 52, 130
certainty, 90
children, 46
Christ
    attestation to, 74, 75
    and community, 120–21
    doctrine of, 20, 21, 146
    as epistemic principle, 101, 102
    experiential encounter with, 57, 125, 126
    as God's word, 70, 72–75
    God's work in, 42
    incarnation of, 11, 86, 94–96, 99
    as Judge, 8
    mediation of the historical, 43, 44, 47

185

Christ (*continued*)
    mystical relationship with, 57, 120–22
    preexistence of, 119
    presence of, 119, 124, 131, 133
    primacy in world and church, 74
    as Redeemer, 146
    relationship with, 38, 43, 44, 46, 125
    revelation in, 34, 82
    righteousness of, 30, 31
    salvation work of, 82, 144
    uniqueness of, 122, 125, 132–33, 137,
        144
    as word of God, 70, 72–75
    See also Jesus; Jesus Christ; Jesus of
        Nazareth
Christ present. *See Christus praesens* (Christ
    present)
Christian discourse, 134
Christian faith, 24, 93
Christian worldview, 15, 16, 61, 89, 103–5
Christianity
    core/center of, 135
    global, 136, 147
    history of, 13, 45, 46, 139, 141
    living, 130, 132, 134
    and mysticism, 44, 45
    positivity of, 134
    as universal religion, 45, 46
    as worldview, 100–103
Christian Faith, The (Schleiermacher), 27, 49,
    53, 56, 57, 76, 114, 115, 122. *See*
    also Glaubenslehre (Schleiermacher)
Christmas hymn, 12
Christology, 73, 128, 132, 133, 141, 142
Christus praesens (Christ present), 43, 57, 119,
    134, 145
church
    and academy, 6
    and belief, 97
    Christ's relation to, 73, 121
    communities' up-to-dateness, 25n8
    conserving memberships in, 3
    and creed, 102, 104–5
    history of, 13
    identity of, 3, 7, 15, 18, 23, 25, 92, 93, 97,
        102–3, 104, 112
    linguistic-literary idioms of, 15
    practice, 16, 17

    Scripture reading of, 95
    teaching and preaching of, 98
    theology practice, 16
    vitality of, 13
    See also church identity
Church Dogmatics (Barth), 62, 70, 72, 75, 81,
    82, 84, 88
church identity
    as Bible-reading community, 104
    and Bible to Trinity relation, 92
    doctrine securing, 23, 25
    one revelation defining, 103
    as singular, 93
    specific beliefs needed for, 97
churchly element, 121
coherence of beliefs, 97–99, 100, 102–3
communal reading, 95, 96
communication, 135
community of love (*Liebesgemeinschaft*), 43
community's identity, 96, 97
concept formation, 126, 137
Confessing Church, 72
confession of faith, 24, 60, 90
conformity, 138
conscience, crisis of, 9, 66n14, 143
consciousness, 50, 122–23, 130
consolation, 13n13
Constantinople, Council of, 112–13
construction
    of doctrine, 90
    social, 145, 150–51, 159–60
    of theology, 141–46
content
    and church-creed analytic, 105
    of doctrine, 76, 180
    epistemology and, 131
    of the faith, 106
    of revelation, 82
    of word of God, 79, 81, 87
conversion, 103–5, 125
Council of Constantinople, 112–13
Council of Nicaea, 112
creeds
    as Christian belief statements, 94
    and Scripture/Bible, 95–96, 102
    and the Trinity doctrine, 112–13
crisis
    of conscience, 9

of faith, 2, 8
God's speech precipitating, 65–66, 88
criterion, 79
cultural sciences, 33
cultural system religion, 25, 151
Cur Deus homo? (Anselm of Canterbury), 86

darkness, 45
Das Heilige (Otto), 154, 155
deconstruction, 156–57
determination, 135
Deus dixit (God has spoken), 70–72, 81, 82, 87, 90, 105
Deutsche Christen (German Christians), 72
Dialectic (Schleiermacher), 114
dialectical theology, 48, 49, 78, 79, 105
dialectics, 114, 115, 116
Die christiliche Vollkommenheit (Fabricius), 44
Die Mystik und das Wort (Brunner), 47, 48
Ding-an-sich (thing in itself), 35, 36
disciples, of Jesus, 118, 125, 130
discourse, 134
discourse analysis, 157
Discourses (Schleiermacher), 154
diversity, 150
divine freedom, 85, 87
divine judgment, 61, 67, 68
divine objectivity, 51, 52. *See also* objectivity
divine righteousness, 64. *See also* righteousness
docere, 24
doctores ecclesiae (doctors of the church), 24
doctrina (teaching), 24
doctrine
    academic disciplines and, 4–5
    the aim of, 10
    changes in nature of, 6, 7
    of Christ, 20, 21, 146
    and Christian identity, 5–6, 17
    connotations of, 23–27
    construction of, 90
    content of, 76, 160
    and dogmatic theology, 13
    the end of, 6, 7, 19, 105, 150
    and experience of Christ, 131, 134
    as grammar of a worldview, 16, 61
    history of, 162, 163
    according to Hütter, 16
    isolation of, 1

and living God, 107
as normative faith statements, 13, 23, 61–62, 89
as normative of truth, 7, 23, 111
origin of, 131–34
purity of, 23
range of, 100–101
reception of, 17, 19, 111–12, 131
relationship with lived experience, 13, 61
and root assertion, 90–94
as rules informing an identity, 16
of sanctification, 31
and theological epistemology, 131–34
theology and, 1–20
of the Trinity, 2, 20, 72, 75, 82–83, 142
truth claims of, 23, 105, 165
understanding of God's word and, 59–62
of the word of God, 72, 75, 76
See also epistemic advantage model of
    doctrine; production of doc-
    trine; Trinity, doctrine of
dogmatic theology
    development of, 141–42
    history of, 28
    and inquiry, 79, 80, 81
    Lutheran, 31
    Schleiermachers's definition of, 13
    system of, 87
    task of, 76, 79, 84
dogmatics, 77

ecclesiology, 133. *See also* church
economies, neo-liberal, 3
ecumenism, 15, 25, 92, 149
education, theological, 3
Ego te absolvo (I forgive you), 15, 16
*Ein Wort zur Controverse über die Mystik in der
    Theologie* (Reischle), 41
empirical sciences, turn to, 35
end of doctrine, 6, 7, 19, 105, 150
Endzweck (purposiveness), 37
Enlightenment
    assault on faith by, 6–7
    European, 110
    German, 2
    and the Trinity, 163
epistemic advantage model of doctrine
    and assertions, 60–61

epistemic advantage model of doctrine
  (*continued*)
    and categories, 89
    coherence of beliefs in, 97–100, 102–3
    and ignoring of historical difference,
        150, 162
    and Scripture, 95–96
epistemology
    of ascent, 9
    to content, 145, 146
    and doctrine, 19, 131–32
    and dogma's development, 142
    theological, 11, 113, 128–30
Epistle to the Romans, The (Barth), 64, 65, 69,
        70, 73, 81, 88. *See also Römerbrief,
        Der* (Barth
Erkenntnis (human knowing; realization), 36
essential beliefs, 96, 97
essential righteousness, 29–31, 39
eternity
    doctrine pointing to, 11
    God and, 9, 10
    history and, 12
    theology's attraction to, 8, 9
eternal perfect, the 71
ethical action, 34, 35, 41, 42, 44
ethics, 32, 33, 35n32, 52–53
ethnography, 160, 161
European Enlightenment, 110
experience
    of Christ, 57
    of God, 19
    human, 155, 168
    and knowledge of God, 7
    and language, 17, 124–30, 135
    lived, 13, 152, 161–62
    mystical, 27
    novel, 137
    religious, 155
    of surprise, 19
    and theology, 17
experiential expressivism, 26
external word (*verbum externum*), 16, 91, 112,
        144

faith
    assertions, 92
    Christian, 21, 93

    and Christian belief, 92
    content of, 90
    in the gospel, 8n4
    and justification, 32
    knowledge of Christian, 24
    obedience of, 74
    personal, 42
    righteousness and, 30
fascism, 61, 64
"Father," 141
Father and Son controversy, 10
fear, 8, 140
feminist theology, 140
finitum capax infiniti (finite capable of the
        infinite), 12
forensic righteousness, 29–31
forgiveness, 30, 37, 39, 45
Formula of Concord, 35
fragment controversy, 118
Fragmente eines Ungenannten (Reimarus), 118
freedom, 51, 52, 85–86, 87

Galilee, 120
Geist (spirit), 50, 51
genocide, 64
genres, of theology, 77, 78, 88
Gentiles, and Jews, 66, 67
Gerechtigkeiten (righteousnesses), 65
German Enlightenment, 2
German Evangelical Church, 72
German Idealism, 27, 50
German Lutherans, 74
German political history, 61–64, 72–73
German Protestantism, 72, 136
German theology, 18, 27, 63
gift-giving, 89n89
Glaubenslehre (Schleiermacher), 154
global Christianity, 136, 147
God
    as the Absolute, 52
    of Christianity, 139
    concept of, 154
    concreted and humanized, 67
    eternity and, 9, 10
    experience and knowledge of, 7
    expressing the truth of, 8
    as first cause, 103
    freedom of, 85–86

as gracious, 8
hidden majesty of, 94
judgment of, 61, 62, 65–68
kingdom of, 34, 35
knowledge of, 14, 34, 38
living, 19
love of, 46
Luther's concept of, 154
male-female determination of, 140
mercies of, 12
omnipotence of, 10
as Redeemer and Creator, 70
and relationship with humans, 169
revelation of, 36, 42, 46, 99
righteousness of, 29–31, 64–68
self-knowledge of, 98
source of doctrine, 23
spoken word and, 81–82
truth of, 8, 14, 23, 81, 106
word of in relation to human words, 60
and the world, 11
See also reality of God; truth: of God;
      word of God
God Is Not a Story (Murphy), 165
God's word, 86, 88, 104. *See also* word; word
     of God
good works, 35
gospel, 64, 74, 91, 93, 101–2, 143
Gospels, 118–20, 129
grace
    and judgment, 68
    the presence of God as, 77
    reception of, 48
grammar of the faith, 16
Greek language, New Testament, 128
ground
    of Barth's theology, 83–85
    of the soul, 43, 53
    and Trinity, 89

heretics, burning of, 10
hermeneutics, 114–15, 116
hidden majesty, of God, 94, 96
highest good, 34, 37, 38
historical disciplines, 13
historical mediation, 38, 44
historicism, 11–14
historiography, 162, 163, 164, 166

history
    Christian, 10
    as a discipline, 3, 12
    of doctrine production, 162–65
    of dogma, 28
    and eternity, 12
    of Germany, 61–64, 72–73
    God in, 19
    of religion, 67
    of religious studies and theology, 159
Holocaust (Shoah), 63
Holy Spirit
    as Bible's divine author, 75
    and conversion, 104, 105
    enlivening of Christianity, 139
    gift of, 30, 31
    as mother of Christ, 106
homo faber (man the worker), 144
homoiousios (of a similar substance), 10
humanities, 12, 33
human words, 76
humility, 165
hymn, Christmas, 12

Idealism, German, 27, 50
identity
    for Christ, 128
    Christian, 5–6, 17
    community, 95, 96, 97
    hidden, 50
    metaphysic of, 50
    philosophy of, 20
    rules for informing, 16, 25
identity conditions, 97
illuminatio (illumination), 32
imagination, 159
imago dei (image of God), 48, 52, 74
immanence, 158
immediate self-consciousness, 18, 53, 123
incarnation
    according to Barth, 11
    as contingent divine policy, 96
    mystery of God in, 94, 95
    necessity and, 86
    new reality of Christ's, 99
indwelling, 31–32
inquiry, 79, 80, 81
instantiation, 140

intensional logic, 126–27
interpretation, 69, 70, 83, 110, 115, 128
Interpretation of Cultures, The (Geertz), 15
intersubjectivity, 167, 168
Israel, 112

Jesus
    as bread of life, 132
    experience of, 118, 126, 161
    historical relationships of, 118
    personal presence of, 129, 132
    and relation to God, 141
    resurrection of, 91
    story of, 112
    transformative work of, 120, 137
    uniqueness of, 132
    as the vine, 129, 132
    See also Christ; Jesus of Nazareth
Jesus Christ
    as cause of redemption, 146
    encounter with, 146
    as God's word, 67, 69–75, 84–86
    lordship of, 81, 82
    new ways of predicating experience of, 147
    revelation in, 34
    as righteousness of God, 68
    See also Christ
Jesus of Nazareth
    encounters with, 125, 158
    God's word in Christ, 71
    the historical, 117, 119, 124
    and redemption, 114, 119
    Schleiermacher's understanding of, 116,
        124, 127
    and transformation, 125
    See also Christ
Jews, and Gentiles, 66, 67
John (Gospel of), 119
judgment
    act of, 126–27
    divine, 61, 67, 68
    of God, 61, 62, 65–68
    and grace, 68
    on human constructions, 61
    and language, 133, 139–40
    synthetic, 37–39, 95, 96
justification
    ethical dimension of, 35

    and faith, 37
    indwelling and, 31, 32
    and kingdom of God, 36
    mediation of, 27, 28
    and mysticism, 40
    and reality, 39, 40
    righteousness and, 29–31
    according to Ritschl, 32–39
    role of, 35
    synthetic judgment of, 37–38
justification *pro te* (for you), 2, 78

Kantian terminology, 153. *See also* neo-
        Kantianism
kingdom of God
    as the final end, 37
    as highest good, 38
    and individual experience, 45
    justification and, 35, 36
    transformation of world into, 34
knowledge
    and dialectic, 114
    doctrinal, 24
    and experience, 7
    of God, 14, 34, 38
    stability of, 9
    theology of, 4, 57
krisis (crisis), 65n12, 66, 68, 69

language
    of Christian community, 15
    Christian confidence and, 8
    doctrine and, 18–19
    and experience, 17, 124–30, 135
    about God, 106
    grammatical structure of, 135
    new, 99, 101, 129–30
    and philosophy, 15
    predication and, 128–30, 133, 134
    and the real, 152
    and reality, 20, 111, 114, 120, 167, 168
    of repetition, 86
    signification, 99
    as social construction, 103
Latin American politics, 160
law, 66, 67, 74, 143
Lectures on Dialectic (Schleiermacher), 49
Lehre (teaching), 24

liberalism, 3, 29, 151
liberation theology, 160
Liebesgemeinschaft . See community of love
  (*Liebesgemeinschaft*)
listening, 138
lived experience, 161–62
lived religion, 131
loci communes (commonplaces), 24
logic
  intensional, 126–27
  medieval, 100
  and predication, 125–28, 129
  and theology, 9
logos theou (word of God), 63
Lutheranism, 23, 25, 27, 29–31, 136
Lutheran orthodoxy, 32, 34, 35
Lutheran-Roman Catholic ecumenism, 25,
  92, 149
Lutherans, 15, 149
Lutherrenaissance, 153

materialism, 157
mediation
  through Christ, 43, 44, 47
  of God's word, 55, 59
  through gospel proclamation and sacra-
    ments, 30
  historical, 43, 44
  of justification, 27, 28
  Ritschl's language of, 39
medieval logic, 100
metalinguistic stipulation, about gospel, 91, 92
metaphysic of identity, 50
metaphysics, 35–36, 40, 57, 143, 165
modalities, 83–88
modality of necessity, 85, 86, 87
modality of possibility, 84, 85
modality of reality, 85
modernity and biblical interpretation, 110,
  111
Moravian piety, 56
mother, applied to Mary, 99
mysteries, 166, 168n28
mysterium tremendum et fascinans (the holy), 154
"mystical" as term, 121–22
mystical element, 121
mystical orientation, 42
mystical union, 32, 35, 39, 40, 41, 43

mysticism
  in encounter with Christ, 122
  historical element in, 42, 166
  and justification, 40
  rehabilitation of, 43, 44, 46
  Ritschl's polemic against, 34, 35, 40,
    41, 42
  Schleiermacher and, 120–21
  of self-relation, 53
  and word, 54, 56, 57

nachdenken (think after), 52
National Socialism, 2, 45, 73
natural and spiritual categories, 35
naturalism, 7, 157
natural sciences, 37. *See also* science
natural theology, 48n69
nature
  causal determination of, 51, 52
  conflation of metaphysics and mysticism
    with, 59
  spirit distinct from, 55
  vs. word of God, 27
nature and spirit
  distinction between, 50–51, 56
  mysticism and, 41, 44–45, 46, 47
  in neo-Kantian metaphysics, 33, 36
  orientation of word to, 62
  pullling apart of, 37, 48–49, 52, 54
  and reality, 39–40
Nature of Doctrine: Religion and Theology in a
  Postliberal Age (Lindbeck), 15, 18, 25
necessity, 84, 85, 86, 88
neo-Kantianism, 21, 27–28, 33, 35–36, 39
New Testament
  earliest layers of, 21, 124, 125, 130
  Gospels, 118–20, 129
  Greek and Hebrew, 128
  and Jesus, 119, 129
  production of, 113, 115, 116, 119, 145
  Schleiermacher's claims concerning, 120,
    145
Nicaea, Council of, 112
Nicene Creed, 94
"No metaphysics, no mysticism" dictum, 29, 41
normativity
  and authority for enforcing, 138
  of beliefs and practice, 13, 61

normativity (*continued*)
    of Christian world view, 100–103
    diversity and, 150
    and reception, 17
    as view of theology, 151
    in a worldview, 103
novelty, 105, 113–15, 130, 132, 137
numinous, the, 154

obedience, 55, 74
obedience to God's word, 86, 88
objectivity, 50, 51, 52
Old Testament, 116–17
omnipotence, 10
ordo salutis (order of salvation), 31, 32, 33
orthodoxy
    Christian, 6–7
    hard forms of, 10
    Lutheran, 32, 34, 35
    Protestant, 31–32, 75
    reason and, 6–7
otherness, 55

package of beliefs, 97, 99, 102
Palestine, first century, 129
Paul, 64, 66, 67, 69
performative justification, 30
personal faith, 42
personal relationship with Christ, 43, 44, 46,
    122
Peter (apostle), 125, 133
philosophy
    and eternity concept, 9
    of identity, 20
    and language, 15
    linguistic turn in, 14–20
    Schleiermacher's enterprise as, 52
    separation from theology, 99
Pietism, 2, 29, 34
piety, 43, 56, 64, 66
plural predication, 136, 137, 139, 142–44
pneumatology, 154
polemics, 10, 16, 29
political theology, 5, 160
politics, 2, 156, 160
Pontius Pilate, 11
Positive Christianity (Fabricius), 45
positivity, 134

possibility, 84, 85, 86, 88
potentia ordinata (ordered power), 86
power, 10, 11, 156, 168
practical theology, 3
practice, 16, 17, 161, 167
predicates, 140, 141
predication
    dogmatic appeal to, 138
    global, 136–37
    language and, 128–30, 133, 134
    and logic, 126–28, 129
    ongoing, 135
    plural, 136, 139, 142–44
    subject of, 126–29, 140, 141
    Western, 137
presence and grace, 77
proclamation, 77, 78, 80, 82, 83, 84, 122
production
    of the canon, 112
    of canonical texts, 112–13
    cultural, 152
    of knowledge, 114
    of New Testament, 113, 115, 116, 119,
        145
production of doctrine
    by historical study, 112, 113
    importance of, 19
    and lived experience, 161
    and reception, 19, 111–12
    and theological epistemology, 131–32, 146
prolegein (things that are spoken before), 75
prolegomena
    to Barth's system, 62, 76, 77, 84
    to Christology, 72
    to Schleiermacher's *Christian Faith*, 114
    of theologians, 88–89
promissio (God's promise of forgiveness), 14
propositions, 100
prosperity gospel, 140
pro te (for you), 2
Protestant Reformation, 54
Protestantism, 136, 158
Prussia, 28
psychology, 18
purity of doctrine, 23
purposiveness *(Endzweck)*, 3

rationalism, 6–7, 154, 155, 166

reality
    of Christianity, 11
    divine, 62–63, 103
    eternal, 10
    and history, 162
    human, 40, 68, 74, 169
    justification aspects of, 39, 40
    and language, 20, 111, 114, 120, 167, 168
    lived, 11
    loss of, 106
    modality of, 85
    and necessity, 86
    new, 99
    in terms of spirit, 49
    transcendent, 87, 150
    and word, 21, 131
    and word of God, 47, 49, 62–63
reality of God
    connection with, 7
    and contradiction to doctrine, 106
    and doctrine, 165
    the external, 103, 152
    and history, 166
    and religious experience, 21
    simplicity of, 98
    and theology, 65
    the transcendent, 60, 87, 145
real presence, 158
reason, 6–7, 9, 53, 155, 166
reception, 17, 19, 111–12, 131, 145
reception of grace, 48
reconciliation, 38
Redeemer, 126, 132, 146
redemption, 46, 114, 119, 120, 123, 128, 146
referent, 106
reflection theory, 50
Reformation breakthrough, 8, 66n14
Reformers, 54
regeneratio et conversio (regeneration and
        conversion), 32
regional theologies, 142
regula fidei (rule of faith), 95, 102, 103, 104
relationship, 38, 39, 46
relationship with Jesus Christ, 38, 43–44, 46, 125
relativism, 151
religion
    Christianity as the universal, 46
    comparative, 155
    as cultural system, 25
    deconstruction of, 156
    experience of, 122
    goal or end of, 34
    Kant's reduction of, 33
    lived, 131
    modern *vs.* apostles and Reformers, 54
    Ritschl's concept of, 37
    the self's capacity for, 53
    subject of, 160
    and theology, 150
    and transcendence, 155
    See also religious studies
Religionsgeschichtliche Schule, 153
religious events excess, 158
religious feelings, 123–24
religious studies
    as academic discipline, 4–5, 156
    boundaries of, 158
    deconstruction and, 157
    and doctrine production, 21
    and historicism, 12
    in modern understanding, 153
    and theology, 154, 156, 158–59, 160,
            163, 169
    See also theology, and religious studies
repetition, 86
response, 37
resurrection, 91
revelation
    content of, 82
    of God, 36, 42, 46, 99
    and Jesus Christ, 34
    the priority of, 64
    tangent touching circle metaphor for, 68
    of Trinity, 83, 84
rhetoric, 70, 72
righteousness, 29–31, 38, 64–68
Roman Catholicism, 15, 25, 149
Roman centurion, 125
Romanticism, 2
Römerbrief, Der (Barth), 62, 64
root assertion, 90–94
rules for informing church practice, 16, 17

"Sabellian" position, 141
sacra doctrina (sacred doctrine), 23
sacredness, 23, 24

salvation, 66n14, 67, 82, 137, 144. *See also* soteriology
sanctification, 31
Schleiermacher problem, 26, 40
science, 24, 33, 35, 37
Scripture, 75, 77, 78, 82, 95, 145. *See also* creeds; Bible
Second Vatican Council, 15
secularism, 151
secular universities religious studies, 4–5
Seelengrund (ground of the soul), 43, 53
self-consciousness, 18, 53, 122, 123
seminaries, 3
sensible self-consciousness, 122, 123
Shoah (Holocaust), 18, 63
simplicity, divine, 98–99, 102
Small Catechism of 1529 (Luther), 10
social construction
    all the way down model of, 151
    problem of, 159–60
    theological language and, 103, 152
    theology as, 149, 150, 151
Solid Declaration of the Formula of Concord, 30
Son, likeness of, 10
soteriology, 120, 121, 124, 134
soul
    care of, 13
    function orientation of, 36, 42, 43–44
    ground of, 43, 53
    transformation of, 124
    and will, 39
speculation, 143, 144
"speech act," 15
Speeches on Religion (Schleiermacher), 54, 154, 155
spirit
    and body, 46
    historical mediation of Christ and, 44
    objectivity and, 51, 52
    and word, 51, 59
    See also nature and spirit
spirit (*Geist*), 50, 51
St. Mary's Church, Wittenberg, Germany, 8
subject, 126–29, 140, 141
subjectivity, 50, 51, 52
summa (comprehensive treatise), 24
Summa theologicae (Aquinas), 93
surprise/the unexpected, 19

synthetic judgment, 37, 39, 95, 96
systematic theology, 13n13, 161
systematization, 141

teaching and preaching, 98
temporal self-consciousness, 122, 123
theologians, 1–2, 9
theological education, 155
theological epistemology, 131–35, 141, 145
theology
    as academic discipline, 4, 5, 13
    assertions of, 60, 61
    according to Barth, 70
    benchmarking in, 144
    Christian, 136
    as church practice, 16
    construction of, 141–46
    deconstruction and preservation of doctrine in, 6
    definition of, 2
    dialectical, 48, 49, 78, 79, 105
    epistemology of, 57–58, 113, 114
    eternity and, 8–10
    feminist, 140
    genres of, 77, 78, 88
    German, 18
    God and the world in, 11
    ground of, 87, 89, 105
    historicist, 11–14
    as human task/enterprise, 76, 149
    as intellectual practice, 61
    as knowledge, 4, 57
    liberation, 160
    as living practice, 106
    and logic, 9
    as object of gospel, 91
    polemics of, 10
    political, 5, 160
    as positive science, 13
    practical, 3
    presupposition of, 76
    regional, 142
    religion and, 153
    and religious studies, 154–56, 159, 160, 169
    in the seminary, 4
    separation from philosophy, 99
    as social construction, 151
    systematic, 13n13, 161

twentieth century shift in, 61
ways of conceptualizing, 18–19, 106
and women, 140
word-oriented, 14–20, 54–56
See also dogmatic theology
Theology and Metaphysics: Toward Comprehension and Resistance (Ritschl), 33, 34, 37
thing in itself *(Ding-an-sich)*, 35, 36
thinking, feeling, and willing, 36
"to hold together," 101
totality, 123–24
Tractatus logico-philosophicus (Wittgenstein), 14
traditions, 113, 135–36, 138
transcendence, 67, 105, 139, 141, 144, 145, 150
transformation
    Christ subject of, 125, 126
    experience and witness in, 130
    and justification, 10, 36, 39
    as lifelong process, 31
    person-forming, 124, 132
    of the soul, 124
    of the world, 34
Trinitarian content, 81
Trinitarian indwelling, 31, 32, 35
Trinity
    Athanasian form of, 119
    and Christology, 142
    construction of, 141
    divine hidden majesty and, 96
    modalities of, 83–85, 88
    production of, 112–13
    reason and, 166
    revelation of, 83, 84
    root of, 71–72, 82, 84
    as unfinished history, 106–7
Trinity, doctrine of
    and assertion, 83
    as foundational in theology, 62
    and historical criticism, 163–64
    and word of God, 2, 72, 75, 76
Trinity and Truth (Marshall), 96, 101
trust, 90
truth
    of Christianity, 137
    condition, 102
    decisions about, 101
    divine, 14, 97–98
    doctrinal claims to, 23, 105, 165

doctrine as norm of, 7, 23, 111
    and experience, 7, 161
    of God, 8, 14, 23, 81, 106
    and historical interpretation, 167
    mistaking power for, 168
    new perspectives on, 2
    of propositions, 100
    pursuit of, 11, 80
    theological, 10, 11, 144
"turtles all the way down," 150–51, 152
typology, 155

unity, 73n37, 74
University of Berlin, 12

vera doctrina (true doctrine), 23
Verbum caro factum est (The Word became flesh), 99
verbum externum (external word), 16, 91, 112, 144
Vermittlung (mediation), 43
Vernunft (reason), 53
Versailles, 64
Vertrauen auf Christus (trust in Christ), 92
Virgin Mary, 11
vocatio (vocation), 32

war, 18, 27, 28, 61, 63, 64, 65
Weimar Republic, 64
Wilhelm I (King of Prussia), 28
will, divine, 44
Wissenschaft (science), 24, 33
witness, 77, 78, 130
Wittenberg, Germany, 8
women, and theology, 140
word
    concepts associated with, 26
    and experience, 27
    human consciousness and, 54
    mediation of, 59
    and mysticism, 54, 56, 57
    ontological difference from nature, 55
    spirit and, 51, 59
    theology of, 54–55, 56
    threefold, 71, 77–80
word of God
    autonomy of, 67, 68, 69
    Christ as, 70, 72–75
    content of, 79, 81, 87

word of God (*continued*)
    criterion of, 84
    doctrine of, 72, 75, 76
    and doctrine of the Trinity, 2, 72, 75, 76
    God's initiative in giving, 51
    history of, 28
    opposed to experience, 27
    and reality, 47, 49, 62–63
    in relation to human words, 60, 69, 71,
        73, 77–79, 104
    in Scripture, 75, 77–78

world, 16, 73, 74, 100
worldviews
    Christian, 15, 16, 61, 89, 103–5
    doctrinal, 7
    religious, 150
World War I, 27, 28, 64
World Wars, 18, 61, 63

Zwischen den Zeiten (journal), 48

CPSIA information can be obtained at www.ICGtesting.com
Printed in the USA
LVOW10s0415301214

420831LV00011B/363/P